HUMAN RIGHTS, TRIBAL MOVEMENTS AND VIOLENCE

HUMAN RIGHTS, TRIBAL MOVEMENTS AND VIOLENCE

Tribal Tenacity in the Twenty-first Century in Central Eastern India

DEBASREE DE

MANOHAR
2023

First published 2023

ISBN 978-93-94262-87-4

Published by
Ajay Kumar Jain *for*
Manohar Publishers & Distributors
4753/23 Ansari Road, Daryaganj
New Delhi 110 002

Typeset by
Kohli Print
Delhi 110 051

Printed at
Replika Press Pvt. Ltd.

To my teacher

PROFESSOR (DR.) AMIT BHATTACHARYYA

Contents

List of Tables

Acknowledgements

Tribal movements during the colonial period and its consequences have been documented by the colonial anthropologists in detail. But the tribal movements that are hitting the news everyday in neoliberal India have only made their way in the television debates, newspaper reports and litigations. They are needed to be studied in a historical context and with potential analytical tools. This is the reason why the present monograph deals with the tribal resistance from a holistic standpoint and records their success and failures from the tribal notion of collective mobilization.

First and foremost I would like to convey my gratitude to Mr. Ramesh Jain who encouraged me to write a book on the tribal movements of India. Later I developed this idea and combined it with my ongoing post-doctoral research that was funded by the Rashtriya Uchchatara Sikshya Abhiyan or RUSA 2.0 Post-Doctoral Research Fellowship under the Faculty of Arts at Jadavpur University. I am indebted to my respected supervisors Dr. Anuradha Roy and Dr. Sudeshna Banerjee of the Department of History for their thoughtful observations, suggestions and insights. I thank Dr. Amit Bhattacharyya who has always been a constant source of inspiration and guidance. I am thankful to Dr. Kaushik Roy, Head of the Department of History, for his timely support. I am most grateful to my colleague Prof. Krishnapada Das who stood by me during my hardest times, guiding and helping in every possible way. Lastly, I am grateful to all the adivasi respondents who entertained my queries and participated in the survey. I am certain that if my father, Late Asim Kumar De were alive, he would definitely appreciate my effort and bless me. My heartfelt gratitude goes to my mother Mrs. Sonali De for always being there for me.

Kolkata
14 August 2022

DEBASREE DE

Abbreviations

AAY	Antyodaya Anna Yojana
ADB	Asian Development Bank
AES	Advanced Encryption Standard
AKMS	Adivasi Kisan Mazdoor Sanghathan
AMARM	Adivasi Moolvasi Astitava Raksha Manch
AMS	Adivasi Mukti Sangathan
ASSSS	Adivasi Samaj Sudhar Shanti Sena
AWC	Anganwadi Centres
BALCO	Bharat Aluminum Company
BBJM	Bisthapan Birodhi Jana Manch
BCKU	Bihar Colliery Kamgar Union
BP	Baghua Irrigation Project
BIP	Badanala Irrigation Project
BJA	Bharat Jan Andolan
BJSM	Bhita-mati Jivan Jivika Surkhya Manch
BPD	Business Partners for Development
BPL	Below Poverty Level
BRO	Border Roads Authority
BSP	Bhilai Steel Plant
CAVOW	Committee against Violence on Women
CBAA	Coal Bearing Areas (Acquisition and Development) Act
CIL	Coal India Ltd.
CMAS	Chasi Muliya Adivasi Sangh
CMM	Chhattisgarh Mukti Morcha
CNT	Chota Nagpur Tenancy Act
CPI (ML)	Communist Party of India (Marxist-Leninist)
CRPF	Central Reserve Police Force
CSRs	Corporate Social Responsibilities
DFID	Department for International Development India
DVS	Dalit Vikas Sangathan

EIR	East Indian Railway's
FDC	Fisheries Development Corporation
FDI	Foreign Direct Investment
GVT	Gramin Vikas Trust
HAL	Hindustan Aeronautics Ltd.
HINDALCO	Hindustan Aluminium Company
HIP	Harabhangi Irrigation Project
ICDS	Integrated Child Development Services
IDCO	Industrial Development Corporation of Odisha
IFFDC	India Farm Forestry Development Cooperative
IMFA	Indian Metal Ferro-Alloys
INTUC	Indian National Trade Union Congress
IPRs	Intellectual Property Rights
IPS	Institute for Policy Studies
IRBs	Indian Reserve Battalions
ISFP	Integrated Shrimp Farming Project
ISP	Indira Sagar Project
JADS	Jagrit Adivasi Dalit Sangathan
JBSS	Jameen Bachao Samanway Samiti
JFM	Joint Forest Management
JKMU	Jharkhand Krantikari Mazdoor Union
JMM	Jharkhand Mukti Morcha
JSPCB	Jharkhand State Pollution Control Board
JSPL	Jindal Steel and Power Plant
KAMS	Krantikari Adivasi Mahila Sangathan
KBK	Kalahandi-Bolangir-Koraput
KBSS	Karanpura Bachao Sangharsh Samiti
KMCS	Khedut Mazdoor Chetna Sangath
LPG	Liberalization, Privatization and Globalization
MCC	Maoist Communist Centre
MISA	Moscow Institute for Steel and Alloys
MMDR	Mineral Development and Regulation
MMSD	Mining, Minerals and Sustainable Development Project
MNCs	Multi-National Companies
MoEF	Ministry of Environment and Forest

MoEFCC	Ministry of Environment, Forest and Climate Change
MoU	Memorandum of Understanding
MPSFDC	Madhya Pradesh State Forest Development Corporation
MPSS	Mali Parbat Surakhya Samiti
MRD	Ministry of Rural Development
MSL	Maharashtra Seamless Company
NALCO	National Aluminium Company
NDA	National Democratic Alliance
NGOs	Non-Governmental Organizations
NIPCCD	National Institute of Public Cooperation and Child Development
NMDC	National Mineral Development Corporation
NREGS	National Rural Employment Guarantee Scheme
NTFPs	Non-Timber Forest Products
NTPC	National Thermal Power Corporation Ltd.
NWDTA	Narmada Water Disputes Tribunal Award
OMC	Odisha Mining Corporation
PAs	Protected Areas
PAPs	Project Affected Peoples
PESA	Panchayat (Extension to Scheduled Areas) Act
PLGA	People's Liberation Guerrilla Army
POSCO	Pohang Steel Company
PSSP	POSCO Pratirodh Sangram Samiti
PSU	Public Sector Utility
PWG	People's War Group
RIP	Rengali Irrigation Project
R&R	Resettlement and Rehabilitation Policy
RSS	Rashtriya Swayamsevak Sangh
SAIL	Steel Authority of India's
SAP	Saranda Action Plan
SECL	South Eastern Coalfields Limited
SEZ	Special Economic Zone
SGSY	Swarnajayanti Gram Swarojgar Yojana
SIIL	Sterlite Industries India Ltd

SIP	Sponge Iron Projects
SMHPCL	Shree Maheshwar Hydel Power Corporation Limited
SMP	Subarnarekha Multipurpose Project
SPO	Special Police Officers
SPTA	Santhal Parganas Tenancy Act
TISCO	Tata Iron and Steel Company
TPS	Tata Power Solar Systems
UAIL	Utkal Alumina International Limited
UCIL	Uranium Corporation of India
UNICEF	United Nations International Children's Emergency Fund
URDS	Utkal Rural Development Society
VAL	Vedanta Alumina Limited
WIRFP	Western India Rain fed Farming Project

Introduction

> The mining that is taking place in the forest areas is threatening the livelihood and survival of many tribes. . . . Let it not be said by future generations that the Indian Republic has been built on the destruction of the green earth and the innocent tribals who have been living there for centuries. . .
>
> K.R. NARAYANAN, 25 JANUARY 2001

Tribal movements of India have a long and glorious history to be documented. During the colonial period there were frequent uprisings by the tribals in almost all regions, be it in Bihar or Andhra or northeastern India. The British government tagged the movements as 'insurrection' and 'rebellion' against the lawful authority. For the British, the tribal movements were violent, seditious and barbaric. They employed several brutal means to gag them in order to restore 'peace and tranquillity'. During the colonial period, the tribal movements were mostly against the outsiders, called the *dikus*, landlords, moneylenders, dishonest shopkeepers and the like. Later when the territorialization of forest areas took place by completely overriding the customary rights causing massive exploitation of forest resources, especially timber for shipbuilding and the construction of railway tracts, the tribals could realize the real intention of the Britishers, who used to humiliate them and their womenfolk. This caused some really strong protest on the part of the tribals leading to one of the biggest movements, called the Santhal *hul* in 1855-6. Gradually, the tribal movements started acquiring the character of an anti-imperialist and anti-colonial movement.

Tribals constitute 8 per cent of India's total population. More or less 44.7 per cent of India's tribal people were below the poverty line in 2011. Interestingly, after the Independence of India, the tribal movements could not have been placated, as was thought. The first Prime Minister of India, Pandit Jawaharlal Nehru perceived the idea of tribal development on the basis of massive scale of industrialization as planned in the First and Second Five-Year Plans. Unlike his advisor Verrier Elwin, his notion of tribal development was that of assimilation and not isolationist. But there was a serious flaw. Tribal consent or participation was out and out ignored when it came to prepare the road map of the tribal development. Nehru once said, the 'dams are the temples of modern India', which still haunts the tribals.

It was this mentality that ruled the country since Independence and became the linchpin of capitalist model of development after the introduction of liberalization, privatization and globalization (LPG). Big fat industrialists, multinational corporations, giant trans-national companies erected and are erecting factories, dams, housing complexes at the expense of natural resources. The traditional wealth like water, land and forest (*jal, zameen* and *jungle*) are being thoughtlessly exploited leaving the earliest citizens as destitute and cheap unorganized labour force in these factories. Their culture, religion, customs and most importantly human rights are being threatened grievously. The market forces and corporates have been given unrestricted access to exploit tribal resource base. This seriously affects the indigenous knowledge and wisdom which have never been safeguarded by any institutional and legal measures and thus grossly violate the Intellectual Property Rights (IPRs). Tribal art and craft have been marketized in the name of preservation and documentation. Governments, both the central and the states, are not interested in establishing centres for exclusive tribal art and culture. It is nothing but affront to tribal dignity and derogatory to the core.

Binay Bhushan Chaudhuri in his analysis of tribal movements in colonial eastern India marked three features of tribal movements and they are: dismantle the domination of the *dikus* (hostile aliens), birth of a radical ideology and finally revaluation of tribal tradition which, according to him, are subject to change over the years. According to him, these three features of the radical tribal resistance are absent in peasant movements of that time. Later, with the arrival of Gandhi a potent alternative was found which could replace the British. Gandhi had a more enduring impact on the tribals as his image created a powerful radical political temperament among the struggling tribals (Chaudhuri 2009). He said that the cultural revitalization movement was a crucial part of the radical political agenda of the tribals and millenarianism constitutes the other inseparable part of it (Chaudhuri 2010). Sinha once stated,

> These tribal movements, *ulghulan*, agitation, rebellion, et cetera formed part of the whole, that is, the Tribal wrath against the system which was thrust upon them. They were mainly against the economic exploitation, territorial encroachment, cultural imposition and social domination. Some of them could at best be movement for entry into existing power structure or movement for generation of alternative power structure or movement for entry into existing structure of prestige without visualizing any alternative structure of power. (Sinha 1990: 180)

Having said that, it is also true to say the tribal movements during the neoliberal era are not influenced by these features of the colonial era. The tribal movements of neoliberal regimes, if tried to be brought under subheadings, can be broadly divided into three categories: movement against land acquisition and displacement, environmentalist movements and movements influenced by extremist ideology of Naxalism. Apart from this, tribal movements can also be categorized as social movements and women's movements. The radical ideology of the colonial period has been radicalized by a more extreme form of violence and insurgency. If the tribals did find an alternative in Gandhi to the alien powers like *dikus* and British authorities, then the tribals of today are trying to find out an alternative either in a separate statehood or in Naxalism. Another distinctive feature of tribal movements of today is that tribals have been mobilized under their own leadership and banner. These leaders are not charismatic leaders like Birsa or believe in a supernatural being who comes in dreams and instructs what to do. The leaders are more pragmatic and lead the movement in a more systematic way in order to achieve their goals, though tribals still have a great faith in their religion and god as one has seen in Niyamgiri where they fiercely resisted the selling of Niyam Raja. Filing petition, moving the court, the media are more common today. Unlike the tribals of the colonial period, tribals are today negotiating their demands, asking for proper compensation on their own terms and not nodding meekly or obstructing thoughtlessly. What they ask is whether the development is sustainable or not. Tribals are wrongly portrayed as anti-development, anti-science or technology. Unlike the colonial times when tribal movements were considered local and regional which did never gain nationwide coverage, today the movements against POSCO, Vedanta and Narmada Bachao Andolan have gained international support and media coverage extensively, although they are still considered as law and order problems as they were by the British. Tribals have successfully secured constitutional and legislative safeguards and judgements of courts like Samatha Judgement of 1997 in their favour, though not always maintained by the state, are some of the protective shields against exploitation which they did not have under the colonial domination. Tribals are more conscious about their rights which are reflected in their movements that are in no way spontaneous but well organized. The single most important factor that has remained unchanged even in this neoliberal regime is the process of cultural revitalization or Sanskritization movement which has been deepened and getting more impetus under the Hindutva ideology lately.

The struggle of the original inhabitants for their own homeland was once called the *mulk ki ladai* during the Munda *ulghulan* of Birsa Munda. Since then the fight has been going on unabatedly and is still unrecognized. The tribals have risen again against all injustices and this time they are fighting not against any alien people like the British, but their own countrymen, the state, the corporate encroachers, and the extremists, who do not treat them as equals and violate their human rights. This time their struggle is not only against the corporate imperialism or state violence, but also against internal colonialism and structural violence that has propelled them into the darkness of poverty and deprivation. Internal conflicts are also visible within the tribal communities themselves. For example, merger of other different tribals into larger Gond identity is a case in point in Bastar. Muria and Maria once used to refer to themselves with the distinctive name of their tribes and rebutted any claims of being Gond. But lately they have started referring to themselves as Gonds to make a broader community to gain benefits. On the other hand, the Dandami Marias displaced the Hill Marias and got displaced by other tribes and non-tribes on account of resources extraction. Extremists started an agency of representing the tribal voice for justice, but gradually became too self-centred, hierarchical, conflict-ridden and contradictory in nature which failed to promote the tribal cause. The Naxalites were not violent till about 1984-5. Violence started erupting due chiefly to the intensification of police brutality and only then the Naxalites started punishing the informers. Bastar Naxalites were not connected to the Charu Majumdar group; rather they followed the path of Satyanarain Sinha who always advocated abdicating violence as far as possible and resort to only limited violence under extreme provocation. Antipathy against the Naxalite is a more recent phenomenon which is gradually developing among the tribal youth (Dubey 1998).

The state does not consider the tribes of India as nationalities in the dominant sense of the term. This notion has been prejudiced by standpoints to the national question of a top-down approach of development and progress to a large extent. Tribal issues are considered as the most glaring examples of how state betrays its own sons and daughters of the soil. This has made them visible in the dominant discourse in which they were once viewed as voiceless, historyless and faceless grey mass. The tribal cause has given a new light in which the propositions like development, eviction, autonomy and indigeneity are being debated and discussed. During the colonial era the tribals were defined as primitive, savages, cannibals and insurgents who reside at the lowest rung of the society in dire poverty and who are excluded from the mainstream subject category of the colonized as a whole. Their primitiveness and resultant marginalization made them feel unproductive, although the British used them to make lands cultivable and revenue-generating. The colonial administration and its policies towards the tribals were formed on a concept of capitalist modernity where tribals have been visualized as exotic, promiscuous, exclusive, homogeneous and exceptional with enigmatic features which are to be protected and reserved in a museum or archive. It does not portray tribes as politically conscious, heterogeneous and hierarchical category which has its own contradictions and complexities. Tribes are time and again explained in the context of a binary of tribe-caste relationship and like a unilinear community which is still at the stage of primitive accumulation without the knowledge and participation in the modern mode of production and modern history. It is not documented that the tribes not only rebelled against the feudal lords, moneylenders, dishonest shopkeepers and later the British, but also took part in the Gandhian movement.

The tribal cause, in the present world, is replete with land related issues, be it land alienation, displacement or adequate rehabilitation. Land for the tribals does not connote just a territory or means of livelihood, but it constitutes their *mulk* or country where they are free, where they live with dignity and where they rule themselves. Often one cannot comprehend this very idea of a tribal territory or space. Land right is intrinsically connected to the history of tribal autonomy, political consciousness and ethnic identity. Tribal movements for land rights or autonomy have some specificity. They make one conscious about the core questions of social alienation, structural violence, land grabbing, deprivation from the right to access to natural resources, in short the cultural *harakiri* that is going on unchecked. Tribal movements are also aiming to make us question the relationship between the state and the citizen, leaders and the masses, law and customs, politics and violence, dominance and subjugation, justice and dignity and the like. The major causes of tribal unrest lie in the dichotomy of social justice and political violence. On the one hand tribal land has been designated as inalienable and tribal areas have been brought under PESA, the growing violence in form of extremist insurgency is gaining support among them and challenging the establishments on the other. If one is to differentiate the characteristics of the tribal unrest in the pre- and post-colonial era one will see that there is hardly any qualitative difference as the basic grievances like land, livelihood and dignity are still unredressed. *Jal, zameen* and *jungle* still hold the principal place when it comes to identifying the factors responsible for the tribal tenacity at large. Movements for autonomy are not new and have roots in the colonial period, thus performing an inseparable part of tribal cause. But separate statehood has been granted not always on the basis of autonomy movement which is often confused with counter-nationalism; rather it is a fact that the creation of Chhattisgarh was very much due to the granting of concessions to the multinationals and big corporates for facilitating the loot of the natural wealth which has nothing to do with secessionism. The obnoxious forces of tribal deprivation unleashed by the state and its machineries play a vital role in mobilizing the collective resistance and organizing the spontaneous fight against all injustices being perpetrated against them since time immemorial (Rupavath 2019). Tribal tenacity, therefore, should be judged by its demands of proper recognition of tribal rights and representation, dignity and identity, agency and existence which did not change at all in the postcolonial times.

Tribal resistance is viewed in the context of the penetration of capitalistic commoditization of tribal life and subsistence economy. Their everyday forms of resistance (Scott 1985) have various causes embedded in the politics of displacement, deprivation and commercial exploitation of natural wealth. The colonial Land Acquisition Act of 1894 empowered the state to acquire private land on the pretext of eminent domain for 'public purposes'. Though the coercive act originated during the colonial era it was widely used in independent India in the Nehruvian era of development which took little time to get converted into the era of displacement. Even after Nehru's modernization drive, the act was quite in force to acquire land more extensively in the post-liberalization period for inviting private capital. The act has recently been replaced with the Right to Fair Compensation and Transparency in Land Acquisition, Rehabilitation and Resettlement Act, 2013 which has rationalized and legalized different mechanisms of land grabbing. After losing the means of livelihood and way of life, the displaced tribals often go through trauma and insecurities which let extremism breed and this is the reason why Naxalite outfits are so much active in the tribal areas and often take up the leadership of tribal movements like Narayanpatna movement of Odisha or Lalgarh movement of West Bengal. But the state, instead of mitigating the actual cause of tribal dissatisfaction, is more involved in how to crush their movement which eventually clears the path of the upsurge of multinational takeover in the name of development and curbing 'disturbances' in the tribal heartlands (Musalaiah 2008).

The tribal identity has emerged after a long and protracted battle against the modern forces of capitalism and modern state as tribals have always been sacrificed for the so-called 'national interest' and they are the ones who suffered most by eviction due to the large industrial and dam projects which in a way prepared them to be at the forefront of resistance since time immemorial. Their struggle revolved around right to natural resources, equal participation in decision making, political autonomy and justice. Their presence as 'primitive' is contrary to the discourse of capitalist modernity that tends to reject their agency, representation and voice of dissent. But tribals are up in arms against all hegemonic political powers that be, irrespective of local chiefs, national leaders or global corporates, to undo the attempts of the selling of indigenous property and human resources. The so-called mainstream political ideologues however, do not acknowledge their movement as environmentalist, but just an anti-displacement agitation. It is the fact that when the whole world is striving for lowering the global pollution, it is the tribals who are playing the role of a vanguard against unplanned industrialization and ecological depletion, desiccation and deforestation through their radicalism and indigeneity (Banerjee 2006).

This led to the outbreak of tribal resistance to indiscriminate dispossession that later on matured into broader anti-establishment conflicts with the rise of extremism. The colonial state was always at the epicentre of tribal resistance movements and after independence tribal movements were against state led industries, dams, real estate, sanctuaries, mining projects and later the same under corporate ownership. Initially the state used to acquire land for the private companies, but later the big multinationals were given the right to acquire land on their own which changed the nature as well as the course of the tribal movements. Michael Levien rightly observed that, agitation at the national level takes place mostly against projects that involved the acquisition of forest land, for example Vedanta and POSCO in Odisha which needed approval from the central government, or sporadically where agitators joined hands together to oppose national land acquisition acts. At the transnational level, tribal activism is identified more with projects funded by the World Bank. At the local or regional level tribal activism is less supported and rarely effective, if not limited to issues where it is often termed as an indigenous rights movement. The neoliberal regime of development-induced displacement, where the state becomes just an agent of land acquisition for growing investment-driven private capital and proves itself less convincing because of which the tribal movements are more vigorous and persistent (Levien 2013).

The terrain of tribal activism has extended from local to global today. They are no more segregated, isolated or meant for the museum. Greater access to the outside world has opened up new vistas for them and transformed their worldview and they have become tactful and strategic in their decisions and actions in order to achieve voice and visibility which can help to create a better political space for themselves. Tribal activism at the grassroot level has used the expertise to gain a more dominating role in politics. The politics of assertion and recognition has made tribal tenacity tangible. They are aware of their vision, empowerment and coping mechanisms. They emphasize more on the collective agency and dialogue to get a wider platform and legitimacy before starting a battle against injustice. Proper recognition and space (political or otherwise) are the two most important demands of the battling tribals. The tribals are no more passive recipients of the mainstream development programmes. The collective mobilization in the form of tribal activism or tenacity has improved their communication skills, enhanced the power of articulation of shared grievances, given the transparency of their cause, addressed various issues, created a common narratives of resistance, strengthened their capacity to negotiate and placed them on a better footing to make their voice better heard as well (Lund and Panda 2011).

Writing the history of the tribal movements has a severe shortcoming as one really does not know what tribes think of history or what constitutes the tribal notion of history writing and what exactly makes the history of tribal movements a comprehensive and holistic account of their own thought process and outlook. One does not really know how the tribes themselves define their movement—whether they call it an unrest or insurgency or a Fight for Right. What one realized during field visits is that tribals do not even consider their protest a movement. For them, it is to convey their dissatisfaction and that is also through a very constitutional way. Tribals never think of killing the police, bureaucrats or counter-insurgents for that matter, they always try to keep it non-violent and propose discussion unless the opposite causes terror. Those who take up arms are mostly not for offensive attacks. Their perspective of resistance is definitely defensive. Tribes whom I have interviewed are very much interested in attending the *gram sabha* meetings where their fate is to be discussed when tribal land is in question. But unfortunately *gram sabha* meetings are being manipulated by the powers that be and public hearings have been turned into mockery. Prathama Banerjee has rightly observed that,

In many states, for example in Orissa, if decisions taken by local assemblies appear to go against state laws 'currently in force', state laws are given precedence over community decisions. Even in areas such as Madhya Pradesh and Chhattisgarh, where Gram Sabha decisions are taken more seriously, 'due regard' to existing relevant laws are demanded from village assemblies, apart from their being 'in harmony' with the constitution. Needless to say, not just around PESA, the current debate around the Land Acquisition, Rehabilitation and Resettlement Act of 2013 and its various amendments also involve the same issue of autonomy of the Gram Sabhas as a unit of self-government. (Banerjee 2016)

The present book has been planned chiefly to highlight the tribal situation of today. The book illuminates the causes, nature and consequences of the tribal movements of twenty-first century India in a fresh light. It has covered several tribal movements, some of which are ongoing, in four states—Madhya Pradesh, Chhattisgarh, Jharkhand and Odisha. The study area has been selected on the basis of its geographical situation. There is a rich history of tribal movements in western, northern, southern and also in the northeastern parts of India and those can be covered in the subsequent volumes, if possible. The book is a holistic account of tribal movements going on in the central-eastern India which were hitherto unrecorded and it has chronicled the history of tribal deprivation and resistance with analytical tools in order to evaluate and assess their nature, achievements and failure. B.B. Chaudhuri, K.S. Singh, Nandini Sunder and colonial anthropologists and administrators wrote extensively on tribal movements of colonial India. But as far as the postcolonial and neoliberal period is concerned, not much study has been conducted on tribal resistance. Walter Fernandes, Felix Padel, and few others have studied tribal movements but they are all case-specific studies. This book includes annals of tribal movements in the neoliberal era in that respects.

It has documented various tribal movements in Madhya Pradesh which are mainly against the deprivation and the denial of basic needs.

Food, shelter, employment are some of the demands of the tribals raised during their movements. Tribal struggle against structural violence has shaken the entire country. It should be remembered that the poor have not invented poverty, but it has been created by the policies the state has orchestrated and the institutions by which they have been materialized (Yunus 2011). In Jharkhand two movements are under study—Pathalgadi and Koel-Karo. Pathalgadi movement is a movement for championing the human rights of the tribals by erecting stone slabs and inscribing constitutional provisions on them by the tribal themselves. This movement has become the cornerstone of the people's rights movement in India. Then comes the save river movement, i.e. Koel-Karo. The movement started a long time ago and can be appreciated for successfully stopping the proposed dam on the river.

Odisha is the hotbed of the tribal movements against multinational and corporate exploitation. Kashipur, Kalinganagar, Jagatsinghpur, Narayanpatna, Sundergarh, Kandhamal and Kalahandi are burning with the tribal protests which have created international news. On the one hand, the tribals are fighting against the displacement and on the other, demanding the right to have adequate resettlement and rehabilitation programme. It is because of their movement that the Indian government has passed mining and mineral act, land acquisition act and resettlement and rehabilitation act. Last but not the least Chhattisgarh is the most troubled area as it is termed as the red corridor due to the presence of the Maoists. Maoists initially played the role of a voice over of the tribals making their grievances heard. The state also created anti-Maoist squad called Salwa Judum with the local tribals to counter the Maoists. Between these two elements the innocent tribal people were getting sandwiched. Gradually, it was found that the tribal issues have taken the back seat as Maoists are not paying attention to their demands. Thus, the tribal movements of Chhattisgarh have become a very complex and problematic issue today.

It is interesting to compare the patterns of conflicts in the study area which sometimes bear similarities to each other and sometimes they are diametrically opposite in nature. For example, when it comes to the pattern of the tribal movements of the neoliberal era they are very organized, well-led and have a clear vision of what they want to achieve. Most of them have been mobilized under a banner and leadership who are conscious about their predicaments and firm on their stand, be it Pathalgadi, anti-Vedanta, anti-POSCO, Narmada Bachao, Jhabua or Betul. The existing patterns are also to be recognized as non-violent and maintaining strictly a constitutional direction. The tribals rely on the democratic system, resort to legal options, participate in the *gram sabha* meetings, stretegize their further move in the meetings of their own organizations and so on and so forth. The only glaring exception is Bastar which is a unique situation to be studied separately and not to bring into any comparison with other tribal movements of other states. Violence in form of revolutionary violence and state-sponsored repressive violence are the dominant patterns of tribal Naxal movement in Chhattisgarh. Odisha also holds a special place as the gigantic greed of the multinationals is more detrimental there than in Jharkhand and Madhya Pradesh. It is chiefly because Odisha is rich in mineral and natural resources. Madhya Pradesh, on the other hand, has a long history of organized struggle under several banners which have been working there for decades. What is important to note is that, Naxalism has not impacted tribals either in Odisha or in Madhya Pradesh. Narayanpatna is a notable exception as Naxalism was quite active here. Violence erupted in the tribal populated distrct of Kandhamal as well, but that was a communal strife and thereby has been kept outside the purview of the present work.

Madhya Pradesh also has its distinctiveness. Hinduization has done its best to bring the tribals into the Hindu fold which is absent in Odisha and Jharkhand. Rashtriya Swayamsevak Sangh (RSS) activists have gained a widespread local support by giving tribals access to biomedical treatment and proper prices for selling *tendu* leaves. During 1990s RSS, the radical Hindu nationalist organization shifted its attention towards the Christian tribals. They increased cultural and educational campaigns in the tribal villages of Madhya Pradesh in order to spread the ideology of Hindutva. The Oraon Christian tribals migrated to the southeast Madhya Pradesh during 1970s when the Catholic mission converted them to Christianity through their philanthropic activities. The RSS civic activists, with the aim of

Hinduization, started working among the disenfranchized tribals and gradually made a support base for them. Their effort was highly appreciated by the tribals who were suffering due to unaccountable state machanisms (Froerer 2009).

There are multiple trends identified time and again in the tribal movements in terms of their typology, structure and operational systems. Druing the colonial era tribal movements were categorized as revivalist and reformist where religion and tradition played a crucial role. Syncretism and secularization were two dominant trends of tribal movements in those days which were functionally connected to each other. There were other trends as well, for example, millenarianism, messianism, etc. But during the neoliberal times the tribal movements are categorized with a generic interpretation, like anti-dam movements, anti displacement movements, environmentalist movements, women's movements or simply social movements. It does not mean tradition or religion has ceased to exist. In Bastar, the current trend of growing Naxalism has received copious attention which is a bit different as the targets have been the security forces, SPOs and Salwa Judum militia. There is a constant victimization of the ordinary tribal people. On the contrary, in Jharkhand, Odisha and Madhya Pradesh tribals are essentially battling against the corporates, police personnel and land mafias. Here the trend is democratically strategic and state intervention is also systematic. The current trend is also about territorial autonomy which is intimately related to the search of identity, participation in the governance and development and control over resources.

According to K.S. Singh, there are limits of prognostication, yet some recent trends are seen in tribal movements in India. For example, agrarian laws are being strengthened, environmental and human rights issues are getting more attention, threat to the resources and displacement are becoming principal agendas, conflict with modern institutions are being deepened, protective discriminations are widening the scope of inequality and polarization, ethnic movements are getting stronger and most importantly demand for self-rule is surfacing which can give birth to many other tribal states as the tribal issues are being globalized. Singh has further stated that, there is a revival of interest in totemism and a belief system which is being manifested in the tribal tradition of oral culture (Singh 1997).

In fine, the book will discuss the tribal movements of the neo-liberal times and will look into how these movements have raised awareness and consciousness among the tribals about their plight and also about their rights, given them agency and representation and what their achievement and success story are. The tribals are still lagging behind all the castes and communities of our country. They do not need charity, but legal protection of their constitutional rights so that they can move forward searching for a better future for themselves.

REFERENCES

Banerjee, Prathama, 2006, 'Culture/Politics: The Irresoluble Double-Bind of the Indian Adivasi', in *The Indian Historical Review*, vol. XXXIII, no. 1, pp. 99-126.

——, 2016, 'Writing the Adivasi: Some Historiographical Notes', in *The Indian Economic and Social History Review*, vol. 53 (1), pp. 131-53.

Chaudhuri, Binay Bhushan, 2009, 'Revaluation of Tradition in the Ideology of the Radical Adivasi Resistance in Colonial Eastern India, 1855-1932—Part I', in *The Indian Historical Review*, 36(2) 273-305.

——, 2010, 'Revaluation of Tradition in the Ideology of the Radical Adivasi Resistance in Colonial Eastern India, 1855-1932—Part II', in *The Indian Historical Review*, 37(1) 39-62.

Dubey, K.C., 1998, 'Tribal Uprisings and Social Movements in Madhya Pradesh', in K.S. Singh (ed.) *Tribal Movements in India: Antiquity to Modernity in Tribal India*, vol. IV, New Delhi: Inter-India Publications, pp. 205-317.

Froerer, Peggy, 2009, 'Activists and Adivasis: Hindu Nationalist Militants in Chhattisgarh, Central India', in David N. Gellner (ed.), *Ethnic Activism and Civil Society in South Asia*, New Delhi: Sage, pp. 57-80.

Levien, Michael, 2013, 'The Politics of Dispossession: Theorizing India's "Land Wars"', in *Politics & Society*, 41(3), pp. 351-94.

Lund, Ragnhild and Smita Mishra Panda, 2011, 'New Activism for Political Recognition', in *Gender, Technology and Development*, 15(1), pp. 75-99.

Musalaiah, Jadi, 2008, 'State, Civil Society and Draft National Tribal Policy:

A Critical Evaluation', in *Indian Journal of Public Administration*, vol. LIV, no. 4, pp. 811-22.

Rupavath, Ramdas, 2019, 'Tribal Alienation and Conflict in India: A Perspective from Below', in *Contemporary Voice of Dalit*, vol. 11(2), pp. 194-209.

Scott, James C., 1976, *The Moral Economy of the Peasant: Rebellion and Subsistence in Southeast Asia*, New Haven: Yale University Press.

——, 1985, *Weapons of the Weak: Everyday Forms of Peasant Resistance*, New Haven: Yale University Press.

Singh, K.S., 1997, 'The Emerging Tribal Scenario', in *India International Centre Quarterly*, vol. 24, no. 1, pp. 85-91.

Sinha, S.P., 1990, 'Tribal Leadership in Bihar: Genesis and Development', in S.P. Sinha (ed.), *Tribal Leadership in Bihar*, The Bihar Tribal Welfare Research Institute for the Government of Bihar, Welfare Department, Ranchi, pp. 71-187.

Yunus, M., 2010, 'Towards Creating a Poverty Free World', in U.R. Ananthamurthy (ed.), *Re-imagining India and other Essays*, New Delhi: Orient BlackSwan, pp. 44-64.

CHAPTER 1

Fight for Human Rights

Tribal Movements in Jharkhand

Tribal movements in Jharkhand have a deep root in the history of colonial oppression and subjugation. Chota Nagpur region in the former broader Bihar witnessed a series of tribal movements during the Gandhian era as well. This chapter records the story of tribal movements waged for the human rights issues and thus accounts for the narration and explanation of two great movements—Pathalgadi and Koel-Karo along with some other major and minor struggles, such as Nagri anti-land grabbing movement, Subarnarekha anti-dam movement, Badkagaon anti-mining movement, movement against Arcelor-Mittal, etc., going on for the violation of tribal rights over natural resources, especially minerals. Right to life and livelihood are inscribed in the Indian Constitution, but things which are inseparable from life and livelihood are under threat in the tribal regions holding colossal deposits of natural wealth. This is the reason why thoughtless and indiscriminate extraction of these resources should be reckoned as the violation of fundamental rights and fight against such attempts should be considered as a fight for human rights. Jharkhand, the land of the bushes and wilderness, is the best example of tribal movements of this kind.

British rule introduced many land settlement acts and revenue reforms in Chota Nagpur region, but could not buy peace. One of the examples of land tenure prevalent among the Mundas is known by the name of *khuntkatti.* According to this system, land belongs to the lineage, but the owners can extend to others the right to till. Since there was substantial land during the British rule and cultivation was usually extended in the forest areas, there was no objection to transfer the tribal lands to the newly arrived traders and moneylenders in

Chota Nagpur. Gradually, they registered the land in their names as private land and thus the tribals were robbed by the *dikus*. When the distress became acute, the tribals rose in rebellion. This led the British to take interest in the tribal land tenure systems and laws and customs prevalent among them (Bose 2019).

Two acts—the Chota Nagpur Tenancy Act (CNTA) in 1908 in response to the Munda *ulghulan* and the Santhal Parganas Tenancy Act (SPTA) in 1949—regulate and largely prohibit the transfer of tribal land to non-tribals and protect the community ownership. The Wilkinson's Rule (WR) 1837 for Ho and Kolhan areas was also one of those legislations made to prevent tribal land alienation. Adivasi displacement in Tatanagar took place during the colonial period. The Tata required land for iron ore mining and realized that the CNTA could hamper the land acquisition, mining and the construction of the Tata Steel Plant. Then Jamshedji Tata requested the British to not implement CNTA until Tata finished the land acquisition. The Act was implemented in 1908 before which the Tata got the required land (George and Bose 2013).

After India's independence many changes were added in the existing land laws including Chota Nagpur Tenancy Act, 1908. Other than development projects, land alienation is also occurring due to the land fragmentation following the increase in population. Under Chief Minister Raghubar Das's leadership, the Jharkhand assembly passed amendments to both acts in late 2016 to acquire tribal land for 'development projects', but widespread protests compelled the government to withdraw the bills (*EPW Engage* 2019). As a strategy to break the unity of the tribes, the Jharkhand Freedom of Religion Bill was introduced and passed in 2017. A few months later, an ordinance was passed introducing the amendment to the Right to Fair Compensation and Transparency in Land Acquisition, Rehabilitation and Settlement (Jharkhand Amendment) Bill, 2017. The ordinance has been awaiting assent of the Governor and President (Xaxa 2019).

With the advent of mining and industrial development the inmigration into the Chota Nagpur became a regular phenomenon. Mining in the Giridih colliery belt has been going on for more than hundred years now. First the Eastern Railway, then National Coal

Development Corporation and then Central Coalfields Ltd. took over the mining operation. Displaced people in the Giridih Open Cast project rehabilitation colonies in Premnagar and Gandhinagar are living in dire poverty. Coalfields in Giridih and Hazaribagh and mica mines in Kodarma helped to increase the flow of migration as well. With the acceleration of industrialization Manbhum and Singhbhum became the targets of exploitation of mineral resources. The outsiders crowded the region in search of work in the mining and industrial sectors as a result of which tribals were subjected to unbridled exploitation and humiliation. It led to the outbreak of a long series of unrest during the colonial era which later intensified during the postcolonial period (Bandyopadhyay 1999). The investment boom has become like a resource curse for the tribals as they are getting alienated from their community ownership of land and primary source of livelihood as well. Around 60 per cent of the large dams constructed for irrigation and hydro-power are situated in the tribal areas (Haldar and Abraham 2015).

The destruction of ecology that was started during the colonial rule aggravated during the postcolonial era of development. The period during 1960-1 is regarded as the inception of industrialization in Chota Nagpur region, when the mega project of Heavy Engineering Corporation started at Hatia near Ranchi. In the 1970s, a fierce conflict began between the adivasis and the forest department. According to Areeparampil, the main reasons of this conflict were: encroachment by the forest department on adivasi customary rights of forest, harassment of the adivasis by the forest department officials, commercialization of forest and destruction of forests by the contractors (Areeparampil 1992). Finally in 2001 the new Jharkhand government brought back the Joint Forest Management System. Jharkhand has abundance of natural wealth of mineral and forest resources because of which it has become one of the hotspots of development projects.

SUBARNAREKHA ANTI-DAM MOVEMENT

The anti-dam movement against Subarnarekha began with the commencement of the project. The Subarnarekha Multipurpose Project

TABLE 1.1: TOTAL LAND ACQUIRED FOR DEVELOPMENT SCHEMES IN JHARKHAND, 1951-95

Category of Project	*Private Land and % of the total land acquired*		*Common Land and % of the total land acquired*		*Forest Land and % of the total land acquired*		*Total Land and % of the project type land acquired*	
	Land Acquired	%	Land Acquired	%	Land Acquired	%	Land Acquired	%
Water Resources	364,646.00	71.7	94,808.00	18.7	48,498.00	9.6	507,952.00	34.0
Industries	98,525.59	56.1	63,768.68	36.3	13,435.91	7.6	175,730.18	11.7
Thermal Power	2,598.45	43.1	2,534.38	42.1	894.04	14.8	6,026.87	0.4
Mines	184,169.00	35.7	156,341.19	30.4	174,614.40	33.9	515,124.59	34.4
Defence Estd.	22,543.61	20.1	11,134.93	9.9	78,610.57	70.0	112,289.11	7.5
Misc. Schemes	152,000.65	85.0	8,941.21	5.0	17,882.43	10.0	178,824.29	12.0
Sub Total	824,483.30	55.1	337,528.39	22.6	333,935.35	22.3	1,495,947.04	100.0
Missing Schemes	27,550.00	55.1	11,300.00	22.6	11,150.00	22.3	50,000.00	
Grand total	852,033.30		348,828.39		345,085.35		1,545,947.04	

Source: Ekka, A. and M. Asif, 2000, *Development-induced Displacement in Rehabilitation in Jharkhand*, New Delhi: Indian Social Institute, pp. 110-11.

(SMP) was first broached in 1973. The estimated cost of the project initially was pegged at Rs. 129 crore, though later it escalated at Rs. 1,500 crore. The project included two big dams in Chandil and Icha, several small dams, three command area storage reservoirs, two barrages at Galudih and Ganjia and seven canals. The river basin was a repository of bauxite, iron, uranium and copper. The planning of the project gained ground in 1978 with the arrival of the World Bank funding in 1990. Although it was envisaged and promulgated that the principal aim of SMP was to ensure supply of water for irrigation of fertile lands in three states, i.e. Bihar, Odisha and West Bengal, a World Bank report revealed that the land was not fitted to canal irrigation. Therefore, the actual purpose of the project was to provide water to the industrial and municipal sector of Singhbhum, generate hydel power amounting to 400 megawatts and flood control. SMP thus followed the footstep of Roro Canal Irrigation Scheme located in Chaibasa which snatched away vast stretches of tribal lands leaving them destitute. The Hos of Singhbhum could not be convinced about the project as they were well aware of the requirements of the land they cultivated for generations. They knew that the project would submerge thousands of acres of farmland, homestead, forest and grazing land. Other than the irrigation purpose, SMP also acquired thousands of acres of such land for flood cushion at Chandil Dam area causing another blow of submergence. SMP gave birth to more than a lakh displaced, the majority of whom belonged to the Ho, Santhals, Mundas and Bhumij tribes, who have lived in Kolhan for time immemorial. They were uprooted from their Ho Dissum due to inundation and villages namely Ruani, Borabinda, Gopalpur, Kashipur, Harsundarpur, Keshavgaria and many more were shifted to other places. After being deprived and dispossessed, the tribals launched a resistance movement led by the Visthapit Mukti Vahini formed by the Chhatra Yuva Sangharsh Vahini in Chandil. On 25 March 1975 when the survey work began, the tribals blockaded Chandil block office with the demand of immediate stoppage of the SMP work, but the work continued as emergency was declared. The tribals wrote to the Prime Minister, but were soon asked to vacate. On 26 March 1978 they organized a rally which was joined by more than a lakh people followed by an indefinite hunger strike on 23 April.

The police invaded the tents, beat and apprehended the demonstrators. On the next day 8,000 tribals along with women and children assembled to protest against the police brutality, but the police ruthlessly opened fire on the unarmed masses killing four tribals. The tribal resistance got a huge support from Belipal Bhitamati Andolan, Koel-Karo Jan Sanghtana and Narmada Bachao Andolan as well (Chadha 1993).

Tribals also protested in Icha Ganga, but were suppressed by the inhuman police tortures. Shankar Sunde led the Icha Kharkai Bandh Visthapit Sangh in Icha. Gangaram Kalundia, an ex-army man helped mobilizing the tribals under Icha Kharkai Bandh Sangarsha Samiti to fight for their right to have a fair compensation, was killed in police custody on 4 April 1982. The police also gunned down two of the protesting students at Tinaldih. More or less 500 non-violent movements were organized by the local organizations in protest against the proposed dam. The tribals organized a demonstration at the dam site in order to put a halt to the work underway for the Icha dam on 5 April 1991 which displaced 30,000 people without any compensation. The deputy police commissioner arrived on 9 April with a huge force to move the demonstrators. When the tribals refused to budge the police started manhandling them along with the women and children. The police vandalized the camps erected for the dharna and then the protesters were taken to Seraikela police station (Singh et'al 1991). On 13 May 1991 a huge rally was held to protest against the arrest of Kumar Chandra Mardi and 450 tribals. After the procession, a meeting was held which was attended by a lot of grassroot organizations such as Narmada Bachao Andolan, Chatra Yuva Sangharsh Vahini, Bhartiya Jan Andolan, Visthapit Mukti Morcha, All Jharkhand Students Union, Kolhan Raksha Sangh, Lalmatia Bachao Andolan and Lok Jagrit Kendra. The tribals vowed to fight against SMP which favoured the big industries and consumerists at the cost of tribal people (Singh 1991).

The tribals again sat on fast from 2 to 11 July 1991 under the leadership of Visthapit Mukti Vahini and Icha Kharkai Bandh Visthapit Sangh and withdrew the fast only after getting a written assurance by the project authorities to fulfil their demands soon. The government under the pressure of the movement announced rehabilitation package, but many tribal villages were deliberately left out of the package coverage and rampant corruption foiled the purpose. The rehabilitation plan framed by the SMP failed miserably due to irregularities and dearth of proper estimating procedures. The tribals of Durri, Baksai and many other villages refused to take the scanty compensation amount offered by SMP, but were intimidated and forced to accept it by the project authority. Thousands of tribals were evicted without any compensation (Singh 1991). In a survey conducted in three tribal villages namely Burlung, Bamundi and Dum affected by the Chandil Dam it was found that the people were made victims of the complete submergence due to gross negligence, faulty survey and technical carelessness. The tribals felt that they were cheated as the amount and payment of compensation was insignificant with which they would not be able to buy cultivable land. Since the tribals did not have any legal titles of their lands, many of them have been denied any compensation so far. The amount which was forcefully imposed on the tribal families was abysmally low compared to the existing market value of the land because of which no displaced family could purchase even half of the land they owned before they were evicted (Upadhyay 1999).

With the introduction of neoliberal economy in the 1990s, the scale of displacement doubled rapidly when the Jharkhand government initiated the Jharkhand Vision 2010 and Jharkhand Industrial Policy. Despite the Scheduled Areas Regulation Act of 1969 the government indulged in rampant tribal land alienation, ensuring a speedy transfer of land to the multinationals at a lower price. As many as 66 MoUs were signed in last couple of years which gave 3,000 acres of land to Jindal Steel at Ghatshila and more than 25,000 acres to Tata Steel for Green Field Project at Manoharpur and Chandil in East Singhbhum (Ekka 2011). This displaced more than ten lakh people. There was going to be a massive land acquisition for the infrastructural development of the Greater Ranchi in the coming years.

Another source says that the government signed 102 MoUs for setting up steel plant, power plant, mines and other associated industries with an estimated investment of Rs. 4,67,240 crore. Tribals are continuously protesting against displacement. The villagers attacked

Kohinoor Steel Plant at Jamshedpur on 1 October 2008 against land acquisition without any compensation. Villagers also attacked the surveyors of Bhushan Steel in East Singhbhum on 11 September 2008. Jupiter Cement Factory workers were attacked by the local tribals on the same day at Kharsawan. Tata Steel was not allowed to acquire land for its Green Field Project by the villagers. People are fighting not only for their means of livelihood but also against environmental degradation, pollution of water bodies and public health related issues (*Update* 2010: 54-6).

ANTI-MINING MOVEMENT

Tribal land alienation in the wake of mining can be traced from the history of Jharia-Raniganj coalfield operation which eventually paved the way for cultural disaggregation and the assertion of tribal autonomy movement. Jharia happens to be India's single most productive coalfield without which railways and machine industries cannot function. The struggle of the workers in the coalfield was interlinked with the tribal solidarity movement in independent India which reinvigorated the demands of a separate autonomous Jharkhand state. The exploitation of coalfield started in Raniganj in 1814. The Jharia field had been surveyed in 1866 and 1887 but developed only after the East Indian Railway's (EIR) survey of 1890 and the track extensions of 1894-5. In six years, Jharia's output rose from 1,500 tons to 2 million tons, after which it became the most productive field in the country. Gradually coalmines became a site of ceaseless exposure to exploitation and intimidation. But the formation of unity among the resisters took a lot of time as the workforce was dominated by the *dehatis* or outsiders. The strike movement of the late 1930s and early 1940s achieved the recognition of a popular union called the Congress-led Chota Nagpur Mazdur Sangh. In 1946 Jharia witnessed 57 strikes involving nearly 66,000 workers with demands going beyond the issue of food supply to union recognition, reinstatement of discharged hands, wage increases and bonus payments. Police repression and arrests of frontline left-wing leaders disabled the movement. This led to the establishment of Indian National Trade Union Congress (INTUC) in 1948. During 1960s, the coalfield was disturbed by the ruffians called the Dhanbad mafias. A new union led by A.K. Roy was formed in 1969, called the Bihar Colliery Kamgar Union (BCKU), which exercised a strong influence in the region for over a decade. The growing demand for Jharkhand state was coupled with tribal grievances of land alienation and industrial hazards, which gave birth to Jharkhand Mukti Morcha (JMM) in 1972. The extremist phase came to an end in 1975 with the declaration of emergency.

In recent times, coalfields have been leased out to the private mining firms (Simeon 1999). The Jharkhand Minor Minerals Concession Rules were adopted in 2004. It gave special powers to the *gram sabha* in granting mining leases and prospecting licenses. Pachwara of Pakur district has a rich coal deposit which was granted to Pachwara Central Block to Panem Coal Mines in 2001. Panem Coal Mines is a joint venture between Punjab State Electricity Board and Eastern Minerals Trading Agency. The project displaced 9 villages, but their cash compensation was much less than what has been proposed by Coal India Rehabilitation Policy of 2000. The Santhals conveyed their grievances in the *gram sabha* meeting but none responded. The movement was led by the local tribes who were falsely booked under several criminal cases by the Panem Coal Mines. In a similar way East Parej Open Cast Coal Mines of Hazaribagh district is a World Bank supported project under Coal India by which East Parej and Duru Kasmar villages were evacuated and 227 families were dispossessed. The tribal leaders who were leading the movement against the project were implicated by false criminal cases. But the movement forced World Bank to review its policies by which it became evident that there were serious violations of its own policy. Movement against ESSAR and Dempo Goa escalated when tribals of Manoharpur of West Singhbhum came to know that the project would evict 7 villages in order to acquire 3,000 acres of land following which ESSAR withdrew the proposed steel plant (George 2014).

In 2011 Saranda forest division of West Singhbhum was designated as a Saranda Action Plan (SAP). In this forest region Rs. 250 crore plan sought to prepare a package of development and security. The MoEF sanctioned lease to Steel Authority of India Ltd. (SAIL) of Chiria, a public sector company, in February 2011 under the clause of 'national interest'. Saranda happens to be India's largest iron ore deposit site which is being exploited despite national-level Forest Advisory Council having recommended against it. SAIL's existing lease on the Gua iron ore reserves located in Saranda lapsed in June 2011 and was renewed in April 2012 (Sareen 2016). A recent report found that, 42 large-scale mining leases were in progress and a further 19 waiting for environmental clearance from the Forest Department in the Saranda forest division of West Singhbhum which has become mandatory for acquiring land for their projects (Shah Commission 2013).

Coal is a very important mineral wealth as far as the overall 'mining boom' of our country is concerned as it is one of the major mineral resources according to the Mine and Mineral Development and Regulation Act of 1957 (MMDR was amended first in 1988 and then in 2003). The Coal India Limited (CIL) symbolized 'public interest', and Acts such as the Coal Bearing Areas (Acquisition and Development) Act (CBAA) was enacted to dodge the protective legislation for adivasis. Undoubtedly, Jharkhand was abundant with coal deposits in pre-colonial era and continues to be a resource periphery in postcolonial India. Jharkhand accounts for 29 per cent of India's coal reserves and holds the largest number of collieries in the country, contributing 21 per cent of India's entire coal production in 2004-5 (Bhushan and Hazra 2008) which is why it is called the 'museum of mineral resources'.

Coal India started a whole series of mining in the Upper Karanpura Valley and the Upper Damodar Valley of which Piparwar and Ashoka were the most controversial as the authority was compelled to reduce the pace of work due to resistance from the local tribals. Land acquisition for mining led to a massive degradation of forest cover in the region and fertile lands were destroyed. Tribals were mobilized under the leadership of the Bharat Jan Andolan (BJA) in opposition to the mining. Maoist Communist Centre (MCC) also played an active part in organizing tribals against the mining-induced-displacement and subsequent land grabbing (Roy 2001).

Thirty-four companies were allocated captive coal mining blocks in 210 villages in the Karanpura Valley alone, between 2005 and 2009 (Lahiri-Dutt and Ahmad 2012). On 8 October 2005, Arcelor-Mittal Company, the world's highest global steel corporation, signed a MoU with the Jharkhand government for setting up a steel plant at an estimated investment of Rs 40,000 crore. The company started mining operation by 2012. The major project acquired 12,000 acres of land and got 1,500 megawatt power plant for consumption. The mega steel project and a power plant were situated in the Kamdara block in Gumla district and Rania, Torpa and Karra block in Khunti district. The central government leased out the Karampada iron ore mines situated in the Meghataburu Mauja reserve forest in West Singhbhum for the steel plant. The company was allocated the Seregarha coal block as well with an estimated reserve of 160 megatonne. The mega project is also using the water of Karo River. Though the company allotted Rs. 1,250 crore for rehabilitation package made for the displaced, the villagers could not be persuaded to give up their lands (Basu 2008). According to Srivastava, Arcelor Mittal required 25,000 acres of land and 20,000 units of water per hour for its steel plant and the township at Gumla and Khunti. The company offered to erect an Industrial Training Institute reserving 50 per cent seats for the tribal students, sponsored a hockey tournament joined hand with social service work done by the Church, but failed to allure the tribals who demanded food, not iron (Srivastava 2018).

During the survey, the government identified a total of 1,025 acres to meet Arcelor-Mittal's requirement of land. Much of this is communal land; at Torpa-Kamdara block of Gumla district, the communal land around 10 villages have been given to the company. The adivasis under the leadership of Adivasi Moolvasi Astitava Raksha Manch began an agitation against the industrialization in the area. AMARM said that this was a brazen violation of community rights vividly inscribed in Khatiyan Part II of CNTA. Dalit Vikas Sangathan (DVS) workers and Karanpura Bachao Sangharsh Samiti (KBSS) claimed that the police were stopping activists from demanding their rights (Lahiri-Dutt and Ahmad 2012).

Dayamani Barla, who led the movement against Arcelor-Mittal wrote a book called *Ek Inch Bhi Zameen Nahi Denge* (We will not part with an inch of our land), which became the bible of the movement. She was threatened for her strong stand. Tribals were mobilized by showing Barla's speeches and messages and some documentary films based on the tribal rights, such as *Ek aur Ulgulan, Kis ki Raksha, Loha Garam Hai*, etc. AMARM organized several demonstrations on 4, 7, 10 and 25 March and a rally on 29 May 2008. Tribals took *tangi* and brooms with them when the project authority called a meeting on 20 August. They, along with the tribal women, gathered and sloganeering their objection against mining and demanded their land rights (Basu 2008).

A very recent case is the land acquisition for coal mines in the Barkagaon block of Karanpura valley, Hazaribagh district by the National Thermal Power Corporation Ltd. (NTPC). The Barkagaon project was allocated coal mines in 2010. This is held to be one of the biggest coal blocks of the continent. In 2016 NTPC, out of the proposed 17,000 acres acquired nearly 2,500 acres of land from the department of forest and did not take prior permission and consent of the concerned *gram sabha.* It also cleared the rights of prospective beneficiaries as mentioned in the Forest Rights Act of 2006 without informing the *gram sabha.* 26 villages were first evacuated and later another 12 villages were displaced by the project. The government applied Section 17 of the Land Acquisition Act in case of Nico Jaiswal's Moitra Coal Mining Project in Barkagaon for acquiring land. Section 17 or better known as emergency provision gives special power to the state to occupy any land under the pretext of 'public purpose'. Eastern Mineral and Trading Agency held a public hearing in 2005 at Badam village in Barkagaon which was attended by 7,000 men and women carrying the banner of Karanpura Bachao Sangharsh Samiti. People started halting public hearings again and again (George 2014).

The local tribals objected to the way in which the entire process was carried out without their consent and opposed land acquisition of their cultivable lands without any compensation. The NTPC and district administration were held responsible for the misdeed. The tribals organized a procession in Chirudih village near Hazaribagh on 1 October 2016 when the police opened fire on the peaceful protesters causing death of the 4 people and 40 people were wounded (Sahu 2021). Though NTPC and other private companies offered compensation, the amount ranging between one to five lakhs per acre in Barkagaon the tribals were unwilling to take one-time cash compensation for a permanent loss. This has caused division among them (Lahiri-Dutt and Ahmad 2012).

The Union Coal Ministry allotted three coal blocks to NTPC in Jharkhand in October 2004 and they are Punkhri-Barwadih, Chatti-Bariatu and Keredari. The government is engaged in land acquisition under the Coal Bearing Area Acquisition and Development Act, 1957. Punkhri-Barwadih in Jharkhand is now resounding in resistance against land alienation for industrialization. NTPC and Coal India Limited in their joint venture started an opencast coalmine in 2007 through Punkhri-Barwadih project, the total cost of which stands as around Rs. 40,000 million. The project displaced 14,000 families by 2009. In November 2006, hundreds of thousands tribal peasants demolished NTPC's office at Barkagaon project site. The tribals organized themselves under the banner of the Karanpura Bisthapita Morcha (KBM) for further struggle which they knew was going to be long drawn as the government backed the project. The tribal lands which have been acquired till date are called Gair Mazurwa (GM) which means state is the owner of those lands but they are under the possession of tribals since a long time. On this pretext NTPC has denied the tribals their right of rehabilitation and compensation in spite of the fact that they have usufruct rights over these lands (Meher 2009).

Another case of forcible displacement and land acquisition took place between 2016 and 2018 when Adani Power Limited started acquiring land for its 1,600 megawatt power plant in the tribal villages of Godda in Santhal Paraganas. The tribals were denied their rightful rehabilitation and instead their resistance movement was brutally suppressed by deploying police force. Adani Power Limited acquired nearly 551 hectares. of land from 10 villages in two blocks of Godda a vast portion of which was common land, without consulting the concerned *gram sabha*. Tribals since then have been protesting against the unlawful land acquisition and the arbitrary method through which the procedure was going on (Sahu 2021).

Another glaring example of gross violation of existing acts is the Chitarpur Coal and Power possessed by the Abhijeet Group of Industries in Balumath block, Latehar district. The company purchased the land through fraudulent means and with the increasing protest the company has withheld the mining operation for the time being and offered some jobs which are unskilled in nature. It is reported that Chakra Opencast Mines project in Latehar is going to displace at least 12,000 people from five villages. The Abhijeet Group offered company shares at a fixed price, job to one family member and community development projects to the land givers. But tribals are suspicious about their intention (Lahiri-Dutt and Ahmad 2012). Adivasis are also protesting against Neelanchal Ispat in order to protect their customs of community ownership of land. On 25 July 2017 the entire state came to a halt following a strike called by the CPI (ML) against land grabbing. At least 21 organizations including the Moolnivasi Chhatra-Yuva Sanghatan, Adivasi Jan Parishad, Ulghulan Mahila Manch, Sarna Prarthana Sabha and the Nagdi-Chaura Zameen Bachao Morcha actively supported the strike. On 5 July 2018 witnessed another *bandh* against forcible land grabbing. In 1994 a non-violent tribal movement against Netarhat Field Firing Project managed to halt the land acquisition for more than two decades.

During fieldwork in Gumla, Latehar and Hazaribagh districts I interviewed few adivasis who said that there was no land survey conducted before the acquisition took place. Vishnu Murmu from Gumla vividly stated that,

> Neither the government nor the company authorities met the affected adivasis to discuss their hardships. In spite of having acts, they do not even bother to inform the gram sabhas before acquisition.

The last but not the least is the case of uranium mining industry introduced in Jaduguda, Bhatin, and Narwapahar in the late 1980s. The Turamdih Uranium Mine was commissioned in 2003, Banduhurang Mine was commissioned in 2007 and Mohuldih Uranium Mine of Seraikela Kharsawan was commissioned in 2012. The radiation of these uranium mines wreaked havoc on the tribal children who are dying due to its poisonous effects. Tribal workers of the mines are suffering from lung cancer. The untreated waste water from the mine is contaminating Subarnarekha and Kharkai rivers and affecting crops. Besides, areas like Jaitapur, Kudankulam where the nuclear power plants are being planned to be opened, the Department of Atomic Energy is aiming to acquire land from the local tribals. Banduhurang, Purihasa, Kerwadungri, Turamdih, Nandup, Mohuldih villages are going through a massive land acquisition process. The public hearing procedures have been kept crippled so that the villagers cannot raise their objection to the illegal land-grabbing. Tribals have mobilized themselves under the banner of Turamdih Vistapit Samiti. There have been rallies, dharnas and blockades organized by the Samiti but police repression, indiscriminate arrests, infliction of false cases, custodial violence and overall violation of human rights are breaking the backbone of the tribal movement in recent years. Jharkhand Krantikari Mazdoor Union (JKMU) was formed for the welfare of the tribals who are working in Uranium Corporation of India Limited (UCIL), but it has threatened to terminate labourers for joining the trade union. JKMU has organized road blockades and demonstrations leading to the reinstatement of workers. Growing dissatisfaction over land acquisition by UCIL for Turamdih mines the tribals came on the street in October 2010. Villagers blockaded the road due to which senior officials of UCIL and Jharkhand State Pollution Control Board (JSPCB) were forced to go back without attending the public hearing held by JSPCB which was mandatory for availing the no-objection certificate for expanding the company's mining capacity (George and Bose 2013).

MOVEMENT AGAINST LAND ACQUISITION

Land acquisition in Nagri is another case in point. The government occupied tribal land in Nagri in 2010 for setting up educational institutions. Nagri is situated 15 kilometres away from Ranchi consisting of more than 500 Oraon families. But a powerful coalition of tribal intellectuals and the regional politicians like Bandhu Tirkey, Salkhan Murmu and Shibu Soren supported the movement against the land-grabbing and forced the government to cancel the forceful acquisition of tribal land (Kumar 2015). Nagri is important due to the fact that the laws once enacted for the protection and safeguarding of the tribal land alienation were randomly violated and contorted by the state itself in order to grab 228 acres of cultivable lands from the poor tribals comprising 35 villages for building campus of IIM, Triple IIT and Law College (Srivastava 2018).

The tribal movement in Nagri village took place on 23 November 2011 against the provisions of 'public purpose' and 'eminent domain' popularized by the Land Acquisition Act. The government of Jharkhand declared the required land as 'eminent domain' which was owned by the tribals. But the government said that the land had been sold by the previous generation in 1957-8 under section [17] (4) 6 of the Land Acquisition Act. It was then decided to ask the tribals to hand over their land to the government for setting up the Birsa Agricultural University and Seed Bank. The tribal land was acquired for the construction of a National Law University as well. The tribals, on the other hand, claimed that, the government had already seized their lands under the aforementioned Section 17 of Land Acquisition Act of 1894 without paying any compensation so far. According to the emergency provision, the displaced have to be provided with a temporary residence and a minimum allowance on monthly basis, though it cannot be considered as a one-time compensation package that is meant to be given at the time of any type of dispossession. It was reported that, Rs. 155,147.88 was allotted as compensation but out of 153 tribal peasants 128 had rejected to take the compensation money amounting to Rs. 133,732 which went to the government treasury without even informing the affected and 25 peasants who took it. The tribals filed a case at the court demanding proper rehabilitation and compensation following several protests launched to restore tribal lands which were eventually transmuted under the carpet of 'public purpose'. The movement could not attract much media attention and gradually lapsed into the darkness of oblivion (Ranjan 2017).

Jameen Bachao Samanway Samiti (JBSS) launched a strong resistance movement against a sponge iron project (SIP) proposed to be set up by Sri Sai Sraddha Metallic Pvt. Ltd. in Kotgarh of West Singhbhum. JBSS was formed to protest against the land acquisition in Lampaisai village of Jaitia panchayat and also to challenge any issue of land-grabbing. When the officials of the Department of Mines and Geology visited the place for assessing the limestone deposit at Lampaisai, the villagers for the first time came to know about the project. They resisted following which the authority slapped a criminal case on the tribals at the local police station. Later a petition was filed against the company in 2010 which questioned the validity of land acquisition in an area which falls under Schedule V. The Ranchi High Court accepted the petition in 2014 in spite of which land acquisition is going on unabatedly (Kumar 2016).

TABLE 1.2: DISPLACEMENT CAUSED BY LAND ACQUISITION (AS DECLARED BY MINING COMPANIES)

Company	*Annual Capacity of Coal (in million tons/year)*	*Land Requirement (in hectares)*	*Estimated Displacement in EIA (Number of People/Families)*
Essar Power Jharkhand (Chakra Opencast)	4.5	900	211 families
Neelanchal Ispat Nigam	1.3	383	1,737
Chitarpur Coal and Power (Abhijeet Group)	0.68	1,378	149
Eastern Mineral Trading Agency	3	491	1,158
Nico Jaiswal	1	294	Not available

Source: Various EIA reports submitted by the companies to PCB and MoEF, Government of India, New Delhi.

KOEL-KARO MOVEMENT

One of the pertinent instances of anti-dam movement was Koel-Karo movement which went on for more than 30 years. The movement was not organized by any social activists or NGOs. It did not get any media attention or coverage either. This was the reason why the movement never had worldwide propaganda and thereby international support. Nevertheless, the movement has already left its mark as one of the successful movements that could stop a monstrous dam building on tribal lands which would be remembered forever. It has set a strong and powerful example of resistance against displacement. The movement has given indigeneity its appropriate space in the discourse of globalization by securing an exclusive participation of the local tribal communities without any outside support of the NGOs.

The Ministry of Environment and Forest of the Indian government directed the National Hydroelectric Power Corporation to prepare a well integrated rehabilitation plan for the tribals hitherto evicted by the Koel-Karo Project in what was Bihar (presently Jharkhand). Different newspapers of Patna wrote that, this was the final nail in the coffin of Koel-Karo. Koel-Karo was among those numerous anti-tribal projects most of which were either stalled or are moving at a slow pace due to ongoing movements. The displaced were not even given the economic compensation, let alone social or cultural rehabilitation.

The Koel-Karo Project was first initiated in 1955 during the Five-Year Plans. After that, Bihar State Electricity Board announced the project in 1973. It said, it would acquire 55,000 acres of land for producing 710 megawatt (later 732 MW) hydroelectric power by damming south Koel river and its tributary north Karo river (Madhukar 1992). For executing the plan two dams would be constructed, one in Basia of Gumla district with a height of about 44 metres and another in Tapkara of Ranchi district with a height of about 55 metres. Two reservoirs would be connected through an inter-basin channel with a length of 34.7 kilometres. As a result of this, two gigantic hydroelectric power centres would be erected in Ranchi and Singhbhum. Initially, the cost of the project was estimated at about 390.4 crore in 1981, but later the expenditure stood at 600 crore in 1986, 1,200 crore in 1990 and 1,338.8 crore in October 1991. It was reported that every day the cost was increasing at a rate of 25 lakhs for various reasons. But the electricity department got the necessary permission from the Public Investment Board and the finance committee of the cabinet also approved the increased budget.

It was said that, when the project work would be completed the tribals would definitely be benefited and tribal development would be expedited. Not only Bihar, but West Bengal, Odisha and Sikkim would also receive electricity. But needless to say the entire electricity was thought to be produced for the industrial sectors. So, the question arose, whose development they were talking about? Jharkhand is already producing 90 per cent electricity of the state of Bihar and 7 per cent of the country. A major share of the necessary coal for producing thermal power for the entire country comes from here. But unfortunately its benefits do not go to the people of Jharkhand. The ratio of electricity supply in the villages of Jharkhand is probably the lowest in the country.

Later it came to light that when the project would be completed both the dams together would submerge 115 villages in Ranchi, Gumla and Singhbhum. Fifty thousand tribals of 7,063 families would be displaced in Ranchi, Gumla and West Singhbhum (Ghosh 2001). According to Koel-Karo Jan Sangathan, the project would affect 256 villages comprising of 10,739 families. Meanwhile 37,600 people were ousted from 17,764 acres of land by the proposed project amongst whom 32,954 or 87.92 per cent were tribals. They would lose 50,000 acres of lands amongst which 25,000 to 30,000 were cultivable lands, 10,000 acres were forest lands, 300 acres were *sarna* lands or sacred groves and *sasandiri* or cremation grounds, 175 churches, 110 temples and 1,400 acres of barren lands. Another source claimed that, the project would affect 200 villages and 45,000 acres of cultivable lands would be submerged. The available data indicated that after the construction of the dams 1,50,000 to 2,00,000 people would lose their home, hearth and livelihood either directly or indirectly. Tribals had traditional and customary rights over these lands. According to the Bihar Sampurna Kranti Mancha, 85 to 90 per cent people who were jeopardized by the project were tribals. On the one hand they had to live in fear of losing their lands and on the other the denial of forest rights—mainly these two factors compelled the tribals to oppose the project. The irony of fate is that, when the Bihar State Electricity Board began Koel-Karo project in 1973, they promised that the local tribals would support it wholeheartedly when they would enjoy its benefits.

The project work was commenced by keeping the tribals totally in darkness. But when the government officials came to acquire land, tribals prevented them. They formed Jan Sanjojan Samiti to give their movement a formal and organized shape. The tribals of Keol area formed Jan Sangharsh Samiti. In 1976, both the organizations were merged and thus emerged Koel-Karo Jan Sangathan. This is to be remembered that the Sangathan was not against the project. Rather, the memorandum they submitted to the government in 1977 clearly mentioned that the tribals were ready to welcome the project. But for this the project authority must initiate welfare measures which means those who would give their lands must be compensated with land. Their only demand was 'land for land'. But the government did not agree with their demands.

Therefore, having no other alternative the tribals started 'stop work' campaign in 1977. After this, a tripartite meeting was called with the

Sangathan, project authority and the representatives of the state government. It was resolved that, in order to know the socio-economic condition of the evicted, a joint survey would be conducted. The survey was done in two or three villages and after a few days surprisingly the reports of the surveys went missing from the government offices. The Sangathan proposed a charter containing 16 points which dilated in detail the stories of distress and hardships of the displaced and a proper rehabilitation package was demanded. All social, economic and cultural resettlement measures were included in the charter. But the government lopsidedly pegged the compensation amount for the oustees without holding any discussion with the affected tribals. In 1983, the Sangathan asked the government to choose displaced people of at least two villages and rehabilitate them. But the government did not respond. In 1984, the Chief Minister of Bihar Chandra Shekhar Singh said, if the police had to fire bullets for acquiring land for the dams they would do that. He went on saying that, land acquisition act was not applicable in this case and no 'land for land' demands would be met. The displaced would be given only monetary compensation. In July the Bihar government deployed armed police for acquiring land and ordered to start the project work. This triggered vigorous tribal resistance. In face of the strong tribal opposition, especially tribal women, the government was bound to remove police force. After this incident, Chandra Shekhar Singh announced that, lands would not be grabbed at gunpoint. The project was suspended for the time being. In 1985, the Chief Minister again said that, after the general election he would resume the project work. In 1986, the government proposed to give land as compensation to 5,006 affected families. In 1989, another 2,000 families were included in the process of giving land as compensation. A proposal was passed to give 2 hectares land per head to the landowners and the landless tribal peasants got one hectare land as compensation of losing forest rights. The Supreme Court mandated that the tribals were to be given *khorkar* (the right to clear the wastelands in the village) and *khutkatti* (rights in the new lands).

The Oraon and Munda tribes were dubious about the intention of the government as they had been deprived a multiple times before. They knew that many tribals who had been evicted by different projects before, did not receive a single penny of compensation, for example, MP Saimon Marandi and his wife Sushila Hansda. In spite of being a member of Bihar Legislative Assembly, they were evicted due to the construction of Turai Dam of Sahebganj without any compensation. A few years ago National Hydroelectric Power Corporation promised jobs for the 6,000 oustees, but backed off by showing baseless excuses.

In 1989, the displaced tribals, after receiving no rehabilitation, filed a writ petition in the Supreme Court against the construction of the dams. In August the Court sent notice to the Bihar government and Justice P.N. Bhagwati said that, the Geneva Conference had made it clear that people cannot be displaced without alternative rehabilitation and resettlement package and India has consented. He suspended the project work until rehabilitation was given (Supreme Court of India, V.P. Lakra and Others Vs. Bihar Government and Others, 1989). This was probably the first remarkable judgement of the honourable Supreme Court that, apropos of the recognition of anti-dam movement and the right of rehabilitation of the displaced. At that time the rehabilitation package proposed by the government was pegged at 130 crore of which only five thousand rupees was proposed to be given to each displaced families. Needless to say it was not possible for a family to begin a new life with such a meagre compensation. After the Supreme Court judgement, the government decided to give 20,000 rupees per acre of the best quality land which was threefold higher than the earlier compensation declared in 1974. But the tribals said that, land was the only thing to them to recourse to. It was an integral part of their identity, and mere monetary compensation could neither be a good substitute for it not could it repay the loss. Moreover, for the tribals, loss of sacred places like *sarna* and *sasandiri* were no less important than cultivable lands which fell under the submergence level (Ghosh 2006).

In 1991, Visthapita Mukti Vahini, Koel-Karo Jan Sangathan, Samata Sangathan and all the Jharkhand students' unions took the plunge into the struggle for saving the tribal rights. On 10 November, Visthapita Mukti Vahini held a rally that started from Chandil and ended in Ranchi on 20 November after covering hundred kilometres on foot. After the rally, a public meeting was organized.

From government to politicians—everyone was flabbergasted by this incident, because they did not take the Supreme Court order as mandatory.

In the meantime, the tribals cut off the road going to Lohajimi. This was the place where the project work had proceeded slightly before the coming of the Supreme Court suspension order. Ordinary tribals under the leadership of tribal women, forced the police and paramilitary to leave Lohajimi way back in 1985. Government officials were also prohibited to enter Lohajimi. The deadlock continued until 1989. After that, the government announced a new rehabilitation package which proposed land and job for each and every displaced family and vocational training and loans for those who would be interested in earning independently. It was also promised that 30,000 acres of forest lands among the 90,000 acres of land in the river basin would be brought under the compensatory reforestation. For example, it was estimated that the Koel-Karo project needed 480 million cubic feet stone chips and stone bricks. The cooperative formed with the displaced people could be employed in the supply work of these raw materials. They had also required preliminary skills and experience of such work. If at least 50 per cent of the intended displaced people were employed in the work then they could be provided with a job or rehabilitation much before the physical eviction and they would not have to depend on anyone. The Koel-Karo Jan Sangathan refused to accede to this rehabilitation package as there was no provision of cultural compensation for the oustees.

Therefore, the ministry of environment instructed the project authority that they had to prepare the resettlement package again following the model of Sardar Sarovar package implemented by the Gujarat government. They also said that, they had to take environmental clearance again before commencing the project work. The authority was afraid that there would be an extra burden of around Rs. 900 crore for offering such a resettlement package which was possibly unbearable for them. They were even clueless from where they would adjust the increasing expenses of the budget as the government had already intimated that no foreign investment would be allowed and they had to arrange the money for the project from within the country. Later on when the government began to augment the price of the electricity, the project authority was impelled to cut short the production from 710 megawatt to 580 megawatt. Besides, the enthusiasm of the workers was at the lowest ebb. An official lamented that, there were more or less 200 workers along with a chief engineer and a general manager working in the Koel-Karo project. But the growing protest and unabated demonstrations had damaged their enterprise and capability. Gradually the National Hydroelectric Power Corporation lost interest in implementing the project.

It was still believed to be one of the lucrative projects of the country. When in October 1991 the financial committee of the Cabinet announced a new budget for the Koel-Karo project, a new chapter of the twenty-year long battle against dam construction began. This time Jharkhand Mukti Morcha took over the leadership from Jan Sangathan. The MP of Jharkhand Mukti Morcha Saimon Marandi said that, dam construction might not be stopped, but people would not let the project work begin until they were given proper rehabilitation. So, it was quite clear that all political parties like Jharkhand Mukti Morcha, Congress, The Left and Janata Party believed that dam would invariably be constructed. Now the struggle was for rehabilitation.

The project work commenced again in 1995. On 5 July the Prime Minister P.V. Narasimha Rao was invited at the dam area to attend the foundation stone laying ceremony, when the news came 75,000 tribals had assembled in an empty field from the previous night in order to convey their protest against the dam. Finally, the authority bowed down to the unbending tribal tenacity and put the Prime Minister's visit on hold. But Chief Minister Lalu Prasad Yadav insisted that he would inaugurate the project on that very day. Later he was desisted under the pressure of the movement. On the one hand there was the Supreme Court verdict and on the other tribal movement – both contributed to the stopping of land acquisition process for the Koel-Karo project and ensured tribal victory. The movement inspired and influenced many other movements like Sardar Sarovar. It gave a new ray of hope to the displaced people of other projects that in the battle against capitalism and globalization they will get justice in the end.

But the struggle had to cross perhaps even an unexpected long way. In 1985, the villagers built a small gate or barricade in Derang village on the *kutcha* road stretching from Tapkara to Lohajimi. Its distance from Tapkara was about 7 km. The road was not built on government land, but of the villagers. The gate was built with the *sal* wood. The reason for the erection of the gate was not to prevent outsiders enter the village, rather to slow down by force the pace of the vehicles coming from outside or stop them so that the villagers could get some time to enquire who these outsiders were, what their motives to come to the village were and where they intended to go. In 1995, when the government renewed the project work, Jan Sangathan declared a *janata* curfew here and erected many such gates across the dam area. Since the outsiders like the project authority never intimated and informed the local tribals anything about the project, the villagers invented this small but dignified method to know the aim of the visitors who wished to enter their villages. The construction of the gate was fully democratic in nature, as neither the state nor the corporate powers ever respected the rights of the tribals or considered it important to inform them about their intention. The researchers who visited these villages have accepted that the tribals never prevented them. They never even stopped the police or project authorities. It happened many times that they did not even ask anything and let them enter. Despite the fact, the gate was a symbol of their demands of dignity, information and democratic rights. This was not an ordinary check post, but a sign of tribal resistance.

On 15 November 2000, Bihar was bifurcated and Jharkhand was created. Though the state was created with the tribal populated districts under the leadership of Bharatiya Janata Party and its first Chief Minister was a tribal, most of the ministers were non-tribals. After coming to power, the government cleared the way for big multinational corporate capital. Since Jharkhand is a highly mineral rich state, mining industries became the first target of the corporate capital. Within a span of merely two weeks on 28 November the government promulgated that land acquisition process would begin soon for Koel-Karo project. At the centre the NDA government was planning to amend the provision of the Fifth Schedule inscribed in the Indian Constitution according to which tribal lands are to be protected from private and corporate greed. There was a time when Chota Nagpur

Tenancy Act was born out of the Birsa Munda *ulghulan* and interestingly the place where Lohajimi dam of Koel-Karo project was being constructed was the birthplace of the *ulghulan*. The tradition of the Munda *ulghulan* motivated the tribals to stand by the displaced in their struggle against displacement and destruction. Another thing was that, it was the tribal deprivation which helped Maoists to grow in Jharkhand. The Maoists championed the tribal cause which gave them a strong foothold in the tribal inhabited districts of Jharkhand. It has been recorded that somewhere between US$ 25 and US$ 750 million is extorted annually by the Maoists from the mining companies in Jharkhand alone. The political response came on 30 January 2010 which allowed Operation Green Hunt into Jharkhand. Sendra was formed by Sunil Mahto, a JMM member of parliament from Jamshedpur as a counter-insurgency measure (Miklian 2014). Both the centre and state governments were determined to douse the flames of anger by deploying paramilitary and had no goodwill to search for a solution of the problem. Places where contractors, landlords, moneylenders, dishonest traders were grabbing tribal lands Maoist organizations like MCC and PWG were more active. But surprisingly the presence of Maoists in Tapkara was negligible. The villagers very consciously kept their movement outside the influence of the Maoists, the Police started entering Derang-Lohajimi on the pretext of looking for the Maoists. In October 2000, Tapkara police outpost built two circular bunkers for secret firing. These bunkers played a very important role in the mass *harakiri* of 2 February (Ghosh 2001).

An investigation report published on 3 March narrated the entire story of the genocide which took place on 2 February 2001 and its aftermath. Sarada Gopalan who was a representative of a Bhopal-based organization called Eklavya, Professor Kaushik Ghosh of Centre for Studies in Social Sciences of Kolkata and an activist of anti-dam movement in Ranchi named Meghnad talked to the representatives of Koel-Karo Jan Sangathan and ordinary villagers and prepared a fact finding report. They all went to ground zero just on the very next day of the mass killing, inspected and collected information about the entire episode. We may describe the incident based on the report below:

On 22 December 2000 the *daroga* of Tapkara police station named R.N. Singh crossed the Derang gate and entered Lohajimi village with a big force of constables. First they wanted to know whether any MCC cadres had entered the village. But the villagers said that it was impossible for them to identify who was a Maoist. Then police said, MCC bear guns by which they could be easily identified. But the villagers responded by saying that they had never seen anyone entering the village with a gun except the police. Then the police left for the time being. There were many complaints against the *daroga.* Tribals said that whenever the tribals went to the Tapkara weekly market for selling woods, he used to snatch away the wood from them.

On 1 February 2001 the *darogas* of Tapkara and Rania police stations brought with them 20-25 armed police in two jeeps, crossed the Derang gate and entered Lohajimi again on the pretext of looking for MCC activists (Bhatia 2001). They parked their cars and walked along the bridge over the Karo river and then entered Jiling Sereng surrounded by hills through the forest. They spent one hour there and then collected wood for fuel and came out. On the way back to the police station they suddenly demolished the gate and loaded their jeeps with the *sal* wood with which the gate was built by the tribals. Within a trice the emblem of tribal dignity, information and democratic right was dismantled. A local ex-army man watched them doing this injustice. He went to the Tapkara police station and asked the *daroga* why he had done this. But instead of giving any explanation the *daroga* ordered the *Bihari* constables to beat him black and blue because the tribal constables refused to beat him. They brutally struck his head with the butt of their guns. Those who came forward to save him were also beaten. The entire event took place between 3.30 and 4 p.m. in the evening.

After the incident, representatives of different villages sat together because the gate was built in 1984-5 and it was really very important for the tribals. It was decided that, on the next day at around 8 to 8.30 a.m. in the morning the tribals would assemble in the Shahid Chawk. On 2 February morning a big crowd started gathering in front of the police station. The tribal women sat at the front row. More or less 4,000 unarmed tribals gathered at the *thana.* It was decided that, they would first want to know why the police demolished the gate. If their answer remained unsatisfactory then they would submit their demands in writing. When the police declined to hold discussion with the tribals, they started writing their memorandum comprised of four clauses. These were: one, the *darogas* of Tapkara and Rania police stations had to be dismissed; two, the ex-army man who was tortured by them had to be compensated with Rs. 50,000; three, the area was a tribal area, tribal people or people who know Munda language and culture had to be employed in the police force in Tapkara and Rania which meant tribals should rule tribals; and four, police had to rebuild the gate with its own money with full respect and dignity. The tribals then handed over the memorandum to the DSP of the Khunti police station. But he said that, he had no power to remove the *daroga.* So, he accepted the memorandum and promised to forward it to the higher authority. Then he left. But the tribals could not be placated. They refused to budge. They decided to go to the MP of Torpa named Koche Munda as he happened to be a public representative and most importantly Torpa was also among the affected zones of Koel-Karo project.

The frontline representatives of the Koel-Karo Jan Sangathan took Koche Munda with them to the police station and demanded the removal of the *daroga.* After returning to the village when they started confabulating with the tribals, suddenly the police came from the police station saying, 'we have got the order, kill them'. It was 3.30 p.m. in the evening. The police came out of the *thana* and started to lathicharge the innocent non-violent unarmed tribals. Within few minutes sound of firing came out of those bunkers. At first it seemed that police might have fired empty shells, but actually they fired indiscriminately on about four to five thousand tribals mostly Mundas with rifles and stain guns without even giving them any prior warning to move. There were many women and children in the crowd of the demonstrators. The tribals got really angry and started pelting stones. Then the police fired tear gas shells. Wounded people were writhing and screaming out of agony before the police station, but none were allowed to come forward to rescue them. When the crowd was scrambling a five-month pregnant women fell down on the ground and got injured badly. She was senseless for next two days. The police began to smash the head of the wounded tribals with their boots ruthlessly. After stopping firing they arrested 12 people from different villages and beat them mercilessly; one among them was a Munda. They were released the next day. In the dark of the night police loaded their jeeps with the dead bodies and fled from that place. Those who were languishing in pain remained untreated and went through agonizing torture.

Five were dead on the spot amongst whom three were class X students. Later another three people succumbed to injury. So, the total casualty remained 8. Thirty-five tribals were seriously injured amongst whom five became crippled for life. For the time being the wounded were treated in the village. The next morning they were taken to the Ranchi hospital by a public bus. One of them died on the way to the hospital. All belonged to the Munda tribe except a Muslim resident from Tapkara. All were aged below 40 except two; one was a class IV student and the other was studying at class IX. There were no records of how many people were actually injured and many went missing. According to the police, they were forced to fire 136 rounds of bullets because the enraged crowds were pelting bricks and stones at them. They furnished evidence of a vandalized *thana*, four burnt jeeps in support of their claim and also said that 25 policemen were injured during the clashes (Ghosh 2001). *Ranchi Express* reported on 3 February that police had claimed that the *daroga* of Tapkara police station was severely injured as well. After two days, the police claimed that tribals killed a policeman and set his body on fire. They also stated that the tribals were instigated and backed by the Maoists and the timber mafias. They even accused Koche Munda. Police lodged an FIR against four thousand innocent tribals implicating them in a false case of murdering a constable and burning down a jeep. But the tribals who gathered at the police station also lodged an FIR where they mentioned that Jan Sangathan had no connection with the Maoists and it was the police who looted timber. They also reiterated in the interviews that, the police themselves vandalized the *thana* and set their jeeps on fire so that it could be shown as proof against the tribals and put the blame on them. It was a completely peaceful gathering, yet the police barbarously fired about 150 rounds of bullets on them at a stretch without any provocation.

This incident showed once again the apathy of the state, people's organizations and human rights organizations about the tribal question. The brutal killing was conducted just to disassemble and dismantle the protesting tribals. Tribals had lost their lives to the state earlier too, but in independent India such an unfortunate event happened probably for the first time where a non-violent, peaceful and democratic tribal movement going on for three decades was trampled with bullets and boots. The police aggression in actuality was an expression of the disregard and indifference of the state and the authoritative society towards the marginalized tribals which tactfully keeps the distance intact.

After this grievous incident the villagers buried the dead bodies in the Shahid Chawk. On 2 March 1946 during the Jharkhand Movement, police gunned down five Munda tribals in this very place which is how the place got its name. Notwithstanding the brutal killing, the tribals were determined to not leave the democratic path of the movement and decided to continue the movement peacefully. This has always been the strength and tradition of the tribal movement. The movement was about justice for both the martyred and the wounded. Koel-Karo Jan Sangathan was unperturbed regarding their demands. These were:

- The *daroga* had to be cashiered.
- The government had to give Rs. 15 lakh per family of the dead and Rs. 10 lakh per family of the injured people as compensation.
- At least one member of the families of the dead had to be provided with a job.
- The local police station had to recruit local tribals or people who know tribal language and culture.
- Koel-Karo project had to be repealed immediately.

The Babulal Marandi government of Jharkhand did nothing to provide justice to the deceasad. The Kolkata edition of *The Statesman* published the status of the government on 4 February. It stated, the commissioner of home affairs Mrs. Sushma Singh said that, the Sangathan activists had attacked the Tapkara police station again. But the situation was under control. She refused to reveal the names of the dead and behaved in a way as if the police firing was not an important issue. According to her, in order to disassemble the crowd police fired only nine rounds of tear gas. She said that the police was searching for the Maoists and it was the villagers who caused the trouble. Police lodged two FIRs against the tribals amongst which one was against the general secretary and other 2,000 unknown people of the Sangathan and the other was against the Koel-Karo Jan Sangathan itself.

The year 2002 was rather good for the movement. In January, the National Hydroelectric Power Corporation conveyed that they wanted to withdraw the project because land acquisition was not possible. The department of land acquisition informed that, they did not dare to go to the tribal areas and no officials were willing to visit those regions (Kumar 2002). So, the responsibility of land acquisition remained with the National Hydroelectric Power Corporation. But the tribals said that, since their fight included women and children as well there was no scope or place for violence. Therefore, the tribals who were struggling non-violently for 28 years cannot be held responsible for denying access to the officials. These kinds of excuses were baseless and ridiculous. Anyways, first in 2003 the then Chief Minister of Jharkhand Arjun Munda cancelled the project and then again in 2005 the government announced that it did not want to proceed with the Koel-Karo project. The decision was sent for the official approval in 2010, but no gazette notification stating the annulment of the project was published on the part of the government up till 2012. The leaders of the movement knew very well that the government would come back with a renewed energy after a brief hiatus. The state hoped and aimed at making the new generation ignorant about the traditional values and attracted them towards the consumerism so that they could be stopped from joining the movement.

The leadership had vowed not to let that happen. That was why they had formed vocational groups with the students, children, women and aged through which the story of their movement could be disseminated and could leave a deep and lasting imprint on the collective consciousness and conscience of the youths. To remember the significant episodes of the movement they included them into the everyday living and marked the festival calendars or yearly calendars with them. They were spreading the stories through oral narratives and histories so that they could never be deleted from their memories. The backbone of the Koel-Karo movement was the question of livelihood of the tribals. They wanted to have their means of survival within their own traditional domain which was their fundamental right.

The Koel-Karo tribal movement contributed to a great extent in implementing the National Policy for Resettlement and Rehabilitation. Whenever the project authorities tried to enter Lohajimi, they faced strong and united resistance of the displaced tribals. The project not only wasted a huge amount of money, but also it failed to achieve its goals. After three decades, the government could not manage time to know how the tribals of Lohajimi were doing today. Every year on 1-3 February the tribals of Tapkara gathered at the Shahid Bedi and paid homage to the martyrs of the movement. Anti-dam movements are not new. They happened earlier, are happening today and will happen tomorrow. But Koel-Karo was completely different from all of them because the movement came out as a successful protest against the domination of state and corporate capital. The tribals saved hundreds of thousand villagers from the threats of submergence and gave them hope to live with dignity.

PATHALGADI MOVEMENT

The Pathalgadi movement is political, ethnic and ecological in nature and questioned the notion of the political rhetoric of development in Jharkhand. It has challenged not only the current model of governance but also asserted tribal identity by proposing an alternative of a powerful *gram sabha* as a village agency at the grass root level. The tribal resistance has gained a momentum in recent years as they have started articulating their indigeneity and consciousness in such a manner that could link themselves with the nature and landscape currently under threat of the so-called state-led development paradigm. The Pathalgadi movement in this neo-colonial era is a lesson that revives the memory of the tribal movement during colonial era which claims their authority over their own territory. The movement has fostered the subnational consciousness among the tribals in the country. The Pathalgadi movement in Jharkhand is strong among the Munda and the Ho tribals, who are of Kolarian origin.

Pathalgadi means erecting stones on a dead person's tomb or just to mark any memorable occasion and is a well-known custom of the tribals. Adivasis inscribe messages on these big stones which are called Pathalgadi locally. They are coloured green and measure about 15 ft. by 4 ft. and the messages are written in white, evidently to denote their close relationship with their environment. Mundas use *sasandiri* which was the indigenous term for describing this custom. These stone slabs are erected by the *gram sabhas* of the villages, which purport, on the one hand, to assume powers by drawing legitimacy from the constitutional provisions. On the other hand, they draw on the customary practice of *parha* panchayat (traditional panchayats of the tribals of Chota Nagpur) to assign more power to the *mankis* (head of *parha*) and the *mundas* (head of the village) (Roy 1912: 117-21). British exploitation of the past was the central theme of the movement, by which the tribals demanded a complete ban on the free passage of the *dikus* and making *gram sabhas* the chief authority (Sen 2018: 81). This has led to the revival of the native system of village governance and the notion of the golden past where there was no displacement, no poverty (The traditional system of self-governance is called the *patti* system among the Mundas, the *parha* system among the Oraons, the *manjhi parganait* system among the Santhals, the *munda manki* system among the Hos and the *doklo sohor maha samiti* among the Kharias). The tribals of Jharkhand are in a great crisis as the influx of outsiders is increasing at an alarming rate. Besides, the *gram sabhas* have never been consulted before any acquisition of land in spite of having clear provisions in Jharkhand Panchayati Raj Act (JPRA), 2001, amended in 2010 as well as PESA in this regard. Pathalgadi movement is aimed to strengthen the role of the *gram sabhas* through PESA (*Hindustan* 25 February 2018).

In February 2017, the government of Jharkhand organized a summit in Ranchi for the global investors called 'Momentum Jharkhand'. A lot of MoUs were signed to make the state one of the richest hubs of mining and industrial investments. Companies like Usha Martin Group, RSB Group, Tata Steel Growth Shop (TGS) and others showed interest (*The Times of India* 2017, *Daily Pioneer* 2017). The government declared that it would form a 'land bank' in which a thousand acres of non-cultivable land would be included for the development programmes (*Indian Express* 2018). This was the background of the Pathalgadi movement. After the declaration made by the chief minister tribals got really afraid of being displaced by the development projects. On 9 March 2017 a stone slab was constructed at the frontier of a small village called Bhandra in Khunti district of Jharkhand. (*Hindustan* 8 March 2018). Initially, the Khunti district of Jharkhand was the stronghold of the movement which later spread to neighbouring districts of Latehar and Singhbhum, and the areas of Jashpur in Chhattisgarh (*Dainik Bhaskar* 6 March 2018). The movement first came in the news when on 21 February 2018, 25 policemen were detained by the villagers of Kanki in Khunti district for entering their locality without prior intimation to the *gram sabha* and apprehending the *gram pradhan*. Since then, arrest of leaders of the movement and *gram pradhans* has resulted in *gherao* of police stations, stopping armed policemen for questioning, for trespassing in their area and holding policemen hostage for releasing persons arrested on the charges of Pathalgadi which has become a regular feature. On 23 May 2018, villagers of Baruhatu of Khunti held an anti-landmine vehicle and eight policemen hostage in return for the release of Durga Munda who was associated with the Pathalgadi movement (*Dainik Bhaskar* 24 May 2018).

Several villages of the district—Kanki, Kochang, Jilinga, Udburu and others—erected stone slabs inscribed with the order given by the *gram sabha* for implementing constitutional provisions, such as Article 13(3)(a), Article 19(5)(6), Article 244(1) part(b) Para (5) (1) of the Fifth Schedule. Significantly, the slab set down a similar order by the *gram sabha* foisting curtailment on the coming of outsiders which included police, government officials, medical staff and strangers. This way, the traditional cultural practice of 'Pathalgadi' was employed with political motives, first, drawing legal measures inscribed in the Constitution and second, on its facade declaring their landscape as an independent area (Singh 2019: 28-33).

According to Virginius Xaxa, in spite of the fact that the Pathalgadi movement was tagged as 'anti-national' and 'Maoist' by the state government and mainstream media, it brings to the fore long-standing issues of adivasi land alienation. People who sympathized with and supported the movement were booked under false cases of sedition along with the villagers. A lot of people were arrested. Some were released later on bail while others are still rotting behind the bars. The Pathalgadis have very justifiably claimed that the movement is constitutional (Xaxa 2019: 10-12). The movement is trying to promote indigenous model of education, open indigenous banks, reject the state authority and has conveyed its solidarity with other adivasi movements in the other parts of our country. The schools that they have started for the poor adivasi children are operated by the *gram sabhas* and teach how to resist state oppression (*Dainik Bhaskar* 10 March 2018).

The Jharkhand government considered the movement as a mere law and order problem and arrested the leaders without any provocation. Leaders like Krishna Hansda, Vijay Kujur, Jyoti Lal Besera, and Shaktapado Hansda were booked under secession laws. The government was quite clueless as to what the movement was. Different versions were coming out on their part; sometimes the government said that the movement was to acquire the economic benefit of the opium cultivation in Khunti district by the leaders of the movement, sometimes it blamed the Christian missionaries for inciting the tribals against Hindus (*Dainik Bhaskar* 10 April 2018) and sometimes that there was an attempt to create a separate state with East Singhbhum, West Singhbhum and Seraikela Kharsawan districts under the camouflage of Pathalgadi movement (*Hindustan* 25 May 2018).

The Pathalgadi movement received a huge response from the tribals of Jharkhand. They used to attend all the meetings addressed by the leaders of Tribal Mahasabha with their traditional weapons like bows and arrows. The turnout was really appreciable because as many as five thousand tribals, including a large number of tribal women, were found attending the rallies. On 3 April 2018, the Governor of Jharkhand, called a special meeting of the *gram pradhans, manki munda* and *parha rajas* and felicitated them all to placate the movement (*Hindustan* 3-4 April 2018). Tribal organizations such as Desh Pargana Mahal and Tribal Mahasabha (*Dainik Bhaskar* 25 February 2018) are currently working towards raising awareness of the tribals about their autonomy and complete control over their own landscape called *abua disum, abua raj* (our village, our governance). The movement has spread over Chhattisgarh and Odisha.

Tribal resistance to the neo-colonial development projects has lately acquired a new dimension. Their movement has affirmed their right to exercise control over land and other natural resources. This is called the right to earth. Right to earth is not only a shallow defence of indigenous right to land but is a defining factor to develop a local mode of management of land according to the local people's requirement. The movement is also against the existing inequalities and oppression. They have even attracted international attention, like POSCO, Kashipur and Vedanta movement. Therefore, a new internationalism is coming to the fore and strengthening global cooperation among people's movements. NGOs have often played a crucial role in depoliticizing the protest movements of the tribals which can be defined as a neo-colonialism from below. For example, Action Aid and its offshoots called Action Aid Asia on the one hand played an active part in the tribal movement against Vedanta, but on the other received donations from Vedanta's parent company Sterlite. Action Aid India also has a tie-up with ICICI Bank which is a major investor in Vedanta (Kak 2010: 30-4). After getting stripped of their possession, the tribals are forced to move in search of livelihood to some unknown destination. After moving to the new cities they found themselves in a completely distressing situation. They somehow manage to work as unskilled labourers and the transformation from a free peasant to an unorganized worker is no doubt painful and traumatic. Finally, the development makes the rich richer and the poor poorer. The tribals, the poorest of the poor, are taken just as collateral damage along with the climate.

REFERENCES

Agarwal, P.K., 2010, *Naxalism: Causes and Cure*, New Delhi: Manas Publications, pp. 151-2.

Areeparampil, M., 1992, 'Forest Andolan in Singhbhum', in S. Narayan (ed.), *Jharkhand Movement: Origin and Evolution*, Delhi: Inter India.

Asif, Mohammed, 2000, 'Why Displaced Persons Reject Project Resettlement Colonies', in *Economic and Political Weekly*, vol. 35, no. 24, pp. 2005-8.

Bandyopadhyay, Madhumita, 1999, 'Demographic Consequences of Non-tribal Incursion in Chota Nagpur Region during Colonial Period (1850-1950)', in *Social Change*, vol. 29, nos. 3 & 4, pp. 10-46.

Basu, Moushumi, 2008, 'Arcelor-Mittal in Jharkhand', in *Economic and Political Weekly,* vol. 43, no. 48, pp. 22-3.

Bharti, Indu, 1991, 'Bihar's Dams, Tribals' Woes', in *Economic and Political Weekly* , vol. 26, no. 22/23, pp. 1385-8.

Bhatia, Bela, 2001, 'Resistance and Repression', in *Frontline*, 3-16 March.

Bhushan, Chandra, Anumita Roychowdhury, Koshy Cherail, Anjani Khanna and Madhukar, 1992, 'Koel Karo Battles On', in *Down to Earth*, New Delhi, 15 June.

Bhushan, Chandra and Monali Zeya Hazra, 2008, 'Mining in the Sates: Jharkhand and West Bengal' in *Rich Lands, Poor People: Is 'Sustainable' Mining Possible? State of India's Environment: Sixth Citizens' Report*, New Delhi: Centre for Science and Environment, p. 159.

Bose, Nirmal Kumar, 2019, *Tribal Life in India*, New Delhi: National Book Trust India, pp. 39-41.

Central Water Commission (CWC), 1996, Status of Projects Monitored by the Central Water Commission 1993-4, CWC, New Delhi.

Chanda, Ashish, 1993, 'Subarnarekha Project: Singhbhum's Sorrow', in *Economic and Political Weekly*, vol. 28, no. 41, pp. 2194-6.

Corbridge, S., 2002, 'The Continuing Struggle for India's Jharkhand: Democracy, Decentralization and the Politics of Names and Numbers', in *Commonwealth and Comparative Politics*, 40: 3, pp. 55-71.

Daily Pioneer, 5 October 2017.

Dainik Bhaskar, 2018, Ranchi.

D'Monte, Darryl, 1984, 'A Dam Too Far', in *Economic and Political Weekly*, vol. 19, no. 47, pp. 1986-7.

Ekka, Alex, 2011, *A Status of Adivasis/Indigenous Peoples Land Series-4, Jharkhand*, Delhi: Aakar Books, pp. 65-6.

EPW Engage, 14 October 2019, 'Jal, Jangal aur Jameen: the Pathalgadi Movement and Adivasi Rights', downloaded from https://www.epw.in/engage/article/pathalgadi-movement-nation-autonomy-rights-adivasi-jharkhand on 9 November 2021.

George, Ajitha S., 2014, *A Status of Adivasis/Indigenous Peoples Mining Series-2, Jharkhand*, Delhi: Aakar.

George, P.T. and Tarun Kanti Bose, 2013, *A Paradise Lost Tribes of Jharkhand Fight against Uranium Mining: A Report on the Impacts of New Uranium Mines in Jharkhand*, pp. 1-32, available at https://www.academia.edu/10140481/A_PARADISE_LOST_TRIBES_OF_JHARKHAND_

FIGHT_AGAINST_URANIUM_MINING downloaded on 5 Nevember 2019

Ghosh, Kaushik, 2006, 'Between Global Flows and Local Dams: Indigenousness, Locality, and the Transnational Sphere in Jharkhand, India', in *Cultural Anthropology*, vol. 21, no. 4, pp. 501-34

Ghosh, Kaushik, Sarada Balagopalan, and Meghnath, 2001, 'Massacres of Adivasis: A Preliminary Report', in *Economic and Political Weekly*, pp. 717-21.

Government of Bihar, 1986, 'Rehabilitation Plan for Displaced and Affected Families of Koel-Karo Hydro-Electric Project', mimeo, Department of Energy, Directorate of Rehabilitation and Land Acquisition.

Haldar, Tanushree and Vinoj Abraham, 2015, 'Development, Displacement and Labour Market Marginalization: The Case of Jharkhand Tribal Population', in *Social Change*, 45(1), pp. 45-66.

Hindustan, 2018, Ranchi.

Indian Express, 7 April 2018.

Kak, Sanjay, 2010, 'The Bauxite Mountains of Orissa', in *Economic and Political Weekly*, vol. XLV, no. 38, pp. 30-4.

Kumar, Navika, 2002, 'NHPC Gets Ready to Pull Plug on Koel Karo', in *Indian Express*, 31 March.

Kumar, Sujit, 2015, 'Changing Equations of Jharkhand Adivasi Politics', in *Economic and Political Weekly*, vol. 50, no. 23, pp. 15-16

——, 2015, 'People's Response to Land Dispossession: Comparative Analysis of Movements Across India', in V.B. Ganguly (ed.), *Land Rights in India: Policies, Movements and Challenges*, New Delhi: Routledge, pp. 215-29.

——, 2016, 'Revisiting Anti-dispossession Resistance Movements', in *Seminar*, 682, 43-7.

——, 2018, 'Adivasis and the State Politics in Jharkhand', in *Studies in Indian Politics*, 6(1), pp. 103-16.

Lahiri-Dutt, Kuntala Radhika Krishnan and Nesar Ahmad, 2012, 'Land Acquisition and Dispossession: Private Coal Companies in Jharkhand', in *Economic and Political Weekly*, vol. 47, no. 6, pp. 39-45.

Meher, Rajkishor, 2009, 'Globalization, Displacement and the Livelihood Issues of Tribal and Agriculture Dependent Poor People: The Case of Mineral-based Industries in India', in *Journal of Developing Societies*, vol. 25, no. 4, pp. 457-80.

Miklian, Jason T., 2014, 'Mining, Displacement and Conflict in Maoist India', unpublished PhD thesis, Department of International Environment and Development Studies, Norwegian University of Life Sciences.

Ministry of Home Affairs, 1985, 'A Report of the Committee on Rehabilitation of Displaced Tribals due to Development Projects', mimeo, Government of India, New Delhi.

PUCL, September 2003, 'Pachwara Coal Mining Project', in *Enquiry Report,* Dumka, Jharkhand Unit.

Ranjan, Rahul, 2017, 'Unraveling the Narratives of Adivasi Dispossession: A Case Study of Land Acquisition in Nagri Village, Jharkhand', in *Development,* 60, pp. 227-34.

Roy, Prodipto, 2001, 'Degradation due to Mining: The Piparwar Case Study and Problems of Estimating Costs of Degradation', in *Social Change,* vol. 31, nos. 1&2, March-June, pp. 144-55.

Roy, S.C., 1912, *The Mundas and their Country.* Calcutta: Kuntaline Press. pp. 117-21.

Sahu, Geetanjoy, 2020, 'Implementation of the Scheduled Tribes and Other Traditional Forest Dwellers (Recognition of Rights) Act 2006 in Jharkhand: Problems and Challenges', in *Journal of Land and Rural Studies,* 9(1), pp. 158-77.

Sareen, Siddharth, 2016, 'Seeing Development as Security: Constructing Top-Down Authority and Inequitable Access in Jharkhand', in *South Asia Multidisciplinary Academic Journal,* 13, pp. 1-16.

Savyasaachi, 2012, 'Struggles for Adivasi Livelihoods: Reclaiming the Foundational Value of Work', in *Economic and Political Weekly,* vol. 47, no. 31, pp. 27-31.

Sen, Asoka Kumar, 2018, *Indigeneity, Landscape and History: Adivasi Self Fashioning in India,* New York: Routledge. p. 81.

Sengupta, Nirmal, 1980, 'Class and Tribe in Jharkhand', in *Economic and Political Weekly,* vol. 15, no. 14, pp. 664-71.

Shah Commission, 2013, *First Report on Illegal Mining of Iron and Manganese Ores in the State of Jharkhand,* vol. IV, Ministry of Mines, New Delhi, Government of India.

Simeon, Dilip, 1999, 'Work and Resistance in the Jharia Coalfield', in *Contribution to Indian Sociology (N.S.),* vol. 33, nos. 1&2, pp. 43-75.

Singh, Anjana, 2019, 'Many Faces of the Pathalgadi Movement in Jharkhand', in *Economic and Political Weekly.* vol. LIV, no. 11, pp. 28-33.

Singh, Kavaljit, Anil Singh, Shankar Sundi, Ghanshyam, Arvind Kumar, Ranjan Palit, Vashudha Joshi, Anil Prakash, J. John, Avadesh Kumar, Arjun Kumar and Balram, 1991, 'Police Action against Dam Oustees', in *Economic and Political Weekly,* vol. 26, no. 21, p. 1306.

Singh, Kavaljit, 1991, 'Tribals Protest against Subarnarekha Dam', in *Economic and Political Weekly,* vol. 26, nos. 22/23, p. 1362.

——, 1991, 'Oustees of Chandil Dam', in *Economic and Political Weekly*, vol. 26, no. 30, p. 1770.

Sinha, B.K., 1996, 'Draft National Policy for Rehabilitation: Objectives and Principles', in *Economic and Political Weekly*, vol. 31, no. 24, pp. 1453-60.

——, 2016, 'Irrelevance of Land Reforms Policies to the Tribals of Jharkahnd', in K.B. Saxena and G. Haragopal (eds.), *Marginalization, Development and Resistance*, vol. II, New Delhi: Aakar, pp. 245-75.

Srivastava, Arun, 2018, 'Adivasis of Jharkhand on War Path to Protect their Identity', in *Mainstream*, vol. LVI, no 32, downloaded from https://www.mainstreamweekly.net/article8119.html on 23 January 2020.

The Chota Nagpur Tenancy (Amendment) Act 1938 (Bihar Act 2 of 1938), Bihar Legislative Department, Superintendent, Government Printing, Bihar, 1938.

The Times of India, Kolkata, 5 June 2007.

The Times of India, 19 May 2017.

Update Series 18, 2010, *Adivasi in India*, Kolkata: Update Publications.

Upadhyay, V., 1999, 'Impact of Subarnarekha Multipurpose Project on Three Singhbhum Villages', in *Social Change*, vol. 29, nos. 3&4, pp. 233-43.

Xaxa, Virginius, 2019, 'Is the Pathalgadi Movement in Tribal Areas Anti-constitutional?' in *Economic and Political Weekly*, vol. LIV, no. 1, pp. 10-12.

CHAPTER 2

Fight against the Mugging of the Multinationals and National Corporates

Tribal Movements in Odisha

> . . . several of the mining companies involved in the most controversial Indian projects are based in London or other foreign cities, and all the projects are facilitated by a background situation dominated by financial imperatives which derive from World Bank-orchestrated loans, and policies designed by the DFID (Department For International Development of the British Government). In every country, the World Bank and financially dominant foreign governments play a similar role controlling or manipulating policy and facilitating the entry of multi-national corporations 'behind the scenes'. (Padel 2015)

Odisha has been the breeding ground of tribal movements since the colonial period. Kondh unrest was one of the glaring examples violently suppressed by the colonial administration. Postcolonial Odisha is also cradling various tribal movements in different parts of the state ranging from Kashipur to Kalinganagar to Jagatsinghpur to Kalahandi to Narayanpatna to Sundergarh to Gopalpur (Tata 1995-2000) against mega projects, particularly those based on FDI. With the liberalization of Indian economy in 1991 a new era of neo-colonial loot began which drained our natural wealth for its own development and instead ushered a new era of multinational mugging of indigenous people who are already suffering from hunger and poverty. The state has been advertized and touted as the best destination for investment and the collateral expenses like displacement, ecological degradation and human migration in course of this internal colonialism are taken for granted. MNCs and Indian corporates are taking away the country's biggest minerals like iron ore, coal, bauxite, manganese, dolomite, and the like, causing exhaustion of the treasure troves which will cost the country heavy in the near future. The phrase 'sustainable mining' came into use in 1999, when the world's ten largest mining companies met to launch 'Mining, Minerals and Sustainable Development Project' (MMSD, part of their Global Mining Initiative), to evaluate how the mining industry could help bring sustainable development (Evans 2002).

Modern mining in Odisha began way back in 1909 when excavation of coal first took place in Rampur of Ib valley. TISCO searched for iron ore in Gorumohisani of Mayurbhanj, manganese in Goriajhar of Gangpur in 1910, dolomite and limestone in Panposh and Bisra in 1914 respectively and chromite in Baula in 1942 (Patra 2014: 30-1). During 1980s the Kalinganagar area was designated as

TABLE 2.1: MINERAL RESERVES IN ODISHA AND INDIA, 2002-3

(*in million tonnes*)

Name of the Mineral/Ore	*Reserves in Odisha*	*Reserves in India*	*Per cent of Indian Reserve*
Iron ore	3,567	13,460	26.50
Chromite	183	186	98.39
Coal	51,571	2,11,594	24.37
Bauxite	1,733	2,462	70.39
Lime stone	1,032	75,679	1.36
Dolomite	434	4,387	9.89
Fire clay	108	518	20.85
China clay	157	986	15.92
Nickel ore	175	184	95.11
Vandaiferous magnetite	2.5	11.5	21.74
Manganese	50	167	29.94
Mineral sand	82	266	32.33
Graphite	2.0	4.58	43.38
Pyrophylite	8.6	9.9	86.87
Lead ore	1.8	176	1.02
Talc-Soap stone	0.1	213.7	0.05

Source: Directorate of Geology, Orissa, Bhubaneswar, cited in *Orissa Economic Survey*, 2003-4.

'destination industry' to create a steel city in the public sector. Bauxite mining began at Panchpatmali in Koraput in 1984. In 1984 the demarcation of land started for this purpose without consulting the local inhabitants. After that a corporate unit was set up as Industrial Development Corporation of Odisha (IDCO) for which an estimated 30,000 acres of land was acquired from 1991 to 1995 out of which 13,000 acres of land was *patta* land that means the owner of these lands were eligible for the compensation. The government compensated, though not at market rates, only to those tribals who had legal documents of ownership of their land, which was very few no doubt, and those who could not show any proof were denied compensation. In 1997 the government converted the area into a private sector industrial city where a bunch of companies emerged. Out of the total 327 mines, 284 are under private sector and 43 mines are under public sector. Most of the public sector companies are owned by the Odisha Mining Corporation or OMC (Patra 2014: 32-3).

THE COMPANY RAJ

Rush for aluminium has become like a madness which requires a colossal amount of bauxite available copiously in Odisha. In modern warfare aluminium is regarded as a strategic metal. First world nations like the USA, Europe and Japan have a scarce deposit of bauxite which is the mother ore of aluminium. This is the reason for which Odisha's bauxite has attracted so much attention of the MNCs across the world. Starting with Rourkela Steel Plant in 1959 as the country's first public sector integrated steel mill, Odisha saw a new dawn of steel industry which only precipitated the quandary. When the country's economy was liberalized and it welcomed foreign investments, MNCs and Indian corporates became frenzied to have control the bauxite resources for their steel plants which would bring them a huge profit. For example, HINDALCO, POSCO, UAIL, TISCO, Alcan (Canada), BHP Billiton (UK), Rio Tinto (UK) and VAL/Sterlite—all are competing for the bid to plunder the rich bauxite reserves of the state which is 51 per cent of the country's entire bauxite deposit. POSCO is the first major transnational steel corporation which included India in its global strategy. The steel ministry of India set a target to produce 100 million tonnes by 2020 and all the giant steel firms like Steel Authority of India Ltd., Tata Steel, Rashtriya Ispat Nigam Ltd. and Jindal group have plans for further expansion (Anonymous 2005).

Rio Tinto is currently involved in iron-ore mines in Keonjhar. Rio Tinto Zinc has been engaged in experimenting a joint venture with Steel Authority of India Ltd, with unlawful and unrecorded mines abutting to the PS mines. Panchapatmali deposit in Koraput district is under National Aluminium Company (NALCO); Maliparbat deposit has been granted to Hindustan Aluminium Company (HINDALCO). OMC has tied up with HIDALCO's sister company Aditya Aluminium for Kodingamali in Sambalpur (Reddy 2013); however, HINDALCO got clearance to build a refinery at Kansariguda and also planned to apply for the clearance for mining Kodingamali deposit. During 1970s an extensive survey was conducted of the bauxite mountains (Rao and Rama 1979) which resulted in the construction of a new aluminium company in 1980, NALCO which established an extensive mine on top of Panchpatmali in Koraput, a refinery nearby at Damanjodi, powered and watered by the Upper Kolab Dam which displaced an estimated 3,000 and 14,000 people respectively, mostly tribals and its smelter at Angul linked by a new railway through the south Odisha mountains (Koraput-Rayagada). NALCO and BALCO are a Public Sector Undertaking (PSU), which makes a large profit for the State (Jojo 2002).

Panchpatmali was Odisha's first bauxite mine. The refinery displaced about 3,000 people from 19 villages. Amlabadi is the model rehabilitation colony located at a distance of 7 km. from Damanjodi. NALCO acquired about 10,058 acres of land that caused displacement of 15 villages with about 597 families out of which 440 families were resettled. Every displaced family was given about Rs. 3,000 per acre, one *pucca* house, and one low-paid job per family, but no land. The Amlabadi colony had only three wells for around 500 families, no school, no drainage system, etc. Villages like Kutudi, Jaliamba, Gadati and others are facing acute water contamination problems as natural streams like Pop Jala, Parua Jala, Bagmani Jala and many others have dried up (Patra 2014). Many displaced families did not receive any compensation from NALCO. In Damanjodi and Amlabadi, pollution level is very high. At the Lanjigarh refinery the dust pollution causes severe respiratory problems for the workers. Besides, highly toxic chemicals discharged by the Lanjigarh refinery have contaminated Vamsadhara and Nagavali rivers due to which local people have developed skin and lung diseases. The Bheden river near the Burkhamunda smelter in Jharsuguda is also contaminated with fluoride causing a long term damage of the surrounding ecology. New tarmac roads funded by Prime Minister's fund were built during 2006-9 in Niyamgiri under the supervision of Dongria Kondh Development Agency which is being used by the timber mafias who are destroying the forested mountain.

The major dams taken up in scheduled areas include the Machkund of Koraput (1954, 51 per cent of the displaced were tribals), Salandi of Keonjhar, Balimela of Malkangiri (1,113 tribal families were affected), Upper Kolab of Koraput, Indravati of Kalahandi, Mahindra of Sundergarh, etc. Upper Kolab Dam was constructed during 1977-87 and was completed in 1992. It displaced about 14,000 people between 1984 and 1990 from more than 60 villages. Among 3,171 displaced families 528 were resettled whereas 2,643 accepted cash money as compensation. Balimela hydro-power project displaced about 60,000 people during 1960s. Hindustan Aeronautics Ltd. (HAL) set up a MiG fighter plane factory at Sunabeda in 1966. It forcefully and suddenly displaced 468 tribal families of Chikapur village in 1968 which shocked the displaced as they were denied any compensation. It has been reported that less than a third of the 3,764 hectare land acquired for the plant has been used till date (Dias 2012). The tribals later resettled themselves in the same place from where they were again evicted by the Upper Kolab Dam Project in 1987. Lower Suktel Dam in Bolangir gave birth to a movement spearheaded by the Lower Suktel Budianchal Sangram Parishad in 2005 (Padel and Das 2010).

Starting with the Rourkela Steel Plant it can be said that before industrialization the tribals of Sundergarh were living a sustainable life. But with the introduction of mining and the commercialization of forest they lost their traditional subsistence economy. The project led to the acquisition of 13,185.31 hectares of land and displaced 23,400 people, of whom 11,300 (48.29 per cent) were tribals. Among the displaced only 4,607 (19.6 per cent) people were provided with jobs, whereas the rest were forced to depend on either agriculture in the resettlement colony or as wage labour. Due to unrestricted industrialization and high prevalence of pollution caused by industries like iron and steel, cement, refractory, engineering and chemicals, Sundergarh faces serious ecological problems in recent times. People of Modem India Labour Colony are exposed to toxic gases like benzene, anthracite vapour, carbon monoxide, iron oxide, etc., which are discharged occasionally from the coke ovens and the by-products plants located nearby. In Sundergarh it has been found that pollution-related diseases like tuberculosis and respiratory diseases, dysentery and malaria are on the rise. Tribals who were resettled in the colony are forced to live as squatters and are worst hit by the air pollution caused by the giant steel plant. The entire industrial belt of Sambalpur, Jharsuguda, Sundargarh, Keonjhar, Jajpur and Angul is getting highly contaminated bit by bit. The income insecurity has added more miseries to the existing hazards like social disarticulation and breaking up of tribal community life (Meher 2003).

Odisha government came up with an idea of establishing an extensive industrial complex in Duburi, Dangadi and Sukinda of Jajpur which is endowed with abundant mineral resources in the early 1990s where both iron ore and chromite are available copiously. Aiming at this, the government signed a series of MoUs with more or less ten units covering an area of 13,000 hectares. The complex includes about 13 mineral-based industries like iron and steel, stainless steel, sponge iron and ferrochrome, etc. The giant private corporates like Tatas, Visa Steel, Jindal, MESCO, Neelachal Ispat Nigam and others have already grabbed the opportunity and are about to finish work. Neelanchal Ispat alone displaced 639 families, of which only 53 have been given employment in the company. The MESCO plant displaced 87 families and only five got jobs, whereas Visa displaced 430 families and only 42 have been given employment (Shankaran 2009). Very few of the displaced (25 of the 183 families got a job) are living in a resettlement colony at Gobarghati put up at Mirigachara. The displaced who were not offered jobs have to walk 15 kms. every day to the stone crushers at Rs. 40 per day. Jindal caused dislocation of about 50-60 families, whereas Rohit of 12 families. A corridor connecting the plants uprooted 28 families (Pradhan 2006). The Odisha government granted mining lease and provided land to these companies for speedy accomplishment of their individual ventures. The Aditya Aluminium Project has also aimed at mining 3 Million Ton Per Annum (MTPA) bauxite at Kodingamali in Koraput and to establish 1 MTPA aluminum refinery at the Kansariguda village of Kashipur in Rayagada. Besides, the company has put forward a plan to set up 5 × 130 megawatt captive power plants and 260,000 TPA aluminium smelter plants at Lapanga in Sambalpur. All the families of Kansariguda village, two other villages of Rayagada and four villages of Koraput were dispossessed of their fertile lands in the wake of land acquisition. The tribals formed Sukinda Upatyaka Adivasi-Harijan Ekta and Suraksha Parishad in 1995 in Kalinganagar which was later renamed as Bisthapan Birodhi Jana Manch (BBJM) in order to vent their dissent against involuntary dislocation (Meher 2009).

Vedanta Alumina Limited (VAL) of Mumbai is the Indian subsidiary of London listed Vedanta Resources Plc. Vedanta (formerly Sesa Goa/Sterlite) proposed to mine bauxite from the Niyamgiri hill range, set up a refinery at Lanjigarh jointly with OMC and another bauxite mining at Karlapet. Initially the cost of the project was pegged at Rs. 4,000 crore. The major shareholders in VAL are Barclays, Deutsche Bank and ABN Amro. For Lanjigarh deposit approval for mining lease has been granted in favour of OMC on 5 October 2004. VAL proposed to set up an Alumina Complex that includes a 1 MTPA refinery plant, 3 MTPA of bauxite mining and a 75 megawatt captive power plant at Lanjigarh. The Government of Odisha offered 660.749 hectares of forest land for 240 bauxite mining and its refineries at the foot-hills of the mountains on 28 February 2005. Nearly 102 families were fully uprooted and 1,220 were affected by the project (PAPs) who are mostly the Dongria Kondhs. Three thousand acres of land has been acquired till date. Kondh villages like Jaganathpur, Borobhota, Kinari, Kothduar, Sindhabahali have been wiped out completely and tribals were forced to move out by February 2004. The process of land acquisition went on unabated after that (Pattnaik 2013). Vedanta planned a fresh smelter at Burkhamunda in Jharsuguda and Korba in Chhattisgarh in 2005. The Jharsuguda unit aimed at a production output of 0.9-1 million tonnes whereas the Korba unit's contribution increased from 0.5 to 0.6 million tonnes (*The Statesman* 30 June 2016).

The project was granted SEZ status on 9 May 2007 which means it was given heavy subsidies on land, water, transport and electricity. There are 35 major mining projects to set up steel plants worth over 25 billion dollars which also include Australian BHP-Billiton. Mitsui, the Japanese conglomerate, which through an Indian subsidiary of it already owns mining concessions, has plans for further investments worth 3 billion dollars in Odisha (Devraj 2005). The twelve villages of Lanjigarh which were affected due to land acquisition were: Bundel, Borbhata, Kothadwar, Bandhaguda, Sindbahali, Basantpada, Jagannathpur, Kinari, Kappaguda, Belamba, Boringpadar and Turiguda. Private land of 391 hectares and 628 hectares of common village land were acquired for it (Rout and Patnaik 2018).

It has been reported that Odisha has gotten investment worth Rs. 4,00,000 crore in mineral sector alone. De Beers, the South African diamond company, received the right to explore over 8,500 square kilometres in Odisha (CSE 2008). According to Odisha's Human Development Report, the ratio of poverty in north and south Odisha (districts like Koraput, Malkangiri, Sundergarh, Keonjhar) increased between 1993-4 and 1999-2000. Seventy-five per cent of the poor in Odisha are living in these areas. Keonjhar, which ranked 30 in the list of most backward districts of the country and where mining projects are most predominant, has 62 per cent of its population living below the poverty line, whereas Koraput, which ranked 10 in the list of most backward districts of the country and where bauxite is being extracted at the highest amount, 79 per cent people live below the poverty line and both the districts are tribal dominated constituting 50 to 80 per cent of the entire population. The report says, the northwestern districts (Sundargarh, Keonjhar, and Mayurbhanj) account for 35.3 per cent of Odisha's tribal population and the southwestern districts (Koraput, Kalahandi, Phulbani, and Balangir) account for another 39.4 per cent. The currents of modernization have consciously avoided and marginalized them. It has affected their means of livelihood and alienated them from the mainstream development causing a serious social problem (Human Development Report 2004).

Bauxite mining and aluminium production by the MNCs has transformed the peaceful tribal landscape of Kalahandi-Bolangir-Koraput (KBK) belt of Odisha into a disturbed and tumultuous region since 1990s. The region is gifted with one-third of the country's rich deposit of bauxite. Kashipur and Thuamul-Rampur blocks are home of about a thousand intermittent streams and sizeable forest coverage. The region is also the home of several hills like Bapla Mali, Panchpatmali, Kodingamali, Gandhamardhan Mountain, Niyamgiri Mountain and rivers like Vamsadhara, Baitarani, Mahanadi, Indravati, Kolab and many more. Odisha also has a rich copper deposit for which many foreign companies are competing. In 1993, the then prime minister Narasimha Rao undertook several measures to make KBK a hub of development and within two years launched the Long Term Action Plan for KBK with an investment of Rs. 6,251 crore. But the funds were siphoned off by the corrupt officials and politicians and the tribals remained as underdeveloped and backward as they were (Update 2010). A subservient or compliant state has been conniving actively in order to facilitate the transfer of resources from the tribal territory to the 'great' global and national behemoths in the capitalist wens.

Moreover, rampant violation of environmental norms by the mining companies has been recorded time and again, for example, MoEF has declared the Baitarani River a polluted river. The CSE report has revealed that based on the current steel project of Odisha government, it would need at least 527 million cubic metres of fresh water annually that could be drawn from Baitarani, apart from tapping Mahanadi and Brahmani (CSE 2008). The expansion of Rungta iron and bauxite mines in Sundergarh has altered the flow of six perennial springs and affected the water catchment area of Baitarani. There are altogether 186 mines functioning over an area of 47,338.5 hectares. People were also affected due to the construction of a dam on Salandi river which is one of the biggest tributaries of Baitarani (Pattanaik 2012). The coal mining activities in Chendipada block of Angul also contributed to it. Brahmani is also contaminated by the emission of effluents from iron ore mines of Sundergarh. Ten billion litres of groundwater is taken for Talcher coalfield every year because of which the Talcher-Angul industrial belt is considered today as a living desert.

Graphite and quartz mines of Nuapada are causing damages to forest cover at an alarming rate. Iron ore mines located at Koida block of Sundergarh and Joda and Banspal blocks of Keonjhar are functioning without obtaining necessary environmental clearances. In Joda the forest area has reduced by 50 per cent and in Keonjhar Sadar 70 per cent. Talabira Coal Mines of M/s INDAL Company at Sambalpur is also causing indiscriminate deforestation as the authorities cleared Khinda and Lapanga Gramya forests. The industrial overburden aggravated the problem further. The Barsua and Kolta iron ore mines and allied activities have devastated the wildlife corridors and forest ranges in the Bonai Hills of Sundergarh. The Hadgarh Wildlife Sanctuary has got affected by the Boula Chromite mines as well (Patra 2014).

The government of Odisha has recently announced its 'Odisha Industrial Development Plan: Vision 2025' by which it is supporting speedy expansion of industrialization. For this reason the state has designated four regions as industrial investment clusters and they are: Kalinganagar (Manufacturing Zone), Paradip (Petroleum, Chemicals and Petrochemicals Investment Region), Dhamra (Port-based Manufacturing Zone) and Bhubaneswar (Information Technology Investment Region) (Sahoo and Jojo 2020). Kalinganagar Industrial Complex includes Tata, Maharashtra Seamless, Uttam Galva, Orion, Mittal, Star Light Iron, Rohit, Dinabandhu and others. The total capacity of all is estimated to be around 12 million metric tonnes per annum. IDCO has acquired about 13,000 acres of land till 2013 of which 6,900 acres are private land and the rest is state-owned land. Tribals have been cultivating the state land for generations without any legal titles (Patra 2014). The state has also designed a land bank from the acquired land for the rapid growth of industries. This indicates that the policy of the state government endorses land acquisition in the forested belt, voluntarily or involuntarily, in order to implement its plan further.

The state government is also offering huge subsidies in form of tax concessions and guarantees to the transnational companies and big corporate houses. For example, Odisha government has given POSCO (Pohang Steel Company, a Korean giant) SEZ status, iron ore at a discounted market rate which Brazil and China did not agree, a steady supply of water and other infrastructural facilities. POSCO proposed to set up a 12 million tonnes capacity steel plant at Paradip Port in June 2005 which affected one lakh people of 22 villages in the Ersama block of Jagatsinghpur directly or indirectly (Dash and Samal 2008). POSCO threatened to displace 22,000 people from 3,700 families in 11 villages. The project received environmental clearance in August 2007. Currently, Odisha has a deposit of about 50 billion tonnes of iron ore of which 600 million tonnes have been secured by POSCO for the next thirty years. It produces about 28 million tonnes of steel per annum and by 2006 the other steel factories of Odisha are planning to add another 12 million to the annual supply for the consumption of the world. The state government has also allocated 1,132 acres of land to them for facilitating the process (Kapoor and Chana 2010). Mining would have also affected the Khandadhara waterfall which provides water both for drinking and irrigation. The proposed port to be built at Jatadhari also evoked concerns for coast-line damages and the nesting habitat of the endangered turtle olive ridley (Asher 2006).

Steel is regarded as a decontrolled item which does not figure in the essential commodity list. The Indian government is virtually giving precious iron almost free of cost to the MNCs and making the citizens pay international price for the finished product. It is interesting to note that because of the concealed externalized costs and secret pricing, the companies accumulate a lot of profit, but the state in exchange get a very little share of it especially when the actual costs of production are calculated. For example, NALCO's royalty or tax paid to the government of Odisha reveals that since all the ingredients like bauxite, coal, hydropower, limestone, labour, are available locally it cuts short the expenses to a large extent which does not reflect in their payment of royalty or tax to the state government as it is much lesser than what it should be. Many people are surprised to know that NALCO has not yet been privatized. There was a great pressure against exporting the production of NALCO and to keep it within India. Needless to say, the benefit never trickles down to the affected people (Padel and Das 2010) and would never get translated into development of that area. The same is also true for POSCO as the state bestowed largesse at the expense of public welfare violating Section

13 (1) (d) (i) and (iii) of the Prevention of Corruption Act and Article 39 (b) and (c) of the Constitution. In spite of that, both the centre and the state governments are giving clearance for mining on an effective royalty of mere three per cent which hardly covers the cost to the national treasury for incurring the loss of damages they cause. The Supreme Court has directed that if the state wants it can prevent and take over the country's mineral wealth under Section 17 of the Mines and Minerals (Development and Regulation) Act, 1957 (MMDR Act) and can also override the rights of MNCs under Section 11 (Rajappa 2011). Thus the government has been empowered to not sell the country's highly rich non-renewable mineral resources worth billions of dollars to the foreign MNCs and national corporates who export them to Australia, Brazil, China, Japan, Korea and Switzerland, unless it wants to deplete its reserves.

The World Bank, Asian Development Bank and many G7 countries are backing these companies by providing loans and aided projects which are facilitating the mugging of the multinationals, transnational and other corporate companies. There are also Orissa Water Resource Consolidated Projects supported by the World Bank like Badanala Irrigation Project (BIP), Baghua Irrigation Project (BIP), Harabhangi Irrigation Project (HIP) and Rengali Irrigation Project (RIP) which have caused massive displacement of tribal people. This is depriving the social sector spending which could increase the per capita income and living standards of its half fed tribal people. The anti-poverty programmes have been pushed to the back seat and the profit is fleeing outside the country which in a way is causing resource crunch on one hand and economic crisis in the long run on the other. For example, the Rengali Dam Project, started in 1973 and completed in 1991, alone displaced approximately 11,289 families (around 46,570 people) from 263 villages (Government of Orissa 2000) and inundated around 99,717 acres of land. It was decided that the reclamation cost would be paid as compensation to the oustees, but what was paid did not match the actual valuation of their lost assets and other compensatory measures under the resettlement and rehabilitation policy was too low leaving the displaced languishing in poverty and insecurity (Sahoo and Jojo 2020). The Indravati dam project which displaced about 40,000 people was funded by loans incurred from the World Bank during 1980s and 1990s, 80 per cent of whom were tribals. The project promised electricity to the local villages from the hydro-power to be generated which was never met; instead the deep forest cover got lost forever (Padel 2015). The World Bank is also involved in devising loans from other international financial institutions, like International Fund for Agricultural Development in Kashipur, a Japanese loan for the Upper Kolab project and a Saudi loan for the Rayagada-Koraput railway. The movement against Upper Indravati was led by Indravati Gana Sangharsh Parishad in 1990. But the movement was quelled by a brutal lathicharge by the police injuring 180 people. The displaced who had *patta* received a scanty compensation amount and those who did not have legal documents, got nothing. The irrigation of the dam could not solve Kalahandi's drought problem (Padel and Das 2010).

We can cite a host of example of projects which are being supported by international agencies, such as the World Bank which is financing NTPC's mega thermal power plant and a coal mine at Talcher from 1978, coal sector rehabilitation project, Ib valley coalfield, power sector restructuring, etc. It is also assisting super highway between Gopalpur and Talcher, a highway between Balasore and Kharagpur and a four mouthed road from Rourkela of Sundergarh to Sambalpur financially. ADB has financed the expansion of Paradip Port, power sector restructuring and AES/Ib valley power project. There are also G7 countries which are assisting Odisha's infrastructural projects financially like America which sanctioned loans for the Ib valley coalfield power plant; France provided loans for the construction of NALCO's aluminium smelting complex, Ananta coal mines and Kaniha and Ib valley coalfield power plants; Japan invested millions for the expansion of coal mining in the state, EXIM Bank of Japan is a co-financer of Daitari-Banspani railway line and OECF of Japan is investing millions in the vibrant tourism sector of Odisha; United Kingdom is investing in the modernization of Hirakud dam and privatization of the power sector. According to the Institute for Policy Studies (IPS) report, the major *cestui que* of these loans and aids are different American transnational companies like AES, Dodge Phelps, General Electric, Foster Wheeler, Spectrum Technologies, North-East Energy Services and Raytheon; French companies like

Stein Industries and Aluminium Pechiney; Canadian Alcan; Japanese Mitsui and UK-Australian RTZ-CRA (Singh 1997). Needless to say, 'human development' of the World Bank has generated massive distress and poverty instead of progress.

Public sector companies are also competing to reap the benefit of the marginalized. For instance, the state acquired hundreds of acres of cultivable lands for the Mahanadi Coalfields Limited (MCL) which was a subsidiary of Coal India Limited. Since the mid-1990s, the displaced have been tribals protesting and have organized blockades in front of the Basundhara coal mines for a better rehabilitation package. The Basundhara mines in Sundargarh began operation in early 2000, most of the tribals who got evicted with promises of compensation and jobs did not get anything either from MCL or from the government (Meher 2009). The displaced villagers of Kulhapada under the leadership of Basundhara Surakshya Samiti were compelled to organize a blockade of coal production and transportation from the Basundhara mines which caused a big loss of production amounting to 10,000 tonnes of coal per day (*The Times of India* 1 July 2007).

Odisha has been an exceptionally debt-ridden state. One of the reasons must be the decline in profits and employment. Department for International Development (DFID) which works for the British government to alleviate poverty, is working in Odisha, Madhya Pradesh, Andhra Pradesh and Tamil Nadu. Odisha was the first state that received grants from DFID for the privatization of its electricity which in turn increased the cost of electricity and subsequently for the privatization of water and forest resources. DFID sends its aid through the World Bank's Odisha Socio-economic Development Programme, mainly for Public Sector Reform, Public Financial Management and Improved Service Delivery. It also promotes Odisha Tribal Empowerment and Livelihoods Programme. It helped to make the draft of Odisha's R&R Policy in 2006. It aims at advocating liberalization and privatization in collaboration with the World Bank which is quite evident in the Commonwealth Development Corporation, owned by DFID which aggrandize the private sector in the developing world. One of its partners is JK Paper Mill. DFID is connected to UAIL through Business Partners for Development (BPD) project at the World Bank. It is also connected to the Lanjigarh

TABLE 2.2: MEGA INVESTMENT PROPOSED

Company	*Proposed Project*	*Location India*	*Cost (Rs. million)*
Consolidated Electric Power	Power	Jharsuguda	160,000
Larsen & Toubro Ltd	Steel	Gopalpur	70,000
Tata Steel	Steel	Gopalpur	65,000
Ganapati Exports Ltd	Steel	Duburi	60,000
Hindalco Industries Ltd	Aluminium	Kalahandi	50,000
Indian Oil Corporation	Oil Refinery	Paradip	50,000
Nippon Denro Ispat Ltd	Oil Refinery	Paradip	50,000
MESCO	Steel	Duburi	42,690
Oswal Agro Ltd	Fertilizer	Paradip	42,200
Utkal Alumina	Aluminium	Rayagada	30,000
Ashok Leyland	Oil Refinery	Haridaspur	24,000
Consolidated Electric Power	Power	Ib Valley	20,750
Neelachal Ispat Nigam Ltd	Steel	Duburi	15,250
Indian Seamless and Alloys Ltd	Steel/Pig Iron		13,770
Orind Steels Ltd	Cold Rolled Steel	Duburi	11,500

Source: IPICOL, Government of Odisha cited in 'Industry Flocks to "Backward" Indian State' by Kavaljit Singh https://www.twn.my/title/1907-cn.htm downloaded on 1 November 2021.

refinery of Vedanta through the Trade and Investment website entry of the UK government. The potential partners of British business include Tata, Jindal, Bhusan, Ispat and many other steel and iron industries as well as NALCO other than Vedanta. Jindal has set up steel plants at Kalinganagar and Angul financially assisted by the export credit guarantee department of the UK government. DFID granted 39 million dollars for the renovation of the Hirakud Dam Reservoir in 2003-5 which severely affected the farmers. The smelter of Jindal joined by Bhusan steel plant in 2005, Vedanta, HINDALCO and other 15 factories got the green signal to exploit the water in future depriving the farmers of water they need. In this way the penetration of foreign capital is being directed by the UK through DFID and the USA through the World Bank (Padel and Das 2010).

The forest and the unending water resources have saved the indigenous communities during the lean agricultural seasons by supplying them with substantial supplementary food and forest products. But this subsistence economy has been threatened by the incessant strikes of multinationals and corporate sponsored mega projects which are encroaching on tribal land and natural resources. The new investments have failed even to create job opportunities for the poor. These are capital intensive and the poor and marginalized are being used only as a pool of cheap labour.

LAND ACQUISITION

Tribals were not aware of this plunder initially, but gradually they started realizing the role of the MNCs when it came to the grabbing of their fertile lands. Tribals have time and again made it clear in their slogans that they want grain, not money. Land is not just a means of livelihood; it is their strength, their dignity, a symbol of their self-respect if not indigeneity. In scheduled areas of Odisha an average of 74 per cent of the land is categorized as government land out of which 48 per cent is forest land and 26 per cent non-forest land. The Forest Enquiry Committee Report of 1959 says that 12,000 sq. miles of land were under shifting cultivation (Kumar 2011). It has been recorded that 295 projects were approved of diverting 331.36 square kilometres of forest land. According to some sources, 27,479.65 hectares of forest land were diverted between January 1989 and December 2006 out of which 11,242.08 hectares were cleared for 115 mining projects in Odisha. Around 7,375 hectares of forest land was taken for irrigation projects whereas 2,551 hectares for industrial projects (*National Land Reforms Policy* 2017). Capitalist exploitation has rendered the tribals landless as 95 per cent mining activities is going on in tribal areas of Odisha. According to some conservative estimates, 24,124 hectares land, until 1999, were deforested due to development projects in the tribal areas like dams, mines, roads, railways and industries (Behura and Panigrahi 2006: 192).

As per official records, 81,176 families from 1,446 villages were displaced in Odisha between 1950 and 1993 because of different development projects, which entailed acquisition of 14,82,626 acres of land (Jena 2006). The state government cleared 184 industrial projects between 2002 and 2010 which brought a total investment of Rs. 8 lakh crore. They include 50 plants for the production of

TABLE 2.3: THE SCALE OF DISPLACEMENT IN ODISHA BETWEEN 1951 AND 1995

Projects	*No. of People Displaced*	*No. of People Rehabilitated*	*Percentage*	*No. of People who have not been Rehabilitated*	*Percentage*
Irrigation	3,25,000	90,000	27.69	2,35,000	72.31
Factories	71,794	27,300	38.03	44,494	61.97
Mines	1,00,000	60,000	60.00	40,000	40.00
Others	50,000	15,540	31.08	34,460	68.92
TOTAL	5,46,794	1,92,840	35.27	3,53,954	64.73

Source: Fernandes, Walter and Mohammed Asif, 1997, *Development-Induced Displacement in Orissa 1951 to 1995: A Database on Its Extent and Nature*, New Delhi: Indian Social Institute, p. 135.

83 million tonnes of steel at an investment of Rs. 2,50,000 crore, 30 thermal power plants earmarked production of 37,000 megawatt of power, 4 projects for port, many alumina refineries and few cement plants. The state has already selected 14 sites for the development of ports along the 480 km. coastline. These projects need as much as 50,000 acres of land. Apart from industries thousands of acres of land are also required for mining. The 30 thermal power

TABLE 2.4: REHABILITATION DISPLACEMENT AND SITUATION IN ODISHA, 1951-91

Category	*Displaced*	*Resettled*	*Percentage*	*Backlog of Settled*	*Backlog is Percentage*
Dams	3,25,000	90,000	27.69	2,35,000	72.31
Industries	71.794	27,300	38.03	44,494	61.97
Mines	1,00,000	60,000	60.00	40,000	40.00
Misc.	50,000	15,540	31.08	3,460	68.92
TOTAL	5,46,794	1,92,840	35.27	3,53,954	64.73

Source: Fernandes, Walter and Mohammed Asif, 1997, *Development-Induced Displacement in Orissa 1951 to 1995: A Database on Its Extent and Nature*, New Delhi: Indian Social Institute, p. 135.

plants alone would generate 90 million tonnes of fly ash a year and there is a severe dearth of land for dumping the industrial waste. The government has acquired around 15,000 acres of land and the private companies have been asked to purchase land from the people directly. The state has come out with its own R&R policy, but resistance and repression both continue unabated (*Frontline* 2011).

The former Planning Commission stated that more than 40 per cent of the evicted families are tribals. Koraput, at present, has 18 big projects occupying 50,000 acres of land which deprived 10 per cent tribals from their livelihood. Data also shows that a total of 8,41,916.50 acres of tribal land was alienated in Odisha alone by the end of 1999 which was highest in Koraput 28,901.55 acres followed by Kandhamal 15,864.55 acres (Ambagudia 2010).

RESETTLEMENT AND REHABILITATION

The current industrial and foreign investment boom is going on at the expense of the dislodging the sons of the soil of the central and eastern India and also at the cost of the green landscape. The corporate culture aims only at making profits and nothing else matters to it. The protectors of the environment, the poorest of the poor tribals are challenging the thunder of corporatization with an undaunted will power as the captivating rehabilitation policies and allurement of cash money could not drench the flames of their anger of losing their identity, their land, though International Labour Organization has set land for land as international standards for compensation. But most of the corporate social responsibility programmes are mere eyewash intended to stave off protesters and deceive the affected people.

Between 1951 and 1995, 1.5 million people have been displaced in Odisha alone among whom 42 per cent were tribals. Mining alone has evicted some 5,00,000 people (CSE 2008). While only 32 per cent of the total number of displaced were resettled, the rate is mere 25 per cent when it comes to the tribals (Fernandes 2001: 91), though the actual number is still not recorded and needless to say it is much higher than what is estimated roughly. Data reveals a miniscule part of the whole scenario. MNCs on their part are offering jobs and meeting other Corporate Social Responsibilities (CSRs) through various developmental works as rehabilitation measures, but that is not what is aimed at the development of the tribals. They are offering mostly unskilled jobs which no way fulfils tribal aspirations. Their CSRs include providing mainly vocational training, handicrafts, opening of schools and health centres and stuff like that. The Supreme Court directed Vedanta to pay 5 per cent of their entire profit or Rs. 10 crore for the Community Development Purpose, but the local Dongria Kondh tribals believed that money cannot compensate the loss of their mountain, forests, rivers and most importantly their god Niyam Raja (*Business Standard* 2008). The villagers who were persuaded to receive the compensation money were taken to Vedantanagar in police jeeps, where they were transformed into a chain of cheap labour force surviving without land and caught between the mountain and the refinery.

Chendipada block of Angul houses a sprawling 3,000-acre Jindal Steel and Power Plant (JSPL). The CSR wing of the company is called JSPL, the foundation which has constructed a resettlement and rehabilitation colony for those displaced by the plant. The villagers who lost their land and home were kept in a concrete ghetto next to the green forest around. The concrete buildings of the colony are getting some health services in form of a dispensary with doctor-on-call and also an ambulance facility. The school inside the colony has two rooms where children sit on the floor. The foundation has also started Kishori Express, a mobile van operating in 321 villages of Chendipada and Banarpal blocks in which the adolescent girls are tested for low haemoglobin levels as women of the villages were diagnosed with acute anaemia. This initiative was supported by National Health Mission. Another effort that the foundation took was to procure low-cost sanitary napkins. Jan Jeevika Kendra was a Self-Help Group under the foundation which was promoting hygiene in the area. The women of the group also made soaps, jute bags, incense sticks with the grant provided by the company (Ganguli 2015).

In the case of POSCO, the authorities promised to provide 7,000 jobs to the displaced, but not to the project affected people who are numbering nearly about 20,000. The UAIL formed Utkal Rural Development Society (URDS) and Business Partner for Development (BPD) in 1998. It was an NGO which was holding camps for eye check-up, distributing seeds and building roads, culverts and a nursery. But PSSP dismantled all the initiatives and refused to take any facilities provided through the NGO in protest against land acquisition. They demanded the government to come forward for any developmental work which is not supposed to be delivered by the company (Mahana 2019: 166).

Tata Steel established 55,000 tonnes per annum capacity ferro-chrome plant at Gopalpur of Ganjam with as estimated investment of Rs. 800 crore which would be the anchorage industry for the SEZ. The foundation stone of Gopalpur Steel Plant was laid by Narasimha Rao on 30 December 1995 which was destroyed by the villagers on the very next day. Three villages consisted of more than one thousand families who were forcefully evicted and shifted to the resettlement colony. The Gopalpur Movement against Tata Steel was organized under the leadership of Gana Sangram Samiti. In August 1996 the women's wing called Nari Sena spearheaded the movement, but 6,000 armed forces were sent to crush the resistance. Hundreds of protesters were arrested and brutally beaten due to which two died and many got injured. The project displaced 25,000 people from 25 villages. The movement, however, succeeded to halt a dam on the Rushikulya River, but Tata could not be stopped (Padel and Das 2010). The movement forced the company to provide a comprehensive R&R package during 1996-7. The package was also known for its inclusive attitude towards the project displaced women. Sikta Pati has discussed the R&R policy in detail where she mentioned that, in the rehabilitation township a total of 21 Self-Help Groups were working with the help of Tata Consultancy Services amongst which Radhakrishna Nari Sangha of Sindhigaon had been registered under the Societies Registration Act of 1860. Izzat Mahila Samiti, an apex level body was formed in Tata colony for a speedy implementation of different resettlement plans. But the trick of the Tata's R&R policy was that, no project affected people were considered as eligible for rehabilitation assistance and only the displaced persons got that opportunity. Adult single women were also excluded from the definition of family and thereby were not allowed to receive compensation. Thus the displaced were forced to live with much reduced resources than what they had earlier before getting displaced. The tribals lost the food supplements that they earlier used to get from the forest. Women had to walk longer for the collection of water, firewood and fodder. The hand pumps were defunct. Increasing alcoholism and incidents of crime made the situation worst. Due to the movement the Odisha government and Tata Steel had to come up with a set of additional R&R benefit for the displaced families which are again below expectation (Pati 2012: 103-4, 112-14).

The problems are many when it comes to an unplanned rehabilitation programme providing unjust distribution of benefit. Ib thermal power plant started operation in 1992 and spread over two districts of Odisha, Jharsuguda and Sundergarh. The coalfield is a part of the MCL. It is interesting to note that when the mining started no one objected, rather the villagers acknowledged that the project gave them jobs at a higher wage than agriculture on which they were dependent before displacement. They also received compensation for their land. Yet they had some demands and they varied from village to village. For example, in Bundia village, people demanded steady supply of potable drinking water; in Lajkura, Chharla and Ubuda village relocation was more important than compensation; in Ainlapali village displaced people demanded employment and reduction of polluting coal-dust emission. The tribals of the project area complained that they could not collect *tendu leaf* which was an essential forest product for their supplementary income as their land was filled with dust and *mahua* trees were also filled with coal-dust failing to yield good fruits (Mishra 2009). Thus inequitable distribution of benefit could cause dissatisfaction among the oustees regarding the rehabilitation package.

Tata Steel provided some support to make the displaced tribal women of Kalinganagar self-independent which was availed by 90 per cent of them. Tata provided housing, electricity, gas, educational and medical services and vocational training like mobile repairing and tailoring. But the problem was that the people were threatened to evacuate their lands by the hired goons of Tata and people went through police repression which is why the people were really dissatisfied with Tata's attempts (Mohanty 2016). After the Kalinganagar movement the government of Odisha was forced to present its own R&R Policy in 2006 and a special policy was introduced for

Kalinganagar oustees only, though its implementation was not at all satisfactory because Kalinganagar special rehabilitation package did not include the project affected persons in it and considered only those displaced persons for rehabilitation who had *patta* (59 per cent). More than 80 per cent of the displaced and affected people did not even have BPL cards. Seventy-two per cent of the displaced were marked as encroachers (Padel and Das 2010).

Lack of initiatives for the recognition of tribal rights over land and conferring *pattas* both for farmland and for shifting cultivation land (*dongar*) to them causes a great damage when there is any programme of land acquisition irrespective of public or private companies. For example, the village called Guptaganga located in upper catchment of Baitarani river was inhabited by the Juang tribes. The tribals did not have any *patta* of the land they used to till. During 2007-8 the tribals organized *gram sabha* meetings asking for the recognition of their rights over the land estimated as 270 acres comprised of both forest and revenue land. But the forest department did not pay heed to their demands, rather undertook a massive plantation programme under the Odisha Forestry Sector Development Project funded by the Japan Bank for International Cooperation in the land under cultivation of 57 Juang tribal families which severely affected their livelihoods (Patra 2014: 103-4).

TRIBAL MOVEMENTS

The legitimacy of the movements of the indigenous people against multinationals and corporates have been overshadowed by the petty politics and constantly being diluted in the myopic interpretation of the state authorities as mere law and order issues. There is a conscious attempt to reject the tribal movement as a social movement and a repertoire of organized collective behaviour which fight for saving the national wealth from the monstrous greed of the foreign capital. But tribals never gave up; they were determined to save nature from the clutches of billionaires.

Tribal movements against the big loot of the transnational and national corporates date back to 1950s when they first resisted Hirakud Hydel Project at Burla at Sambalpur. Hirakud displaced nearly

285 villages consisting of 22,144 families, 18,432 houses. A total of 112,038,59 acres of fertile land was submerged by the reservoir which affected the subsistence economy of the tribals. Later, the intensity and frequency of the resistance movements accentuated gradually and the country witnessed movement against Rengali Hydel Project in 1971, Save Gandhamardan Movement of early 1980s in Paikamal of Baragarh to resist the mining of Gandhamardan mountains by Bharat Aluminium Company or BALCO, the Baliapal Movement during 1985-90 against the National Missile Test Range, Netarhat, Enron thermal power, Chilika Bachao Andolan against Tata's Integrated Shrimp Farming Project (ISFP) backed by the government of Odisha in early 1990s, Gopalpur Movement against Tata Steel during 1995-6, the movement against Lower Suktel Dam at Bolangir in 2005, anti-land alienation movement in Nabarangpur and many more coming up. The Supreme Court closed down Tata's Chilika project as the aquaculture project violated the Coastal Regulation Zone. But the goons of Tata invaded the tribal villages to take revenge and destroyed their fishing boats (Kapoor 2012).

Tribals are resisting such attempts of mugging of the MNCs and Indian corporates. The indiscriminate loot of forest, water, land and mineral resources made them fight the insatiable greed of the giant companies leading sometimes to abandonment of various projects like POSCO and failing the profit motif of the MNCs and some of the biggest public sector companies like TISCO, Jindal, HINDALCO (Birla Group), ESSAR, etc. Many of them could not even begin the preliminary surveys in face of strong resistance of the tribals. Many, even tried to suppress the movement by force so that the project work might progress, but failed, like UAIL, VAL, Tata, etc. The fierce onslaught on tribal rights to resources has been time and again withstood by the country's first citizens in an unending battle for right to life and livelihood which were inscribed in the Constitution decades ago. There has grown a recent trend to slap an extremist tag on dissent of any kind and tribals are no exception. Thus under the guise of 'national security threat' the state has unleashed a war of resources in which the worst sufferers are the poorest of the poor, hungry and malnourished tribals who are being maimed, displaced and crushed at the cost of the 'greater good'.

The state neither assesses the negative impact of such multinational and corporate projects nor ensures adequate rehabilitation package, instead it has unleashed brutal and merciless repressive measures to subdue the resistance of the tribals going on in different parts of Odisha. The tribal unrest gained momentum with the growing bauxite extraction projects like BALCO, RSB Metaltech, Larsen & Toubro (L&T) and Sterlite Industries India Ltd (SIIL) in Kashipur. L&T planned to mine Kuturu Mali and Siji Mali in 1990s. But confrontations with local people compelled them to postpone the plan. They later joined Dubal in November 2006 for building another refinery near Kalyan Singpur. Jindal had a plan to mine Mali Parbat as well which will affect about 42 villages under Dalaiguda, Sorishapodar and Pakhajhola gram panchayats. NALCO reportedly has plans to expand its operations onto Deo Mali; Continental Resources, a Canadian company has also managed to get lease for mining Gandhamardan (Padel 2015). From the very inception Mali Parbat bauxite mines of HINDALCO Group in 2006, it faced stiff resistance from the local tribals. In May 2006 trouble escalated when the tribals started demonstrating in Similiguda. But the company hired goons who pounced on the protesting tribals in Maliguda, misbehaved with their womenfolk and injured 10 seriously (*The Hindu* 15 June 2008). The project work got halted frequently in 2012. The resistance gained momentum under the leadership of Mali Parbat Surakhya Samiti (MPSS) in September 2021 as it was seeking a new lease to resume mining. Mecon Ltd., a big engineering firm which has contracts for Ashapura, Jindal and Vanasree group in Odisha is planning for mining Mali Parbat and opening up refineries (Padel and Das 2010).

The tradition of tribal movement in Odisha continued with the outbreak of Kashipur Movement against Utkal Alumina International Limited (UAIL) which proposed for bauxite mining in Baphlimali hill zone in Rayagada of Kashipur. It also proposed to set up a refinery at D. Karol of Doraguda in Kucheipadar village and Ramibeda village for the processing of bauxite. The processed aluminium will be taken to Tikiri and thence to Visakhapatnam for exportation to different countries. The cost of the project was initially pegged at Rs. 4,500 crore, but later revised at Rs. 10,000 crore. UAIL was a consortium comprised of two large national corporates and one multinational company (Tata, INDAL and Norsk Hydro of Norway). The proposed alumina production initially was 1 million tonnes of alumina per annum and was later expanded to 3 million tonnes. When the resistance started during 1998-2000, Tata left the project after which ALCAN (Canada) developed a huge share in its subsidiary INDAL and sold it to HINDALCO. But tribal unrest led by the Integrated Rural Development of Weaker Sections in India, a civil society organization, forced Norsk Hydro to quit the venture. Thus it emerged as a joint venture of the mining giants HINDALCO (Birla group) and Alcan. Tribals of D. Karol, Ramibeda and Kendukhunti villages lost 75 per cent of their land due to the mining project. UAIL had already grabbed 2,500 acres of land and evicted more than 2,000 people (Pattnaik 2013), though conservative estimates say that the number of the project affected people is more than 60,000. The 45 cusecs of water needed for the plant is to be extracted from Golagad river. Only 147 families from the three displaced villages were considered as completely displaced and listed for cash compensation. Kucheipadar was the sole village which denied compensation (Padel and Das 2010).

The displaced and project affected people have organized under the banner of Utkal Alumina Dwara Bisthapita, Kshyatigrasta & Prabhabita Committee to press the government for the benefits they were once promised to be given. It also claimed new and updated rehabilitation package. But after several requests, petitions and dharnas, their demands remained unfulfilled leading to stronger protest against inaction and indifference. The displaced with the help of Prakritik Suraksha Sampad Parishad (PSSP) held meeting at the Nuapada resettlement colony on 3 June 2009 and closed down the factory for an indefinite period of time. Later, however, the factory work began but the grievances of the displaced were never attended with care (Mahana 2019: 200-201). Indian Metal Ferro-Alloys (IMFA) proposed for mining Sasubahumali in October 2007. It aimed to set up a refinery next to its ferro-manganese factory at Therubali and a 250,000 tonnes smelter at Choudwar near Cuttack. Anamani Parbat or Ushabali has already been designated as bauxite-rich mountain in 2008 in Kandhamal. The survey was conducted by Gimpex causing displacement of about 50,000 Christians in the district (Padel and Das 2010).

There were some grassroot organizations formed by PSSP, established on 14 February, 1996, in different blocks and these are: Baplimali Surakshya Samiti formed in 1995 fighting for the protection of Baphlimali hills at Maikanch, Gaon Mati Surakshya Samiti fighting for saving Sasubahumali hills at Siriguda, Sasubahumali Surakshya Samiti fighting against the BALCO and Sterlite companies at Khurigaon, Anchaklika Surakshya Samiti fighting against mining of Sijimali and Kutrumali hills and also against L&T company in Sunger, Basundhara Surakshya Samiti fighting against Aditya Birla in Barigaon and also for saving Kodingamali hills, Bankam Surakshya Samiti at Puhundi and Sunadei Surakshya Samiti at Bagrijhola. The Kashipur movement was led by the PSSP as an umbrella organization under which all these samitis are fighting against mining. Land acquisition by UAIL began in June 1996. The local administration intimidated the tribals, forced them to sign the documents and took the compensation at gunpoint. UAIL started the construction work of its rehabilitation colony at D. Karol in July 1997. Another resettlement colony was constructed at Nuapada. Tribals started protesting and were tortured brutally by the police in 1997-8 for which UAIL was compelled to suspend work for a while (Mahana 2019: 39, 219). On 15 December 2000, a meeting was called at Maikanch to discuss the modes of protest and on the next day, the police fired on the crowd killing three tribals and injuring many. The killing is infamously called the Maikanch firing. On 20 December a road blockade was organized attended by 10,000 people. But police repression could not crush the movement, it continued. From the end of 2004 the state repression was intensified. Kucheipadar became the epicentre of the movement. PSSP organized a rally on 15 May 2005 against police brutality. Tribals of Kashipur and Laxmipur submitted a memorandum to the governor asking for the cancellation of the project. They refused to take the compensation. The police again attacked a meeting called by PSSP on 8 June. Within a year 52 people were sent behind the bars (Sarangi 2005). But the movement could not prevent the refinery which started its trial production in June 2013.

BALCO is a foreign technical collaboration undertaken by the Government of India which proposed to mine the deep forest range on the top of the Gandhamardan hill area located in Bargarh district in the 1976 for its aluminium project which was granted in 1981.

The bauxite reserve of Gandhamardan was estimated to be 213 million tonnes. BALCO began its project work on 2 May 1983 which was aimed to end by April 1985. In the first half of 1985 more than 60,000 trees were felled for the construction of roads and a ropeway for BALCO. But tribals were up in arms to stop the company operations and mobilized under the banner of Nrushinganatha Surakshya Samiti. The tribal women, made a great sacrifice and put their children before the vehicles of the company and the police. They formed Gandhamardan Surakshya Yuva Parishad on 19 August 1985 in Baidapali village. The movement was supported wholeheartedly by the civil society. Suderlal Bahuguna visited the place during 6-12 February 1986. The movement was called the Gandhamardan Bachao Andolan in which many people including women took part. Gandhamardan Jana Paribesh Sampad Surakshya Parishad was formed in Delhi to save the hills from the encroachment of the MNCs. Thus the movement got a huge media coverage. A committee headed by B.D. Nag was formed by the central government on 28 December 1986 when on that very day thousands of people assembled to oppose BALCO following which the Ministry of Environment and Forest (MoEF) denied clearance to the project in 1987 and BALCO was forced to stall the project (Mahana 2019).

Tatas signed an MoU with the Odisha government on 17 November 2004 to set up a steel plant in Kalinganagar. During the protest movement against Maharashtra Seamless Company (MSL) at Kalinganagar 26 tribals mainly women were lathicharged on 9 May 2005 and taken to jail. The phenomenal increase in the incidents of violence impelled the MSL to retreat from the project. Tribals withstood the construction work of Bhusan Steel Company (uranium shell) of Dhenkanal in December 2005. On 20 May 2006 Bhusan security forces opened fire on a crowd of demonstrators. On 7 October 2005 Tata began erecting the boundary wall at Dholpathar village when tribals protested and the police lathicharged the demonstrators. In spite of growing resistance, Tata did not stop but started their construction work at Champakoila. On 2 January 2006, 13 tribals were killed and 1,159 were threatened to be arrested while protesting against Tata Steel in Kalinganagar. The most gruesome chapter of the movement unfolded when the dead bodies were returned with mutilated hands and genitals. The state government shrugged off its shoulder only after declaring an insignificant sum of compensation money, 5 lakhs for the dead and 50,000 for the injured. The amount that was initially given to the displaced tribals (Rs. 35,000 per acre) as compensation of their land was much less than the market price of the land (Rs. 1 lakh per acre) as this land was later sold to Tata at Rs. 3,35,000 per acre which was almost double the price and when the tribals got to know this, they demanded just compensation and refused to give up. The state forced the tribals to give up their land. Moreover, most of the people whose land was taken, were not paid the compensation money till 2010. One reason was the siphoning off the money by the officers and the other one was that the majority of the displaced did not have *patta*. Tata claimed that among 1,195 identified families who were displaced, 912 families received their rehabilitation and resettlement package till May 2011. Tatas also tried to bribe some of the tribals in order to create division among the protesters. They offered an enticing resettlement programme which included homestead land, free ration, financial help for rebuilding the houses, job and training, etc. The poor tribals fell prey to it, received compensation and moved to the rehabilitation colonies located in Trijanga, Danagadi I & II, Sansailo and Gobarghati which is why the Tatas could set up its plant (Mahana 2019). Maniapatala village was added later where 39 families were displaced, taking a total number of evicted families to 1,234 out of which 993 families were forced to receive compensation and driven out of their homes by December 2012 (Mohanty 2016: 79).

The tribals of Bolangir started resisting against Suktel Dam when on 11 May 2005 the police resorted to violence and 70 protesters were detained. They were beaten black and blue in the custody. The dam was constructed to ensure uninterrupted supply of water to the aluminium plant in the Gandhamardan mountainous region of Bolangir. Thirty-four tribal people were arrested in April 2006 in Lanjigarh of Kalahandi while protesting against the forceful land acquisition by Vedanta and demanded proper compensation. Though the Supreme Court later gave green signal to Vedanta, the tribal movement is unstoppable. In the same year tribals of Jagatsinghpur prohibited the POSCO authorities to conduct their survey work in

Paradip and 9 of them were booked by the police under false charges. The villagers in Kujang, Dhinkia and Nuagaon were agitating against POSCO since 2005 under the banner of POSCO Pratirodh Sangram Samiti (PPSS) and successfully stymied the project work.

Tribals of Nuapada were tortured in the same way when they voiced their protest against a sanctuary project as there was no rehabilitation programme announced before the land acquisition by the forest department. Eighteen tribals were arrested during the protest in 2005. According to government sources, there are 104 sponge iron plants located in nine districts of Odisha, namely in Sundargarh (47), Keonjhar (19), Jharsuguda (11), Sambalpur (10), Mayurbhanj (2), Cuttack (4), Jajpur (4), Dhenkanal (4) and Angul (3). Due to interminable discharge of dusts of coal and iron by these sponge iron factories, the land lost its fertility, grains were polluted and thus food production got affected severely in Jharsuguda and Sundargarh (Meher 2009). Tribals of Sambalpur and Jharsuguda are opposing the sponge iron factories which are being operated illegally without any NOCs (Sarengi 2006). On 24 March 2006 more or less 4,000 tribals organized a rally in protest of Nepaz Sponge Iron Company in Kuarmunda block. The police attacked the peaceful procession inhumanly and arrested 118 people mostly women and children. Protests are also ripe against the land acquisition by the JP Power Plant in Angul, TPS in Subarnapur, KVK Nilachal, TPS and TATA in Naraj, TPS in Cuttack district.

Other than transnational and corporates the state led conservation induced pauperization is also making tribals victims of development leading to the birth of indigenous movements. The protest against Kuldiha Wildlife Sanctuary located at the junction of Balasore, Mayurbhanj and Keonjhar (KBK belt) and Sunabeda Wildlife Sanctuary in Nuapada (KBK zone), however sporadic in manner, are significant in the context of the loss of sustainable livelihood of the local tribal people. More than 700 villages are still inside the existing sanctuaries. In the Sunabeda Sanctuary there are 30 revenue villages and 34 unsurveyed settlements which are densely populated by Chuktia Bhunjias, a primitive tribal group. Kotagarh sanctuary and Lakhari sanctuary have faced a similar situation where the villages have not been relocated (Kumar 2011). The forest department has violated section 18B of the Wildlife Protection (Amendment) Act of 2002 and Forest Rights Act of 2006. The settlement of tribal rights and individual or community claims are pending for a long period of time as a complete ban has been imposed on all the development activities, collection of minor forest products by the tribals. The tribals of Kuldiha have organized under the indigenous organization called Bhita-mati Jivan Jivika Surkhya Manch (BJSM) against such injustice. It is also important to note that Nuapada where Sunabeda Sanctuary is situated was a part of the infamous red corridor. But due to lack of experience in democratic movement and support from other grassroot organizations, the movement failed to leave its mark (Ray, 2021).

In recent times the mineral rich Keonjhar district which was comparatively peaceful and did not have any record of tribal unrest became a hub of protest of the displaced tribals. Tribals of nine villages of Mahadeijoda, Raisuan, Janardanpur and Nuagaon gram panchayats of Keonjhar district decided to resist the 5.1 million tonnes Sterlite Steel Plant at Mahadeijoda in June 2007 as they knew that the project might affect more than thousand acres of cultivable lands, water bodies and plantations. BBJM claimed that the project would damage as many as 12 minor irrigation projects, the Hemrada and Machhakandana rivers, nine lift irrigation projects and four streams that currently help growing a large amount of crops and vegetables. The mega project proposed to acquire 1,217.18 acres of government land and 2,160.89 acres of private land. This would cause eviction of 173 families in the affected gram panchayats amongst which Dhatika, Tikarpada and Kedargarh villages were greatly damaged (*The Times of India* 1 July 2007). The state government finally dropped the decision of land acquisition in the face of tribal movement in October 2012. The withdrawal of the land acquisition process for the steel project comes as another blow to the industrial group which is reeling under the closure of alumina refinery of Vedanta Aluminium at Lanjigarh in the state for want of bauxite (*Business Standard* 27 December 2012).

Tribal movements in Odisha have always been non-violent and organized mass movements which have always resorted to the democratic path for airing grievances, sought legal help for fighting for their fundamental rights and Gandhian ideology of civil disobedience. But state violence is unbound and determined to gag and crush the movement at any expense be it by its machineries or by tagging the tribal movements as 'Maoist'. Chasi Muliya Adivasi Sangh (CMAS) is such an organization of Narayanpatna which was banned as Maoist front organization, but which actually fought to recover the tribal land from the hands of the non-tribals. It was also fighting against liquor consumption. On 20 November 2009 two tribal persons were killed and many got wounded in a security force firing. Maoists were championing the rights of the tribals but they did not lead the movement. The local tribals refused to let them interfere in their movement which had a fifteen year long history of struggle. Resistance to the Saptadhara Dam and Thermal Power Project in Jeypore initially came from the Maoists. The ceaseless battle of the tribals against feudalism, imperialism, corporatization, liquor mafias, timber mafias and state oppression is still going on in its fullest force.

Tribal movements have sometimes been viewed as parochial and a reflection of obstructing ethno-territorial aspirations, manifested in different violent forms. But that is not true. Tribal movements are mostly rationally collective and rely on the agency of the affected people who galvanize the state to take steps towards ecological preservation, conservation and harmful impacts of mining and damming. For example, after so many years of fighting against Vedanta, the Dongria Kondhs are still not granted their desired expectations. It is an irony of fate that most tribal movements in Odisha took place in a Scheduled Five area which was also brought under Panchayats (Extension to Scheduled Areas) Act, 1996 (PESA) and where tribal land cannot be alienated legally. Niyamgiri is also protected under section 18 of the Indian Wildlife Act and was declared as an elephant reserve in 2004. Various independent local organizations led the movement like Niyamgiri Bachao Samiti, Niyamgiri Surakshya Abhiyan, Lok Shakti Abhiyan, etc.

Niyamgiri Surakshya Samiti, Kalahandi Sachetan Nagarika Manch, Green Kalahandi and Samajbadi Jana Parishad all these civil society organizations are working here for the tribal cause. Tribals vent their dissent through these organizations. It is unfortunate that in spite of tribal resistance to Vedanta and the legitimate concerns towards destruction of greenery the project was successfully completed which was detrimental to the life and livelihood of the tribals in every respect. The disempowerment of the tribal people has a wider perspective if seen from the glass of the system of decentralized governance. Initially, Dongria Kondhs opposed the land acquisition process vehemently. But when their struggle failed to achieve its goal they resisted the mining of bauxite in the Niyamgiri Hills which is religiously, culturally and symbolically interlinked to their identity, well-being and to the very root of their existence. Since then the tribals have been fighting for a better deal in terms of jobs, education, health and other basic development facilities. Vedanta also stands as a glaring example of how the *gram sabha* consent was made up, manipulated and tribal representatives were made silent and thus disempowered. The aforementioned twelve *gram sabhas* of Rayagada and Kalahandi objected to the mining and refused to give consent to Vedanta in the public meetings convened on 26 June 2002 and again during July-August 2013. Supporters and agents of Vedanta influenced the *gram sabha* decisions and thereby defeated the real intention of local self-governance in scheduled areas (Rout and Patnaik 2014). Similar situation appeared in the case of the Kashipur movement where UAIL with the help of the state government, arranged two meetings in order to obtain the consent of tribals as Kashipur is situated in a Scheduled Five zone where tribal's consent is mandatory. So, the meetings were held on 27 January and 26 May 2004 at a long distance which the poor tribals had to skip as they could not afford to go there. PSSP was not invited; rather people were brought from outside promising food and one-day wage and the meeting ground was cordoned by armed police. Both the meetings failed in the face of strong protest. But UAIL with the help of the police, successfully created a rift between the leadership of PSSP and extracted the required consent by intimidating people for completing necessary paperwork (Mahana 2019). Similarly, tribals in Dhenkanal resisted Lanco when it arranged a public hearing for a 2,640 megawatt power plant which later got permission for only a 1,320 megawatt. Tata held another public hearing for the proposed power plant at Naraj in Cuttack in 2009 with the support of a huge police force (Mishra 2010).

Apart from repression, social exclusion, spatial isolation and economic marginalization of the affected by ignoring their representation can be a strong reason of the failure of their movement such as happened in Vedanta's case in Lanjigarh. On 17 and again on 27 January 2009 two back to back demonstrations were held by the Dongria Kondhs where hundreds of thousands of tribals, both men and women, joined with their traditional weapons and showed strong resistance to Vedanta. When the review committee divulged the detrimental effects of Vedanta on the ecology of Niyamgiri, it was denied forest clearance in 2010 and the environmental clearance was rescinded subsequently in 2011. Vedanta closed down its Lanjigarh refinery in December 2012. With the recognition of the tribal right to worship, Supreme Court ruled the holding of *gram sabha* meeting for tribals' consent in 2013. Tribals conveyed their decision unanimously saying no to Vedanta after which MoEF cancelled Vedanta's mining lease on 9 January 2014 leaving the Dongria Kondhs cheer for their glorious victory over corporate enslavement. Later, though, the government of Odisha decided to mine the adjoining mountain of Khandual Mali at Karlapat on behalf of the Vedanta Resources and petitioned to the Ministry of Environment, Forest and Climate Change (MoEFCC) and to the Supreme Court to resume mining in Niyamgiri. The Karlapat Wildlife Sanctuary was established in 1992 leaving the bauxite deposit outside. Khandual Mali has been leased out to BHP Billiton in November 2005. This tendency is no doubt alarming as the Kondhs of Khandual Mali have vowed to protect their land and lord resolutely (Padel 2015). But the Supreme Court has directed to add 12 *gram sabhas* to the petition as a party.

Tribal movements against MNCs and national corporates have been time and again tagged as anti-development and antagonistic to change, but the real intention of development should not be destructive and should not be based on a wrong notion according to which tribals must sacrifice for the greater good. In Felix Padel's word,

> The minerals up there are not lying unutilized: they play a vital role in the ecosystem. Many people understand how India's water situation is badly affected by industry taking too much and polluting rivers, by dams and over-use of groundwater. We also need to understand the vital role of mountains as sources of the country's streams and rivers. Movements against excessive mining are not 'anti-development' at all. They are safeguarding

the ecosystems that life depends on for future generations. . . . Real development would mean the transformation of decision-making processes leading to empowerment of local communities, and harmonization between priorities of the economy with those of ecology. (Padel 2015)

According to Kundan Kumar, the state-corporate nexus has proved fatal for the tribal movements. It has been found time and again that the powerful national mega corporates with extractive projects are often backed by high offices like the Prime Minister, Finance Minister, Chief Minister and top bureaucrats. The former finance minister, Mr. Chidambaram, was one of the board members of Vedanta Plc. There are such uncountable instances where PMO or the FM's office intervened on behalf of companies like POSCO and Vedanta. Vedanta was alleged to be one of the major funders of the BJD government of Odisha. At the state level, top political and bureaucratic personalities were bribed by various companies and in exchange of necessary permissions they provided jobs to their relatives. Many of the corporate magnates are themselves politicians, such as Navin Jindal (Congress MP and owner of Jindal Steels) and Jaya Panda (BJD MP, IMFA group) (Kumar 2014).

Development must come with the target to improve the living standard and livelihood of the marginalized so that they can taste the fruits of development and not suffer for it. Mega projects always aim at exploiting the natural resources at the cost of tribal livelihood because of which tribals are left with nothing but resisting their plunder. If alternative model of development is initiated in the tribal regions which is suitable to their way of life, provides economic advancement and social development in the true sense, only then the actual purpose of development can be served. And this is not a far cry as the tribals of Putsil village of Koraput district have constructed such an alternative model of development in the form of a mini hydel-power project that caused zero displacement, no environmental depletion and absence of violence. The water is irrigating the land and producing electricity. This is a very small scheme of about four feet of height and owned by the people themselves for their own benefit (Anonymous 2004). Thus tribal resistance is not only about the challenge against the hegemony of corporate capitalism and spectre of state led development, but it is also about providing a suitable alternative model of development that is inclusive, reciprocal and participatory. There is nothing called 'ideal' form of development, rather it should be more pragmatic and is more about what is exactly needed for the community development and not at the cost of the community.

It is unfortunate that the state is inviting the free market economy through the MNC model of development in the land of the tribals. The debate regarding the development-induced displacement ushered by the MNC led mega projects has underscored the importance of tribal rights and representation. In fact, Odisha is one of those states which have been badly affected by poverty and starvation deaths. It has also been recorded that the number of poor in both urban and rural areas have increased manifold during 1993-4 and 1999-2000 (Sen and Himanshu 2004). Hence, it is difficult to fathom why the government is pursuing massive displacement and livelihood loss which is causing more hardships and poverty for the people affected instead of reducing it.

REFERENCES

Ambagudia, Jagannath, 2010, 'Tribal Rights, Dispossession and the State in Orissa', in *Economic and Political Weekly*, vol. XLV, no. 33, pp. 60-7.

Anonymous, 2004, 'Human Rights Violation in the Context of the Displacement of Project Affected People: A Report on Five Case Studies of State-Sponsored Terror in India', in *Social Change*, vol. 34, no. 4, pp. 107-21.

——, 2005, 'POSCO Project, A Mega Deal', in *Economic and Political Weekly*, vol. 40, no 27, p. 2888.

Asher, Manish, 2006, 'Steel Not Enough?', in *Economic and Political Weekly*, vol. 41, no. 7, pp. 555-6.

Behura, N. and N. Panigrahi, 2006, *Tribals and the Indian Constitution: Functioning of the Fifth Schedule in Orissa*, New Delhi: Rawat Publications.

Business Standard, 9 August 2008, 'Tribals May Not Swap Hill for Rs 10 Crore', New Delhi.

Centre for Science and Environment, 2008, 'Rich Lands Poor People: Is "Sustainable" Mining Possible?', in *The State of India's Environment: The 6th Citizen Report*, New Delhi: Centre for Science and Environment.

Dash, K.C. and K.C. Samal, 2008, 'New Mega Projects in Orissa: Protests by Potential Displaced Persons', in *Social Change,* 38(4), pp. 627-44.

Devraj, Ranjit, 2005, *Indigenous Peoples Day: Riches Out from Under India's Orissa Tribals,* http://www.ipsnews.net/2005/08/indigenous-peoples-day-riches-out-from-under-indias-orissa-tribals/ downloaded on 31 October 2021.

Dias, Anthony, 2012, *Development and its Human Cost,* Jaipur: Rawat Publications.

Evans, G., James Goodman, and Nina Lansbury, 2002, *Moving Mountains: Communities Confront Mining and Globalization,* London: Zed.

Fernandes, Walter, 2001, 'Development Induced Displacement and Sustainable Development', in *Social Change,* 31(1-2), pp. 87-103.

Frontline, 17 January 2003, 'Under Public Scrutiny', available at https://frontline.thehindu.com/the-nation/article30215144.ece downloaded on 4 January 2020.

——, 17 June 2011, pp. 16-17.

Ganguli, Abhiraj, 10 May 2015, 'Sailing on a Thin Raft', in *The Statesman.*

Government of Orissa, 2000, Status report on rehabilitation and resettlement and I.P.D.P of Rengali irrigation project, Department of Water Resources, Bhubaneswar.

Human Development Report, 2004, Government of Orissa, Bhubaneswar: Published by Planning and Coordination Department, Government of Orissa.

Jena, Manipadma, 2006, 'Orissa: Draft Resettlement and Rehabilitation Policy, 2006', in *Economic and Political Weekly,* vol. 41, no. 5, pp. 384-7.

Jojo, Bipin K., 2002, 'Political Economy of Large Dam Projects: A Case Study of Upper Kolab Project in Koraput District, Orissa', in S. Tharakan (ed.), *The Nowhere People: Responses to Internally Displaced Persons,* Bangalore: Books for Change.

Kapoor, Dip, 2012, 'Human Rights as Paradox and Equivocation in Contexts of Adivasi (Original Dweller) Dispossession in India', *Journal of Asian and African Studies,* 47(4), pp. 404-20.

Kapoor, Dip and Tejwant Chana, 2010, 'Adivasi Social Movement in Orissa: Development, Marginalization and Dispossession', in Debal K. Singha Roy (ed.), *Dissenting Voices and Transformative Actions: Social Movements in a Globalizing World,* New Delhi: Manohar, pp. 501-18.

Kumar, Kundan, 2011, *A Status of Adivasis/Indigenous Peoples Land Series 2, Orissa,* New Delhi: Aakar.

——, 2014, 'Confronting Extractive Capital: Social and Environmental

Movements in Odisha', in *Economic and Political Weekly*, vol. 49, no. 14, pp. 66-73.

Mahana, Rajakishor, 2019, *Negotiating Marginality: Conflicts Over Tribal Development in India*, New Delhi: Social Science Press.

Meher, Rajkishor, 2003, 'The Social and Ecological Effects of Industrialization in a Tribal Region: The Case of the Rourkela Steel Plant', in *Contributions to Indian Sociology*, 37(3), pp. 429-57.

——, 2009, 'Globalization, Displacement and the Livelihood Issues of Tribal and Agriculture Dependent Poor People: The Case of Mineral-based Industries in India', in *Journal of Developing Societies*, 25(4), pp. 457-80.

Mishra, Banikanta, 2010, 'Agriculture, Industry and Mining in Orissa in the Post-Liberalization Era: An Inter-District and Inter-State Panel Analysis', in *Economic and Political Weekly*, vol. XLV, no. 20, pp. 49-68.

Mishra, Prajna Paramita, 2009, 'Coal Mining and Rural Livelihoods: Case of the Ib Valley Coalfield, Orissa', in *Economic and Political Weekly*, vol. XLIV, no. 44, pp. 117-23.

Mohanty, Aliva, 2016, *Socio-political Harmony and Displaced Women of Odisha*, New Delhi: Abhijit Publications.

National Land Reforms Policy, Committee on State Agrarian Relations and Unfinished Task of Land Reforms, Ministry of Rural Development, Government of India, 8 June 2017, https://dolr.gov.in/sites/default/files/Committee%20Report.pdf downloaded on 30 October 2021.

Padel, Felix, 2015, 'Environmental Justice in a Land of Sacred Animals', in *People in Conservation*, vol. 6, issue 2, pp. 5-7.

Padel, Felix and Samarendra Das, 2010, *Out of this Earth: East India Adivasis and the Aluminium Cartel*, New Delhi: Orient BlackSwan.

Pati, Sikta, 2012, *Industrialization and Displacement: An Economic Impact*, New Delhi: Concept Publishing Company.

Patra, Himansu Sekhar, 2014, *Status of Adivasis/Indigenous Peoples Mining Series 5, Odisha*, New Delhi: Aakar.

Pattanaik, Sarmishtha, 2012, 'Impact of Mining on Water and Human Health: A Case Study of Baitarani River Ecosystem in Orissa', in Anjal Prakash, V.S. Saravana and Jayati Chourey (eds.), *Interlacing Water and Human Health: Case Studies from South Asia*, New Delhi: Sage Publications, pp. 311-32.

Pattnaik, Binay Kumar, 2013, 'Tribal Resistance Movements and the Politics of Development Induced Displacement in Contemporary Orissa', in *Social Change*, 43(1), pp. 53-78.

Pradhan, Pramodini, April 2006, 'Police Firing at Kalinganagar: A Report by People's Union for Civil Liberties (PUCL) Orissa', PUCL Bulletin, pp. 1-4, available at http://sanhati.com/wp-content/uploads/2010/10/pucl-police-firing-at-kalinganagar.pdf downloaded on 7 November 2021.

Rajappa, Sam, 7 May 2011, 'Forced Clearance of POSCO', in *The Statesman.*

Rao, M.G. and P.K. Rama, October 1979, *East Coast Bauxite Deposits of India*, Report by the Geological Survey of India.

Ray, Sthitapragyan, 2021, 'Protest Movements against Sanctuaries in Odisha: Politic with Other Means', in *South Asia Research*, vol. 41(3), pp. 369-83.

Reddy, Gopinath M., Prajna Paramita Mishra and Nagaraju Chikkala, 2013, 'Mining and Displacement in South Odisha: Perspective from a Census Survey', in Sakarama Somayaji, Susmita Dasgupta (eds.), *Sociology of Displacement: Policies and Practice*, Jaipur: Rawat Publications, pp. 192-204.

Rout, Satyapriya and Pratyusna Patnaik, 2014, 'Institutional Exclusion and Tribal Interest Decentralized Government in the Context of Conflicts over Development in India', in *Journal of Developing Societies*, 30(2), pp. 115-43.

——, 2018, 'Neo-liberal Development, Displacement and Exclusion: Tribal Resistance to Vedanta', in Sujit Kumar Mishra and R. Siva Prasad (eds.), *Displacement, Impoverishment and Exclusion: Political Economy of Development in India*, Delhi: Aakar, pp. 206-37.

Sahoo, Uttam and Bipin Jojo, 2020, 'Examining Displacement, Resettlement and Rehabilitation Processes: The Case of Rengali Dam Displaced Communities in Odisha, India', in *The International Journal of Community and Social Development*, 2(1), pp. 29-50.

Sarangi, Debaranjan, 2005, 'Shallow Grave: Orissa's New Labs of Horror', in *Tehelka*, 23 July.

——, 2006, 'Orissa: Paradise for Private Players', in *Frontier*, vol. 39, no. 5, pp. 1-4.

Sen, Abhijit and Himanshu, 2004, 'Poverty and Inequality in India – I', in *Economic and Political Weekly*, vol. 39, no. 38, pp. 4247-63.

Shankaran, Deepa, 2009, 'Like a White Flag? The Gendered Dimension of the Orissa's State Policy on Resettlement and Rehabilitation', in Lyla Mehta (ed.), *Displaced by Development: Confronting Marginalization and Gender Injustice*, New Delhi: Sage Publications, pp. 225-45.

Singh, K., 1997, 'Odisha: From "Backward" to "Investor's Paradise"?' *Corp Watch*, August, http://www.saanet.org/kashipur/articles/kaval.htm downloaded on 1 November 2021.

Update Series 18, 2010, *Adivasi in India*, Kolkata: Update Publications.

CHAPTER 3

Fighting the Structural Violence
Tribal Movements in Madhya Pradesh

> There were more than a hundred women in jail. We continued to protest there. We sang songs, danced and played games. We refused to be intimidated. . . . We learnt how to read and write whilst sitting in protest . . . and we felt a wonderful sense of freedom. . . . But they [the government] still did not give us land. . . . We fasted for 29 days before the government took any notice. . . . We have experienced it all, and we have learnt from our struggle. We have seen how the government behaves when we demand our rights. (Ramkuwar 2009)

The above excerpts have been taken from Ramkuwar's personal testimony of the struggle of tribal women who were ousted by the Man dam as part of the Narmada Bachao Andolan. They demanded land for land as compensation before the submergence of their villages.

Tribal movements in India have a long history of protest against exploitation and repression as they have historically been one of the most disadvantaged sections of the Indian society. Tribals are the most vulnerable community who have achieved almost nothing since Independence. Tribal history is fraught with armed rebellion and violent attacks on the establishments and government machineries, like railroads, shops, police stations and the like. But there are other dimensions of tribal movements, for example, movement without arms and violence, movement for self-representation, democratic rights and right to have constitutional entitlements, movement for proper implementation of Fifth and Sixth Schedules, tribal atrocities act, panchayati raj act, and many more. These movements are for amenities of basic survival, like food security, decent clothing and habitable shelter, if not land, forest and water. It should be noted that Madhya Pradesh has the largest tribal population in India, which is 122.33 lakh (20.27 per cent), of the total population of 603.85 lakh as per 2001 census comprising of 46 Scheduled Tribes, which is much higher than the national average (8.2 per cent). The highest proportion of tribal population is found in Jhabua district (86.6 per cent), followed by Barwani (67 per cent), Dindori (64.5 per cent) and Mandla (57.2 per cent) (Debnath 2010).

The state of Madhya Pradesh is abundantly endowed with natural resources like water, forest, mineral, etc., but has become a symbol of the uneven development. According to S.N. Chaudhary, popularization of the capitalist model of development since British invasion led to the formulations of forest management policies and scheme in such a manner that it has changed the meaning of forest from natural object to natural resource resulting thereby in massive deforestation and erosion of symbiotic interface between tribals and forest (Chaudhary 2008-9). The tribals are dependent mostly on the land, forest and natural resources for survival which has undergirded their traditional way of life. But when these resources are exploited by the state and the multinational corporations the tribals lose their only means of livelihood. Thus starts the chain of deprivation that leads to abysmal poverty, starvation and eventually death. But there is a real dearth of quality research on Madhya Pradesh and this chapter will fill the vacuum to some extent by writing the history of the tribal movement which was hitherto an unexplored area of study. It tries to address the issues related to the structural alienation, if not marginalization of the tribals and analyze different trajectories of today's tribal mobilization in Madhya Pradesh.

There were five backward tribes, i.e., Abujhmaria, Baiga, Sahana, Bharia, and Pahari Korwa who were classified as primitive tribes in Madhya Pradesh during the Fifth Five-Year Plan. During the Sixth Five-Year Plan the Kamar and during Seventh Five-Year Plan the Birhor were added in the list. The nomadic Birhors are a primitive and minor tribal community of Madhya Pradesh whom the government is trying to settle. The state intervention has arrived like an external intervention which to some extent has stopped their life cycle as the Birhors have a long history of nomadism. It was the Nehruvian policy that the tribals should develop according to their own genius, but policies were framed to 'assimilate' and 'uplift' them in order to integrate with the so-called Hindu mainstream society. Birhors are no exception. They have been allotted five acres of cultivable land and houses per family under the Indira Awas Yojna. Needless to say, these measures were hardly enough to 'develop' a community without understanding of their way of life or their adaptation capacities properly. Thus, there remains a host of tribes, including the Birhors, who did not even receive the basic amenities of life (Sinha 1999).

The very first case of structural violence is malnutrition and lack of an awareness drive on the part of the government because of which the underage tribal girls are being married off and when they give birth, the newborn often suffers from malnutrition and different types of deficiency related diseases, like fever, polio, measles, pneumonia, diarrhoea, anaemia, blindness, etc. It has been noticed that the delayed initiation of supplementary nutrition for children as well as pregnant and lactating mothers, lugubrious performance of the Integrated Child Development Programme, Mid-day Meal Programme, Antyodaya Anna Yojana (AAY); complete lack of antenatal care, institutional delivery services, food intake and rest during pregnancies and other nutrition and health services for both mothers and children are some of the reasons for such intense sufferings. Jyotsna Jain and Mihir Shah carried out a survey in seven districts of Madhya Pradesh to assess whether the mid-day meal scheme and the AAY were functioning according to the official guidelines and the interim orders of the Supreme Court in the right to food case. They found that the AAY had contributed significantly to the survival of the poverty stricken people over there. But due to poor outreach of the public distribution system in tribal areas and insufficient coverage within each village, the AAY had failed to provide food security and thereby initiate real development for the tribals (Shah 2005). The most unfortunate thing is that the government does not even take the responsibility of such shameful failures. Even civil society and middle class opinion which starts wringing hands at the mention of starvation deaths, remains impervious to the implications of such findings.

The SATHI team of Centre for Health and Allied Themes in

collaboration with a people's organization, Jagrit Adivasi Dalit Sangathan, a broad-based health committee, Jan Swasthya Samiti and an NGO, Ashagram Trust in Barwani district in Madhya Pradesh, carried out an investigation of undernutrition and suspected starvation deaths in Semli, Verwada and Sipahiduwali village of Pati and Barwani blocks. Barwani is a less developed and chronically drought prone region of the state, with a large tribal population having tribal communities which are chronically undernourished. All the deaths (19 deaths), which occurred during March 2001 to May 2001, were investigated. Six deaths during the six months prior to this period (September 2000 to February 2001), which were strongly suspected to be starvation deaths were also studied. Thus a total of 25 deaths were investigated, seven of which were children, and 18 were adults. Their report is indicative of starvation; and consumption of abnormal or unusual foods (forest leaves/tubers/wild fruits not usually eaten, etc.), also indicative of starvation. Some 84 per cent of the children in these villages were found to be malnourished and nearly 22 per cent were found to be suffering from severe malnutrition, seem comparable to the figures found for the general tribal population of Madhya Pradesh according to National Nutrition Monitoring Bureau which is 20.4 per cent. It should be noted that these severely malnourished children were at significant risk of succumbing to fatal infections if malnutrition was not corrected. The incidents of starvation deaths proved the outright denial of the state to give the tribal people the access to the right to food security (Madhya Pradesh 2003).

The National Institute of Public Cooperation and Child Development (NIPCCD), Indore conducted a study in three tribal districts of Madhya Pradesh namely, Alirajpur, Barwani and Khandwa. The study reveals that there were several factors like timely initiation of breastfeeding, administering first milk of mother (colostrum), exclusive breastfeeding up to six months, timely initiation of complementary feeding, etc., which affect the nutrition and health condition of children. But the tribal women of this region hardly had any knowledge of these factors. They were not even aware of the benefit of breastfeeding to their children's health. One of the reasons is that, most of the tribal women of these areas were either wage labourers or agricultural labourers and they did not get time for breastfeeding their children, discontinuation of which took an enormous toll on their growth. The standard timing of anganwadi centres (AWCs) did not suit the women who worked the whole day. There were no initiatives for propagation of its importance, counselling of the new mothers or educating them or opening up crèches by the local governments. The study also revealed that, the Nutrition Rehabilitation Centres have been established in every district of Madhya Pradesh in joint collaboration of the Department of Women and Child Development, and Department of Health. Under the ICDS programme, children of age group six months-three years are provided *bal ahar* (take-home ration) to supplement their nutritional needs. Children of age group three to six years are provided breakfast and lunch (hot cooked meal) at AWCs. Hot cooked meal (breakfast and lunch) is being prepared by self-help groups (SHGs) under the *Sanjha Chulha* (combined kitchen) programme. But unfortunately due to low coverage, incomplete and faulty growth monitoring records and promotion in some of AWCs, followed by severe dearth of necessary interventions like home visits and community participation, resulted in virtually no impact of government services in reducing malnutrition so far (Mishra 2017).

The second case of structural violence is the denial of livelihood and affecting the living standards of the tribals. Uprooting them from their home, hearth and livelihood can have a deadly effect on their resource use, traditional land use pattern, habitat, inheritance, sustenance and finally existence. It not only changed their surrounding landscapes and traditional patterns of subsistence economy but made them more and more vulnerable in the capitalist consumerist economy as well. Loss of forest cover caused a sea change in the tribal way of life. Kirchali village of Sendhawa Tehsil in Barwani District had a dense forest cover about 35 years ago. But that depleted on a massive scale. The problem is that, though the forest is under control of forest department, the administration and management of the forest did not require the supervision of gram panchayat which was why the collection of timber, NTFPs, fuel and fodder was prohibited by the administration. On the other hand, Pospur village of Pati Tehsil in Barwani District is surrounded by steep hills on all sides. Before three decades it had a deep forest, but now everything is gone. It is surprising to see that the tribals of Kirchali did not infringe on the forest laws and were not that rancorous for the denial of their access to the forest resources. But the tribals of Pospur were more perturbed and disconcerted about their rights being denied by the authority. They frequently protested against such injustice. Pospur-Gupsee gram panchayat had a woman *sarpanch* from Gupsee village in 2003. More than 50 per cent villages in Pati Janpad were outside the control of gram panchayat and governed by the forest department. They were called Van Gram. Those villages which are under panchayat had a long term lease of the land, but in Van Gram villages farmlands were allocated to individual households at maximum 6.25 acres for 15 years and the lease is renewed afresh by the forest department. The forest officers had the power to manage the land, forest and water in the Van Gram. Tribals' access to forest products was a little better in Van Gram than forests under panchayat controlled villages. Tribals were quite aware of their rights and express discontent when it comes to any kind of hardships (Sah 2003).

Many argue that displacement of the tribals and their relocation in a non-tribal area might integrate them with the so-called modern and mainstream society. But in reality this is not the case. Forest dependent tribal people whose livelihoods are based on rainfall reliant agriculture, animal husbandry, wage labour and collection of minor forest products are really vulnerable, thus they automatically tended to be marginalized from the mainstream economy, polity, society and culture. One may cite an example of such case that happened with the tribals of Chainpura. The forest department considered cattle dung as minor forest produce and did not allow the tribal to collect them, not even the owners of the cattle and said that these were state property. After a prolonged litigation the High Court nullified such claims in 1984. According to B.D. Sharma, claiming sovereignty over shit was a colonial thought inscribed in their legislation. It meant the cattle cannot graze in the reserved forest without licence and if they did then the excrement became state property like skin, tusk, horns, honey or wax. When the government offered the tribals pay for collecting the same, the irrationality of the legislation was proved (Sharma 2010: 31).

It was argued that tribals were unable to mobilize themselves collectively. But that is not true as tribals have long been organizing themselves under traditional banners and committees to make their presence felt, voices heard and demands fulfilled. Raising arms in order to resist exploitation by the forest department, corrupt government machinery and usurious moneylenders did not always work—they know. But the state was, and is hell bent to crush their peaceful protests at any cost and for serving this purpose it brutalized the repression even harsher by employing various methods of structural violence and structural constraints. Hunger, poverty, malnutrition, child mortality and starvation are some of these methods that are being unleashed against the innocent tribals to mute their forceful voice of indignation. To deny just compensation, ameliorative policies, basic amenities and above all dignity are the key devices and subterfuges that are being used against the tribals to choke their voice so that they can be compelled to accept any discriminatory proposals, be it resettlement or relocation, compensation, food, healthcare or education. The Green Revolution package led to a steep decline in the water level and created an acute crisis of drinking water in the state. Besides, irrigation development through deep tube wells left a ravaging impact because of which the rates of natural recharge of ground water are severely low in the tribal areas. The fact that about one-fourth of children of schoolgoing age in Madhya Pradesh do not attend schools is shocking and thus substantiates the poor condition of infrastructure. Injustice inherent in industrialization, infrastructure development, mining, dam, conservation induced displacement on forest and land dependent tribal communities and irreparably damaged their livelihood as well as natural systems of the tribal regions. With the shock of dislocation, incidents of migration usually escalate because there is a dearth of potable drinking water facilities at the relocation site which also indicates the lack of irrigation for agriculture. Involuntary migration to the industrial belts leads to the bulging number of urban proletariats in the form of informal labour force where tribals live in congested *bustees* and the womenfolk work as domestic help and sometimes even as prostitutes. This chapter will draw attention to such injustices perpetrated by the state and the dominant society to deprive the tribals the basic human needs of life and this is what one calls the structural violence.

The development experience of Madhya Pradesh can help to fathom the origin of deprivation which underscores the tragic failure of government strategies. For example, Maheshwar hydel private power project on the Narmada had got stuck to a complete financial deadlock. Shree Maheshwar Hydel Power Corporation Limited (SMHPCL) claimed that the project would provide 400 megawatt of peaking power and increase the drinking water supply to Indore and its contiguous areas. It also claimed that it had spent Rs. 2,350 crore and stalling the project would affect the project affected people. MoEF examined their claims and finally stopped the work on 23 April 2010. It was found that the project would affect 61 villages of which 13 would be fully submerged and 9 partially submerged. In 39 villages land would be affected and houses would not be shifted. But the R&R policy made no difference between the fully affected and partially affected people. But after pressures from the PMO, Ministry of Power and Madhya Pradesh state government, the ban was lifted the next year. Another dam called the Omkareshwar dam claimed to generate 520 megawatt of power, which also involved the irrigation of 1.47 lakh hectares of agricultural land. Thirty villages were expected to be submerged at the full reservoir level, i.e., 196.6 m. The dam was completed in 2006 (Venkatesan 2011). Mega dams have been betokening development and industrialization as inevitable when Nehru proclaimed that dams are the temples of modern India. But with the passage of time it has been disproved by the misery of the displaced. Their constitutional right to livelihood has not been given adequate acknowledgement when policies are framed. The state is completely indifferent to the travails of the evicted which convert them into development refugees. Bargi dam has been one of the first completed dams among the chain of thirty major dams on Narmada river. The Bargi dam affected 162 villages and uprooted about 7,000 families without the estimation of the indirectly affected people. The evicted were forced to move to the slums of Jabalpur and eke out living by pulling rickshaws, working at the construction sites and migrate. Among the project affected people 30 per cent were tribals and out of these project affected people who were resettled in Gujarat more than 70 per cent were tribal families (Tripathy 2010).

This official neglect, cruelty and callousness was reflected in Indira

Sagar Project (ISP) (earlier known as Narmada Sagar) at Punasa, in Khandwa district as well. The dam caused displacement of more than 30,000 families and more than 80,000 people in Madhya Pradesh alone. According to the official statistics, more or less 16 per cent of the oustees were tribals. If the project affected people were included among them, the number would be much higher. The Madhya Pradesh government was one of the very few state governments that had enacted its own rehabilitation policy (Madhya Pradesh Resettlement and Rehabilitation Act 1949). But it entails legal entitlements of the owner of the land and in most of the cases condition of update work of land titles in the tribal areas is awful. This causes grave precariousness and controversy when it comes to land acquisition. Apart from this the villagers of Baldi, Jamnia, Jabgaon, Puri and Jhagdia Mal were ousted forcefully without any discussion or intimation which left them in trauma of losing the means of survival. The places where the tribals moved with their handful of compensation money did not have basic amenities like drinking water, drainage and toilets. The resettlement colonies were not even supplied with drinking water, electricity, internal roads, drainage, sewerage, markets, health care facilities, or cremation grounds (Mander 2005). Whatever protection was granted by the Narmada Water Disputes Tribunal Award (NWDTA) and the Supreme Court, was systematically violated by the concerned authorities. Land-for-land policy was out and out violated and not a single displacee of ISP had been assigned a single piece of irrigated land.

The submergence zones of Madhya Pradesh by the Sardar Sarovar Project comprised of Nimad and hilly tribal villages of Alirajpur. Their survival and livelihood strategies were based on resources from land and forest. Although NWDTA declared land-for-land policy for resettlement of the oustees, it overlooked the need for resettlement of those tribals who were submerged by the secondary relocations. Interestingly, neither NWDTA nor the World Bank policy ever included women in the special provision for land allotment (Modi 2012). In this way the state administration through various means denied the rights of the Sardar Sarovar oustees. During the Narmada Bachao Andolan Bhil and Bhilala villages took part actively in the demonstrations and struggle against displacement by the Sardar Sarovar Dam.

They mobilized themselves under the banner of Khedut Mazdoor Chetna Sangathan (Peasants, and Workers' Consciousness Union) to ensure government services and secure forest lands. Narmada Bachao Andolan has thus become a significant space of assertion of tribal identity and resistance against dislocation. The movement was like an eye opener for the government as well because it not only placed its claims to land and forest but also proved the tribals to be the true custodians of the environment, not the state that dispossessed them in the name of 'development'. The fight of the Bhilala adivasis against the dam was seconded by the entire world and gathered praise and support from the urban literati.

Tribal movement against the Haribad minor irrigation project is another case in point. The project was built on the boundary of the two villages of Haribad and Sakad in Thikri taluka of Badwani district on the Kundi river in western Madhya Pradesh. Sakad is a tribal village, 98.4 per cent of its 1,273 population are tribals. Haribad also has quite a good number of tribals, but the non-tribals dominated the village. It has been found that the project benefited Haribad, largely whereas the tribals of Sakad had lost their highly fertile lands. This has led to conflicts between two villages. Water is scarce in this region, both for cultivation and drinking. In 1977 the project was first announced and got the necessary administrative clearances on 5 December 1999. Its estimated cost was Rs. 43 lakh, though later increased up to Rs. 1.66 crore. The tribal village of Sakad is situated upstream of the dam and bore almost the complete burden of submergence, while Haribad is situated downstream and is served by canals. It should also be pointed out that Sakad did not receive direct irrigation, whereas Haribad got advantage from the recharging of ground water. The tribals of Sakad opposed the dam chiefly because they had to sacrifice both their land and resources. They did not even benefit directly by the dam. Initially they proposed to shift the dam further downstream so that it could store more water and the non-tribals could also share the brunt of submergence. Since Sakad was under the Scheduled Areas Act, *gram sabha's* consent was required for the acquisition of the tribal land. In 2003 the *gram sabha* was called and approved the project via secret voting. The displaced tribals objected because according to them the rich people of Haribad influenced the *gram sabha* and suborned other villagers. The displaced tribals boycotted the meeting and later went to the collector, who had reportedly declared the *gram sabha* null and void. Surprisingly, many of the displaced families who were initially resistant to the dam later changed their mind and supported it in exchange of proper compensation. They said that the drought in the last few years had compelled them to yield to the offer. This led to the severe breach of trust between the tribals and non-tribals following the movement against Haribad dam (Dharmadhikary 2006).

According to Nandini Sundar, Jhabua has more or less similar socio-economic and demographic indicators as Dantewada in Chhattisgarh. According to the 2001 census, the population in Jhabua is 85 per cent tribal, with 47 per cent of the population living below the poverty line and only 36.87 per cent literate. But unlike Dantewada, which is the heartland of the Maoist movement, Jhabua has been the site of a remarkable non-violent movement for many decades apart from other local struggles, over land and forests. Similarly, the region of Bundelkhand in central India is one of the poorest areas of the country, and while there is a high degree of stratification, there are no Naxalites. The high poverty stricken areas like Jhabua and Bundelkhand have always been within government control, and nobody has ever prevented the government from implementing whatever welfare schemes it wishes (Sundar 2011).

Tribal movements in Madhya Pradesh have quite effectively equalized the relationship between the state and the tribal society. Unlike its neighbouring states like Chhattisgarh and Odisha, tribals of Madhya Pradesh have successfully curbed the Maoist violence taking over the control of their indigenous protest movements. They have mobilized on their own terms which are not only different in character but also commendable. The orientation of their culture of resistance and politics of protest set a new paradigm of tribal movements which is no less radical than the Maoist guerrillas. During 1970s, tribal movements started gaining ground outside the purview of party politics through various grassroot organizations, local and village bodies. Thus the parameters set for the tribal resistance by the so-called state gradually waned and the tribals put forward new alternatives to the existing power politics both at the regional and state level. They have gradually developed a more conscious, efficient and substantial strategic expertise in allaying the fear of state sponsored organized repression. From time immemorial the democratic struggle of the tribals for emancipation had witnessed brutalities and highhandedness of the ruling authorities, be it colonial or postcolonial. But the state violence could not break their strength and determination though it used all its machineries. There are numerous instances of murder and arrests of the tribal activists who tried to organize people against the coercive measures of the state and non-tribal elites ((locally called 'bazaarias'). One such example is the attempted murder of Shamim Modi of the Shramik Adivasi Sangathan, who was working in Betul and Harda districts.

Tribal rights have never made way into the vocabulary of the constitutional provisions of the elite until it met with revolts. The modern state often ignores the diversities and differences among tribes, or better say, it often tries to widen the distinctiveness and heterogeneity by employing all-inclusive policies and homogeneous representation, that in no way can unify or aim to establish equanimity between the tribal and non-tribal or between different tribal communities. And that causes the tribals to experience a more consolidated form of domination and subjugation that helps to discredit the false propaganda of 'development'. The state fails miserably to enforce law and dishonours the citizens' right to protest. It not only leads to dissatisfaction and disillusionment, but also gives birth to a sense of deprivation which is eventually translated into protracted struggle for justice. Economic inequality and social disparities widen the gap further. And here comes the creation of a wrong perception or criminalization of a tribe which leads to psychological alienation and can be regarded a potential weapon of structural violence.

Once the colonial Criminal Tribes Act of 1871 defined the Bhils as one of the most turbulent and lawless communities in the country. It was part and parcel of the colonial otherization, if not divide and rule policy. The criminalization of Bhils has created a negative notion about the community leading to their segregation and exploitation. Later, after Independence the Bhils were decriminalized but the wrong perception remains unaffected among the non-tribals, like politicians, police and other state bureaucrats, which shaped their imagination while framing policies for them. Thus the identity politics which are very much imposed from above, play a decisive role at the grass root level. It also influences the self-representation of the Bhils. This has given way to land alienation and incidents of dispossession to get doubled during the postcolonial era. It is chiefly due to the ignorance of the Bhils that their land is being grabbed by force, allurement, encroachment, fraudulent means and indebtedness. Since the tribals are barred from selling their land to the non-tribals out of their own wish and will according to the existing law, the cases of forceful acquisition are on the rise. It is a well known fact in the neighbouring districts of Jhabua that the land outside tribal habitats sells for approximately Rs. 20-35 lakh per acre, but within the Bhils land sells at hugely discounted rates from anywhere between 2-25 lakh rupees per acre approximately (Tandon 2020). Talking about the wrong perception circulating in mainstream discourse, one must consider the prevailing notions about the Bhils that are really objectionable. For example, there is a popular notion among the non-tribals that the Bhils are rude, aggressive, ill-tempered, irresponsible, culpable or quarrelsome and wasteful or spendthrift and this is the reason why they oppose welfare schemes in their region. But the reality is something completely different from what the existing perceptions are. The long and unbroken history of ethnic politics and exploitation has the answer to what one calls the tribal resistance to the so-called development projects. Contrary to the dominant representations, the Bhils are quite intelligent and desirable consumers. They like to spend more on luxury goods than basic needs. They are not against development, but want to develop according to their own requirement and rules. They prefer to resist all sorts of powerlessness against all odds through logical dissent. Thus, the Bhil use their power and agency in deciding what suits their genius and what fulfils their needs. They are very much interested in adopting and adapting to the so-called mainstream culture, but they are conditioned by their natural ability and selective attitude. Any attempt from outside to nullify this uniqueness and cultural diversity by tagging them as Maoists could result in creating graver conflict and violence between the tribals and non-tribals.

Another case of structural violence is forceful displacement and involuntary resettlement which have never succeeded in making the dispossessed assimilated or integrated with the people they are forced to live with. Involuntary resettlement is the most incontrovertible manifestation of the adverse inclusion of tribals who are blighted by the persistence of endless poverty. Their cultural behaviour, social norms and ethnic practices are completely different from each other. We can cite an example of the Sahariya, a primitive tribal group displaced by the Kuno Wildlife Sanctuary in Sheopur district. The conservation paradigm has had significant impact on the people who derive their livelihood from designated Protected Areas (PAs). The conservation-induced displacement wreaks havoc on the subsistence oriented agrarian economy of the tribals. The alternative livelihood pattern introduced by the rehabilitation package given for the conservation induced displacement impacted negatively on the Sahariyas.

Kuno Wildlife Sanctuary relocated 24 villages to the outskirts of the proposed sanctuary. Over 5,000 Sahariyas resided in these villages prior to the commencement of the project. No adequate compensation was given to the displaced families for getting access to various livelihood resources lost due to resettlement. Besides, there is no homogeneity in the quality of allotted land and the quality of land is very poor and under degraded forestland, especially when compared to the tracts in their original places. Because of this reason more than 300 families are currently suffering because of low agricultural output. The lack of soil moisture and irrigation facilities caused low productivity. Sahariyas also kept livestock in order to meet their needs of milk, ghee, etc. But after their displacement they were compelled to leave their cattle behind as there was a crisis of fodder at the resettlement colony. When the project was first announced, i.e. in 1981, the tribals used to go for hunting as meat is the principal food of the Sahariyas. But after the notification of the sanctuary, severe action was taken against hunting wild animals. Another significant thing is that, a variety of non-timber forest products such as honey, *tendu* leaves, *sal* gum, 'safed musli', 'ber' (zizyphus), 'bilaiya', 'hadjudi' and so on were harvested extensively. But after the rehabilitation of the forest communities they lost the access to these products which were the alternative, if not additional source of their income (Kabra 2003).

There are innumerable such instances of structural violence whereby Article 21 of the Indian Constitution has been violated rampantly and spectacularly. Tribals have always sacrificed for the greater good and development has been initiated at their cost. Another case in point is the Tawa Dam in Hoshangabad district which was constructed on the Tawa river for serving irrigation purposes. The construction work began in 1960s and ended in 1975. The dam submerged 41 tribal villages along with about 20,000 hectares of deep forest range. Though the dam irrigated a huge area in the district, yet the tribals were not benefited by the project at all as they lived at a higher level and there was no plan of lift irrigation. The dam could not distribute water equally and a lot of places are still suffering from waterlogging, salinity and some face water crisis. Tribals were not only forcefully evicted from their habitat, they were also denied the right to have a just compensation and rehabilitation. They were neither offered land-for-land nor cash compensation nor jobs. Most of the tribals did not have legal entitlement called *patta* of their lands because of which they could easily be ousted without any compensation. Very few of them had *patta*, but then also they were given a meagre amount with which nothing could be done. They were forced to live near the submerged villages on the banks of the Tawa reservoir, called Tawanagar, which lacks drinking water facility, grazing grounds and communication. Before displacement they at least had access to them (Sunil and Smitha 1996).

Madhya Pradesh government established the Fisheries Development Corporation (FDC) in 1979 for managing the production of fish in the reservoir. Ironically the evicted tribals who had sacrificed their land for it were not included in it, rather people from outside were given employment in the project. The local tribals were prohibited to fish in the river and no alternative livelihood was made possible for them. Those who tried to fish were denounced as 'thief'. They were arrested, extorted and their boats and nets were confiscated by the police and goons hired by the corporation. Besides, the wastes of the Sarni thermal power station of Betul polluted the river and caused death of fishes. Thus, the project was a big failure. The tribals were organized by a local grassroot organization called Kisan Adivasi Sangathan which was working on the displaced people in the area for a long time. With the help of the district administration the organization formed 35 primary cooperative societies of the fishermen, 98 per cent of whom belonged to the Scheduled Tribes. This initiative was also aimed at giving some relief to the forgotten displaced tribals in the form of temporary employment. When the project was announced in 1955, the fishermen organized a rally on 6 and 7 September on their boats, broke the law, fished in the river and sold them in the town. This was termed as 'fishing satyagraha' and symbolized their indigenous right over the natural resources. This mass mobilization soon caused dissatisfaction and discomfort for the government and after dallying for a long time, the government finally declined to accede to the claims of the Sangathan in granting fishing rights to the impoverished tribals. The tribals blocked the Kesla road on Bhopal-Nagpur national highway in protest against the decision on 9 December after which repression came down on them. The police resorted to looting their belongings and lathicharged 2,000 tribals including women and aged among whom two hundred were detained and twelve leaders were booked under baseless charges (Sunil and Smitha 1996).

Incidents of chronic and endemic poverty in the central tribal belt are alarmingly high. About half of the tribal households are categorized as poor. This is the reason why seasonal migration plays such an important role as a major coping mechanism in the time of emergencies like crop failure, drought or disease. Tribal migration has always been part and parcel of their culture. They migrate mainly in the agriculturally lean seasons. Migration can also be attributed to the push and pull factors operating in tribal economy. Bhils are the most dominant marginal subsistence peasants in Badwani, Alirajpur, and Jhabua districts of Madhya Pradesh. They work as seasonal migrant labourer in the informal sector in the neighbouring states like Gujarat, Maharashtra and Rajasthan. The agriculture of tribal areas of Madhya Pradesh is heavily dependent on rain. Soil erosion has caused infertility of the soil and all these have contributed to droughts, food insecurity, malnutrition and child mortality (between October 2009 and February 2010, 46 tribal children died of malnutrition in three villages in Jhabua district). Hence, migration has become the principal survival strategy during the dry months for the tribals of the state. Sadguru Water

Development Foundation is working in tribal villages of Jhabua (other than Gujarat and Rajasthan) in order to create alternative sustainable development of common property resources. But such positive experiments could not vouch for a panacea of the ills of tribal society and also built counterproductive process as it was not supported either by institutional structure or the participation of the local tribals and benefited only the privileged few (Sah 2010).

During 1999-2000 which was a drought period and full of widespread distress, tribal migration increased manifold. After the earthquake in Kuchch during 2001-2 tribals flocked in the area in search of work at the construction sites. From Jhabua and Ratlam the tribals even travelled to Kota, Surat or Bhuj for jobs at the construction sites. They were recruited by the local agents called *mukkadams*. It attracted almost 20,000 tribals from western part of the state alone. Later irrigation projects and *rabi* cultivation generated a substantial hike in the earnings which finally led to affect both the volume of migration and income from migration. Department for International Development India (DFID) launched a Western India Rainfed Farming Project (WIRFP) Phase I in 1993-9 in order to support the migrant tribal labourers which set up Palayan Suchna Kendra (PSK) or migrant information centres by which the migrant tribals could register themselves and PSK on their part could also connect to the social justice committees at the *gram sabha* level under the MP government's scheme of *gram swaraj* or village self-reliance (Mosse 2005). Phase II of the project was implemented by Gramin Vikas Trust (GVT) and the India Farm Forestry Development Co-operative (IFFDC) over a seven-year period (1999-2006). It aimed at sustainably amplifying the livelihoods of 675,000 tribal poor in one of the backward, ecologically depleted and drought prone regions of India and diffuse the technologies and approaches developed extensively in the area (WIRFP Final Report 2005). This surveillance can be proved beneficial in getting information about any misdeeds and exploitation of the tribals if conducted with efficiency.

However, subordination and deprivation has not gone unchallenged in Madhya Pradesh. There exists an unbroken culture of grassroot mobilization and resistance in the tribal heartland of Madhya Pradesh. The local state apparatus has denied tribals in the region even the most basic rights and entitlements. There are unending incidents that have occurred time and again to prove this. One of them took place in 1994 in Chikhli village of Dhar when a confrontation broke out between the forest department and the local tribals. The forest department tried to plant trees forcibly on Chikhli's traditional grazing ground by the revenue department. When on 17 May the tribals came to know that men from the forest department had arrived to begin plantation work, they rushed to the spot. The range officer fired in the air to disperse the tribals and the police later booked the protesting tribals on several charges (Shraddha 1994).

The tribals have proved time and again that democratic struggle from below can effectively challenge the adverse incorporation of subaltern groups in a given power structure. And when they speak the language of protest, repression comes down from above that tries to stonewall their advances. There are a series of laws passed to protect the tribals from injustices which fell defunct without proper and timely implementation on the part of the administration and judiciary. The structural violence perpetrated by the state by using its machinery had faced resistance by the tribals of Madhya Pradesh. Established in 1990s, Adivasi Mukti Sangathan (AMS) is one such organization under which the tribals of Barwani and Khargone district in the western part of Madhya Pradesh had launched protest movement against the state repression in the form of low-ranking officials—forest guards, police and revenue officers (patwaris) in particular—who would demand bribes in cash and kind from villagers on various pretexts. Their movement is to challenge the predations and violence of the local state (Nilsen 2015). From 1996 to the early 2000s the tribals of Dewas district formed local organizations like Adivasi Morcha Sangathan and Adivasi Shakti Sangathan in order to vent their grievances against the illegal extortion, corruption, loot by the forest department, police, other government machinery and usurious moneylenders. A lot of tribals joined these organizations which have gained a lot of political influence lately. They have even contested in the panchayat elections and won.

Tribal women are not indifferent towards these corruptions and maladministration rather they have courageously participated in a large number in the movements and proved their strength. Their movement is for negotiating a tolerated space where they could exercise their rights to forest resources, confronting the existing power structure and preventing widespread alcoholism. Once a survey was conducted by an NGO called Arohi Trust which revealed that the average haemoglobin level of the tribal women in Nimad was 7.5 gms per decalitre that means they were severely anaemic. Apart from this the women labourers were also underpaid, debt-ridden and bore the brunt of alcoholism most. The tribal women of Nimad rose in protest when the atrocious government authorities like excise officials and powerful non-tribals like liquor mafias tried to gag the tribal organizations which were actively working in the region for the sake of the downtrodden. Their militant movement remind one about the Lalgarh movement of West Bengal where tribal women were at the forefront of the intrepid struggle against police brutalities. In the early morning of 8 January 1998 a large crowd of tribal women gathered at the police station in Katkut village of Khargone district to agitate against indiscriminate arrests and implication of false cases against the innocent tribals in the region. The women were organized under Adivasi Shakti Sangathan (ASS) which had been spearheading tribal movements for a long time. They were determined to get arrested and did not want bail. But the police arrested only eight women against whom there were some false cases lodged regarding breaking of forest laws and stealing timber. The local administration even clamped down Section 144 in order to halt all the rallies and public meetings called by the tribals to be held in Sendhwa and Barwah on 24-25 November. Before this incident, there was already a huge rally organized by almost all tribal organizations together on 8 September. A massive force consisting of more or less three thousand policemen was arranged from other districts to execute the ban. The tribals were not going to yield and decided to go on according to their plan. At the midnight of 24 November the police arrested both men and women while going to join the rally in Sendhwa. On 27 November, the tribal women under the leadership of ASS demonstrated in front of the police station without caring about the cold and rain and demanded the unconditional release of all the arrested tribals immediately. The confrontation escalated when the tribal women carried on their epic struggle even inside the jail and one tribal woman named Subhadra went on for an indefinite hunger strike demanding the withdrawal of all the false charges pressed against them. Her condition was worsening when she was taken to the hospital but she did not succumb to the injustice. After 11 days of hunger strike the authority gave up and agreed to withdraw charges, released the arrested and transferred the superintendent of police. Thus, the tribal women's movement of Nimad successfully foiled all the attempt of the vested interests and became victorious (Rahul 1998).

In September 1999 a group of forest guards plundered Katukya village in Dewas and gunned down an innocent Bhil called Roopsingh. The raid was a part of state sponsored squelching mission to smash AMS movement which had been under way since 1995. According to the Scheduled Castes and Scheduled Tribes (Prevention of Atrocities) Act, murdering of a tribal by a non-tribal entitles his/her heirs to have compensation. Enraged by the killing, thousands of AMS activists along with the local tribals gheraoed Udainagar police station with his dead body and demanded the arrests of the culprits and payment of the compensation to the family of Roopsingh. But unfortunately in spite of assiduous efforts neither the district magistrate nor the High Court did justice and rejected the plea on some spurious grounds that the murderer was also a tribal. Notwithstanding the fact that the Supreme Court passed an order ruling that the district magistrate should give the compensation to the petitioner in compliance with the Act, the authority never took the initiative (Banerjee 2005).

After this incident the Madhya Pradesh government started realizing the force of the AMS and their movement for tribal rights. Theft of timber was just an alibi. The actual fact was that the government could sense the growing awareness among the tribals. Soon all the state apparatus assembled at a high level meeting that was held in Bhopal on 17 February 2001 to launch an operation which was dubbed as 'Operation Clean' to quell the tribal movements in various parts of the state (Anonymous 2004). It was decided that AMS ought to be demobilized and the tribals were to be persuaded to join Forest Protection Committees organized by the state. In March, Operation Clean confronted the tribals and attacked the village of Kadoriya. Tribal houses were destroyed and all their belongings were taken away.

The stored grains were all spoiled by spreading poisonous chemicals. Over the next four days, police and forest guards despoiled four more villagers. In the morning of 2 April, police and forest guards reached their next destination Mehendikheda village and started vandalizing houses. The villagers started throwing stones at them. On that fateful day, the tribals of Dewas suddenly received notice from the forest department officials of Khargone division which stated that the tribals would be evicted from their forest lands with immediate effect on the pretext that the tribals were encroachers. This is no doubt an excellent example of the mockery of development where the tribals become encroachers in their own land. In Bagli tehsil the district administration of Dewas started destroying tribal houses without informing or giving any prior notice of any kind from 28 March 2001. A recent report revealed that, the administration, police and forest department came in formidable strength with over 400 armed police in about 32 vehicles. Kadodia was the first village that was targeted where four houses were destroyed that day. On 29 March 11 houses in Potla, on 30 March 2 houses in Jamasindh, on 31 March 14 houses in Patpadi (including the house of the sarpanch), on 1 April 21 houses in Katukia and on 2 April 2 houses in Mehendikheda village were knocked down. On 31 March, the tribals tried to protest peacefully by sitting on a mud road leading to the villages. They continued this protest for three days and then on 2 April they assembled at Mehendikheda to stop the demolition of the houses in that village. Unfortunately that village was the target of that day. The police began firing at 9 a.m. and went on without respite till 12 noon in which four men were killed. Wanton damage, looting and plunder took place along with firing (Swaminathana 2001). The state repression came under the cliché alibi that the protesting tribals were Maoists so that the state could easily trample the tribal organizations which were challenging the dominant political parties in elections. It was also because of the fact that the tribals were resisting the corrupt officials and moneylenders from taking money from them illegally.

There are other tribal organizations too which are fighting against the notoriety and brutality of the state officials and police. In 1980s, Khedut Mazdoor Chetna Sangathan (KMCS) emerged in Alirajpur of Jhabua district. During the 1990s Jagrit Adivasi Dalit Sangathan

(JADS) in Badwani district, AMS in Khargone district, ASS in Barwah tehsil, Adivasi Morcha Sangathan in Bagli tehsil and the Shramik Adivasi Sangathan in Betul and Harda districts emerged as powerful tribal movements. During the mid-1990s, the Adivasi Morcha Sangathan started working on the reproductive health of the tribal women in Barwah and Bagli tehsils. But women's reproductive health is very much linked to the broader power structure of gender relationship in the tribal community. It was later understood that to change it one needs to initiate a collective mobilization of both the sexes.

State responses towards these local tribal movements have always been negative and it was often said that these organizations have been formed to hinder government functionaries to implement different schemes. The state has created Adivasi Samaj Sudhar Shanti Sena (ASSSS) to counter the rise of AMS in 1997. This led to the outbreak of an unprecedented era of terror and violent oppression in the strongholds of AMS. Between 1996 and 1998 the conflict between AMS and the Shanti Sena intensified rapidly. But the truth is that these organizations have always campaigned for the speedy implementation of schemes and never obstructed government initiatives. One such scheme was National Rural Employment Guarantee Scheme (NREGS). It was because of these tribal organizations that NREGS has become one of the most successful government schemes in Pati block of Badwani district. But this is not the case in other blocks. For example, a study conducted in 2008 in Gond populated Pathai village of Sahpur development block of Betul district revealed that the purpose of the sub-scheme of Kapildhara of NREGS, which is directed to provide irrigation facility to the marginal farmers as well as wage work, was defeated due to lack of assertiveness of the panchayat representative and rampant malpractices (Chaudhary 2010).

State policies for tribals have an immanent contradiction which is manifested in the conflicts regarding the forest management issues. In 1994, the Madhya Pradesh government, in order to implement directives issued by the central government, took initiative to legalize *nevad* which would give the tribals a tittle to their *nevad* land that they had been tilling for decades. But due to stringent requirements most of the tribals could not even apply for it. The order released by the environmental ministry said that the tribals had to prove that they encroached on the *nevad* land before October 1980 and their landholdings did not exceed two hectares. Since tribals did not possess any such proof of legal documents they remained unqualified for the right of *patta.* What they were supposed to submit was the receipt of fines that they paid for illegally cultivating the forest lands. But here also they were never given receipts by the forest officials who extort them frequently for money. The question remains, if *nevad* was considered a crime why did the government wanted to regularize it? The fact is that shifting cultivation like *nevad* or *podu* (in Odisha) or *jhum* (in Jharkhand) actually helps the forest to regenerate and by taking steps towards legalizing the practice of shifting cultivation, the state had finally recognized the tribals' rights of ownership of forest land. But before this recognition there had been long history of tribal movements for rights over *nevad* land. Amita Baviskar has documented this history in detail.

In 1988, tribals of Jhabua started their battle against the injustice under the leadership of Khedut Mazdoor Chetna Sangathan (KMCS) which compelled the authority to conduct a survey in Mathvad forest. According to the survey, almost every tribal in the region had augmented his legal holdings with a lot of small *nevad* plots. Most of this land had been cultivated since 1970 and sometimes even earlier. KMCS mobilized tribals from around 95 villages to struggle for justice. Violent confrontations broke out when the forest department officials prevented tribals from getting into *nevad* land by digging cattle proof trenches in order to block the entry of the tribals. They were intimidated by forceful confiscation of all their fields and false cases inflicted on them. But the tribals did not cower in fear. Then as an alternative a new scheme was introduced in mid-1980s called the Hitgrahi Yojana which promised forest land to be leased to the landless tribals for growing crops. It was also said that the complete expenditure of afforestation would be borne by the forest department. Tribals would be given the usufruct rights of the cultivated crop. The KMCS convinced the tribals of Alirajpur to join the scheme but after a few months the government terminated the scheme by giving the excuse of shortage of funds. After this the fight was intensified further. Tribals of Attha, Khodar, Gendra, Kiti, Semlani, Pujara ki Chauki, Khodamba, Umrath and many other villages had successfully fought for their legitimate rights which enabled them to have a collective sense of security to take initiatives towards soil and water conservation programmes on a great extent. The KMCS had ensured and safeguarded their access to the *nevad* land (Baviskar 1994).

Alf Gunvald Nilsen has also provided a glaring account of the movement launched by KMCS in Alirajpur. In this town the Irrigation Department planned to construct a pond. Khemla and Khemraj took work there and soon found that the contractor was paying the workers far less than the minimum wage stipulated by the state government. Under their leadership, the workers declared a strike and demanded the wages that they deserved. The contractor hired goons and badly beat up Khemla, but could not stop the movement from growing. Later on the sub-divisional magistrate settled the matter in favour of the workers. Khemraj and Khemla started travelling from one village to another and organized tribals. When Khemraj came to know that several tribals of Gondwani village were being detained by the forest guards and taken to the Range Office in the adjacent village of Attha, he went to the Forest Department seeking immediate action. But the forest guards tortured him and he was badly injured. The angry tribals organized a rally to Alirajpur town and conducted a dharna. The incident spread like wild fire. The chief minister took action and the forest guards were benched. The resounding success of the movement reinvigorated the tribals of the other villages and thus KMCS was formed. The KMCS extended its area of protest from exploitation of the state officials to rampant corruption and demanded constructive planning for health and education for the tribals. They also claimed their constitutional right to join politics and recognition of their forest rights. This led to the outbreak of violent confrontations. The movement was so strong that the Forest Department was compelled to allow *nevad* to proceed in villages that were known to be the strongholds of KMCS (Nilsen 2012). In Nilsen's words,

> In strictly quantitative terms, the AMS constituted a challenge of greater proportions than the KMCS by covering five times as many villages; its organizational reach alone made it a force to be reckoned with in the area. Correspondingly, the repression unleashed by the state against the AMS and the ASS/AMS was also of a qualitatively different kind than that

faced by the KMCS. The AMS and the ASS/AMS faced sustained and co-ordinated campaigns of coercion, violence, and murder, orchestrated in and by the state, with approval from its upper political and bureaucratic echelons. (Nilsen 2012)

Tribal organizations fighting against an unresponsive, unaccountable and predatory agents of the state are often seen as Maoist front organizations and needless to say that this is a very well-planned policy of the Indian state which has unleashed a relentless attack on the basic democratic rights and entitlements of its most impoverished and backward citizens. The tribals who are actually trying to articulate their local grievances and challenge the powerlessness and marginality are facing an enormous amount of coercion due to their just claims and demands. But there are many structural impediments to the limit to which the indigenous people can voice their protest, like institutional, strategic or simply at the grass root level. Poverty is the basic reason of this powerlessness. Tribals have been historically denied agency and thrown out to the margins with some given facilities that the authority feels suitable for them, be it development, recognition or representation, in a very limited way. Their issues were neither politicized nor prioritized till the time they galvanized the state to take action in their favour.

Therefore, it has become the sole responsibility on the part of the state to supress any kind of attempt to raise substantial awareness among the tribals regarding their democratic rights, civil liberties, and constitutional provisions that could translate into defensive measures. The blatant threats perpetrated against the tribal organizations and their representatives are the outcome of a conflict of interest between the tribals' claim of customary rights and state ownership of the forest. For example, the Bhils clear forest land and use it for cultivation which is called *nevad*, is a key survival strategy. Though *nevad* means 'new field', it has now become a symbol of encroached fields. But this also causes the flagrant violation of forest laws that gives the state a potential instrument to criminalize the Bhils as 'encroachers' on government property. Again, the conflict between the forest department and local Gond tribals in Harda district over 'encroachments' generated a debate regarding the Scheduled Tribes (Recognition of Forest Rights) Act. Not only that, the distillation of traditional *mahua* liquor has also become a target of the rapacious police to harass, beat and extort the innocent tribals.

During the 1990s, two developments changed the course of the AMS movement. First, it had expanded its activities across West Nimar. It was active in more than five hundred villages in three blocks of the district by 1996 and established links with other Adivasi organizations too. Within this time the movement was successful in prohibiting illegal timber and liquor trade in the tribal villages. AMS pioneered a wide campaign against the liquor trade in Bhagwanpura block that finally led to the closure of some 250 outlets. This was no doubt a direct attack on the incomes of the liquor traders, agents and the local police as well. Then the AMS moved on from addressing local issues at the local level to articulating a claim for tribal self-rule and coined the slogan *hamare gaon mein, hamara raj* (our rule in our villages). In order to achieve its goals, AMS linked its activities to the Bharat Jan Andolan which was a national network of people's movements led by the former commissioner for Scheduled Castes and Scheduled Tribes, B.D. Sharma and its campaign for the implementation of the Bhuriya Committee Report (submitted in 1995), arguing for the implementation of tribal self-rule in scheduled areas. In 1996, the central government enacted the PESA, which was intended to devolve powers of accountable governance to the level of the *gram sabha* in scheduled areas. What PESA did was to provide AMS with a means of institutionalizing tribal empowerment that was ordained by the legislative powers. In 1997, the Madhya Pradesh Panchayati Raj Act was amended in order to bring it into line with the PESA. This created a new era of tribal mobilization for the AMS. The movement has drawn support from one hundred thousand tribal people which prove that AMS has become a stronger force in the emerging regional political sphere (Nilsen 2016).

In recent times Jhabua has witnessed a sea change in the tribal politics and movement. Sanskritizing elements were always present in the tribal world since time immemorial. It is not new, but what is new is that the response of the tribals towards the Hinduization and especially Hindu fundamentalist activities today. In the history of tribal movements, there were always a division between revivalist and reformist traditions. If Santhal movement was revivalist then Khewar movement was reformist in nature. Both Tana Bhagat and Haribaba movements were influenced by the Hinduization process, better known as *bhagat* cult. But Jhabua and some other parts of Madhya Pradesh remained outside the purview of Sanskritization for a long time. But during the last century several attempts of Sanskritization have been recorded in this particular region. The most striking feature of this movement has been the gradual repudiation of the tribal customary practices and religion in favour of the internalization of the Hindu sects and culture by the tribals. Tribals who have embraced Hindu sects have even started keeping a distance from those tribes who opposed the theory of upward mobility or to be more specific Saffronization. In Jhabua this development started canvassing the tribal scenario way back in 1940s. But the blossoming of the Hindutva culture in this tribal heartland took place during 1990s. In 1997-9 Christian tribals were attacked and their churches were set ablaze. In 2004 assembly elections saffron forces won and formed the government in Madhya Pradesh. According to the census of 1991, Christians constitute roughly around 15,000 in the total population of 13 lakh in the district. Their economic condition was no better than other tribes. In January violence against Christian tribals broke out and several churches, schools and homes were torched by the Hinduized segments of the tribals. This was a cataclysmic departure from the tribal struggle for democratic rights which indicates an eclipse of tribal mobilization against displacement from home, hearth and livelihood (Baviskar 2005).

Structural violence is of many types. Apart from malnutrition, starvation, etc. apathy in creating job opportunities are also regarded as structural violence because it indirectly forces the tribals to take up jobs in hazardous climate of the unorganized sectors as wage labourers with no guarantee of service, social security, health protection or protection of workers' rights so far. Such is the case of the Bhils and Bhilalas of Jhabua and Dhar districts of Madhya Pradesh from where thousands of tribals migrate to Balasinor, Rheda and Godhra districts of Gujarat to work in the quartz rock crushing factories. In the factories like Jyoti, Aman, Gayatri and Narayan, stone is crushed to dust. Different surveys have repeatedly warned the factory owners that air pollution level continues to be above the safety line in the factory areas. But they did not pay heed to it. The tribals inhale poisonous silica while crushing the stone and contact Silicosis which is an incurable disease and causes death. The symptoms are rasping breath, emaciation, profound weakness. Dhar is a predominantly tribal district and has seven tehsils—Dhar, Badnawar, Manawar, Dharampuri, Sardarpura and Kukshi, most of which are rain deficit areas and were affected by severe drought in 2002 and 2008. The land in Jhabua is also arid and both the districts depend heavily on agriculture. But there is an out and out indifference on the part of the government to engineer knowhow for better cultivation and ensure a safe and fair employment for the tribals. The state government's watershed programme failed to generate employment and thus could not ameliorate the condition of the tribals. Unsystematic and thoughtless application of the technology of Green Revolution proved hazardous for the tribals. The district administration has also lagged behind in implementing NREGS. Most of the landless tribals are not even provided with job cards. This has forced the tribals to choose a migrant's life in a precarious and risky job sector. Thus Jhabua became one of the poorest districts of India. In 2006 a survey was conducted by KMCS in cooperation with an Indore-based NGO called Shilpi Kendra that works on public health. The report reveals that the tribals get a meagre amount of fifty rupees per day which is below minimum wage. Their survey of Silicosis in 21 villages of Alirajpur tehsil, Jhabua district contains a thorough compilation of occupational and medical history, together with physical and radiological examinations. According to this report, 489 persons from 218 households were exposed to toxic silica dust of varying intensity and duration. Of these, 158 were dead and another 266 were ill with Silicosis. That is a frighteningly high as 86 per cent are either dead or seriously ill. Of those affected, 92 per cent are the primary wage earners for their family. Ninty-four per cent of the deaths have occurred within three years of exposure to silica dust (Shilpi Kendra 2007). The response of the state is beyond expectation as neither a single factory was closed down nor were the tribals compensated. Nevertheless, the tribals are not ignorant about their democratic rights; they just do not have a political representation that could voice their demands for a just protection and compensation. The KMCS has set a stellar instance of activism and made the issue a public agenda. Their movement has brought the local community organizations, public health professionals and social workers together under one umbrella and established networks with other states in order to raise awareness in media, courts and other statutory bodies about the crisis (Baviskar 2008).

Another aspect of structural violence is indebtedness leading to land alienation as both are interrelated. They are the perils of tribal economy. As land alienation is the nub of displacement and depeasantization, it is regarded as one of the crucial yardsticks of analyzing structural change that has taken place in the tribal economy. There were various legislations introduced in Madhya Pradesh before and after Independence. The Central Provinces Land Alienation Act of 1916 was implemented to check the unwanted transfer of tribal land; Madhya Bharat Scheduled Areas (Allotment and Transfer of Land) Regulation of 1954 (applicable to Madhya Bharat region only) was introduced to restrict transfer of tribal land to non-tribals without the prior permission of collector, sale, mortgage, lease or otherwise; Madhya Pradesh Land Revenue Codes of 1959 was enacted to provide protection to the Scheduled Tribes against alienation of their lands. But the grim scenario of land alienation today says that none could check transfer of tribal land to the non-tribals. As per the document of the Tenth Plan, nearly 9.75 lakh acres of tribal land was reported as alienated in 1999 and a sizeable proportion of it was in Madhya Pradesh. The data on land alienation and restoration of tribal land mentioned in the Annual Report of the Ministry of Rural Development, Government of India (MRD 1999-2000) reveals that land alienation among the tribals in Madhya Pradesh is remarkably high. Besides, a sizeable tribal area of Madhya Pradesh has gone out of the total quantum of surplus land as a result of court decisions as litigations withhold a major part of land (Mohanty 2012).

Similarly, indebtedness is another curse of rural life, especially in the tribal areas where usurers and private traders resort to unscrupulous means to befool the illiterate tribals and grab their lands by taking advantage of their poor repayment capacity and poor asset condition. Tribals fall prey to the debt trap due to a lot of reasons, e.g. unavailability of agricultural resources, absence of micro-credit organizations,

TABLE 3.1: TRIBAL LAND ALIENATION

State	*Area Involved in Litigation*	*Area Reserved for Public Purpose*	*Area Unfit for Cultivation*	*Area not Available for Miscellaneous Reasons*	*Total*
Madhya Pradesh	63.24	19.47	13.31	3.98	100.00

Source: National Institute of Rural Development, Rural Development Statistics, Hyderabad: National Institute of Rural Development, 1999.

displacement, social obligations, consumption expenditure, purchase of capital asset, illness, poor access of the government medical network and the like. Madhya Pradesh had two acts enacted in 1976 and 1982 respectively to check land alienation via indebtedness but it still persists. The contribution of the grain bank and self-help groups is also negligible. A recent study found that the tribals of Shoupur were worst hit by the indebtedness. In villages like Kevlari of Chhindwara and Silpati of Betul, tribals were under constant pressure to covertly transfer their land allotted to them by the government to the moneylenders. Tribals who did not transfer their lands were forced to sell their crops to the lender at a low price (Joshi 2010).

There were numerous government initiatives for poverty eradication. One of them was the Swarnajayanti Gram Swarojgar Yojana (SGSY) introduced in 1999 to provide self-employment. A study conducted among the tribal women members of SHG in Jhabua who work under this scheme found that 80 per cent respondents took loan from the moneylenders and more than 70 per cent could not repay their loans in time. The principal reasons of non-repayment were unemployment and migration. The observations that emerged from the study clearly mention that it is the illiteracy, backwardness, displacement from indigenous resources, alcoholism, migration, absence of modern communication and above all poverty which are the main reasons because of which tribals are unable to take advantage of the government schemes like micro-credits and the like. The study further warns that liberalization, privatization and globalization have aggravated their crisis and exposed them to the larger threats of vulnerability and disempowerment (Tapan 2010).

Tribal economy in Madhya Pradesh is intrinsically related to the forest and that is why forest management plays a crucial role in analyzing the plight of the tribals here. To prioritize people's participation in the development and management of the forest the Forest Department of Madhya Pradesh passed the resolution of Joint Forest Management (JFM) in 1991 and its amendment in 1995 gave more importance to the weaker sections and NGOs. The resolution was revised in 2000 and 2001 which connected JFM with panchayat system. The World Bank had also helped increase people's participation, provide employment, planting non-timber forest produces and finally generate livelihood. But a recent research has unveiled that the tribals are not given opportunities or being oriented in planning, implementation, monitoring and evaluation through the participatory process. It is the forest officials who manipulate their power to run any project and thus control the entire mechanism. Appropriate micro-planning is also absent. Most of the time the disbursement of allotted budget does not appear in time and there is a great negligence recorded regarding the capacity building and skill development. The key outcome of such initiatives towards a sustainable development is an inequitable distribution of share among the beneficiaries which ultimately deprives the tribal people who need them the most (Debnath 2010).

Recently many tribal development programme have been introduced by the central government like national level Vanbandhu Kalyan Yojana, Tribal Education Loan Scheme, Eklavya Model Housing Development to protect the tribal communities from getting impoverished. It has been claimed by the Chief Minister of Madhya Pradesh Shivraj Singh Chouhan that the tribal welfare scheme in the state is also inspired by the vision of the national tribal development which speaks for equal right of the tribals. It includes 24-hour electricity, potable water under Jal Jeevan Mission, construction of roads, coaching and skill development training facilities for students under Mukhyamantri Medhavi Vidyarthi Yojana, facilitating selling of *tendu* leaves, creating employment under Devaranya Yojana, giving free treatments, and celebrating Jhabua Festival every year. All these promises were made on the auspicious occasion of the birth anniversary of Birsa Munda on 15 November 2021. One can only hope seeing those getting fulfilled in the long run (*The Times of India* 15 November 2021).

Next is the case of the role of tribal women in functioning of democratic decentralization programme or panchayati raj system in the state of Madhya Pradesh. It has often been argued that tribals lack a sense of collective mobilization and fail to create an effective demand in political institutional frameworks like the panchayats. But instances can be cited where such claims will be rebutted by the tribal female *sarpanches* themselves. Increasing socio-political consciousness among the tribals about their right and capability generated conflict within the power structure of the tribal society itself. The election of Sunita of Brahmin dominated Tighra village, block Simariya, district Rewa in 2004 as a tribal *sarpanch* was not welcomed by the dominant section of her village. Manju Kapur has recorded her struggle against patriarchal hierarchy and a corrupt system in her village which is a glaring instance of how the socially weak people are threatened and intimidated. She was accused of siphoning off funds allotted for NREGS, framed in false charges, harassed by Section 40, forced to move to the court and when nothing could dissuade her they threatened her to be run over by car. Sunita said to the sub-divisional magistrate,

> Sir, I am an adivasi woman sarpanch for the first time. These are Brahmins who say: give a project estimate for 20,000 rupees . . . to us. Because I don't do this, they are against me. . . . Officers listen to the Brahmins, they do not understand what is true and what is false. (Kapur 2009)

Sunita's achievements include installation of 25 sanitation points, repairing of 12 hand pumps, creation of 100 foot capacity pumps under the Jal Abishek Programme, construction of roads, deepening of village ponds and issuance of 288 job cards under NREGS (Kapur 2009). Shanta Bai Davar, another tribal woman, was the *sarpanch* of the Dikthan gram panchayat in the Nalcha block in Dhar district. She had shown commendable courage in trashing male dominance in her village. She initiated several developmental activities by involving people from the grass roots. She undertook, under her supervision, construction of a police chowki, concrete roads, an Education Guarantee Scheme school, laying of 5,000 ft underground pipeline and lakes to store water. What is also remarkable arc the efforts taken by her to mobilize women *sarpanches* from across the blocks periodically, thereby giving meaning to a collective empowerment of women *sarpanches* (Kumar 2001).

It is hard to believe that after seventy-five years of Independence the status of the tribals in Indian society provides a grim and disappointing picture. Studies have shown that over the years the gap between the tribals and non-tribals has widened. The state response towards their development remained insufficient, dubious and ambivalent. The state neither ensures their participation in the decision making process nor provides answers to their grievances, rather supressed their rightful movements by employing various means of structural violence so that it could subdue their voices in favour of the powerful and dominant.

REFERENCES

Anonymous, 2003, 'Madhya Pradesh: Undernutrition and Starvation Deaths: An Inquiry', in *Economic and Political Weekly*, vol. 38, no. 18, pp. 1751-5.

——, 2004, 'Human Rights Violation in the Context of the Displacement of Project Affected People: A Report on Five Case Studies of State-sponsored Terror in India', in *Social Change*, vol. 34, no. 4, pp. 107-21.

Banerjee, Rahul, 2005, 'Pillar to Post in Quest of Justice', in *Economic and Political Weekly*, vol. 40, no. 31, pp. 3373-4.

Baviskar, Amita, 1994, 'Fate of the Forest: Conservation and Tribal Rights', in *Economic and Political Weekly*, vol. 29, no. 38, pp. 2493-2501.

——, 2005, 'Adivasi Encounters with Hindu Nationalism in MP', in *Economic and Political Weekly*, vol. 40, no. 48, pp. 5105-13.

——, 2008, 'Contract Killings: Silicosis among Adivasi Migrant Workers', in *Economic and Political Weekly*, vol. 43, no. 25, pp. 8-10.

Chaudhary, S.N., 2008-9, 'Human Rights of Tribal Women Engaged in Collection of Non-Timber Forest Produces in Madhya Pradesh', in *Journal of Gender Equality and Sensitivity*, vol. 3, no. 1.

——, 2010, 'Changing Patterns of Tribal Economy and its Implications: Case Study of a Betul Village', in S.N. Chaudhary (ed.), *Tribal Economy Crossroads*, Jaipur: Rawat Publications, pp. 84-118.

Debnath, Debashis, 2010, 'Forest Management vis-à-vis Tribal Economy', in S.N. Chaudhary (ed.), *Tribal Economy Crossroads*, Jaipur: Rawat Publications, pp. 266-87.

Dharmadhikary, Rehmat and Shripad, 2006, 'When Multiple Conflicts Overlap: Haribad Project in Madhya Pradesh', in *Economic and Political Weekly*, vol. 41, no. 7, pp. 603-4.

Joshi, Y.G., 2010, 'Indebtedness and Land Alienation among Tribals of Madhya Pradesh', in S.N. Chaudhary (ed.), *Tribal Economy Crossroads*, Jaipur: Rawat Publications, pp. 119-65.

Kabra, Asmita, 2003, 'Displacement and Rehabilitation of an Adivasi Settlement Case of Kuno Wildlife Sanctuary, Madhya Pradesh', in *Economic and Political Weekly*, vol. 38, no. 29, pp. 3073-8.

Kapur, Manju, 2009, 'Sarpanch Sahib Sunita', in Manjima Bhattacharjya (ed.), *Sarpanch Sahib*, New Delhi: Harper Collins Publishers India, pp. 55-70.

Kumar, B. Venkatesh, 2001, 'Panchayats and Water Scarcity', in *Economic and Political Weekly*, vol. 36, no. 29, pp. 2752-3.

Mander, Harsh, 2005, 'Displacement with State Subterfuge: Case Study of Indira Sagar Pariyojana', in *Economic and Political Weekly*, vol. 40, no. 48, pp. 5056-67.

Mishra, Rajesh, 2017, 'Determinants of Child Malnutrition in Tribal Areas of Madhya Pradesh', in *Economic and Political Weekly*, vol. LII, no. 5, pp. 50-7.

Modi, Renu, 2012, 'Sardar Sarovar Oustees: Coping with Displacement', in Indra Munshi (ed.), *The Adivasi Question: Issues of Land, Forest and Livelihood*, New Delhi: Economic and Political Weekely and Orient BlackSwan, pp. 264-71

Mohanty, B.B., 2012, 'Land Distribution among Scheduled Castes and Tribes', in Indra Munshi (ed.), *The Adivasi Question: Issues of Land, Forest and Livelihood*, New Delhi: Economic and Political Weekely and Orient BlackSwan, pp. 125-51.

Mosse, David, Sanjeev Gupta and Vidya Shah, 2005, 'On the Margins in the City: Adivasi Seasonal Labour Migration in Western India', in *Economic and Political Weekly*, vol. 40, no. 28, pp. 3025-38.

Nilsen, Alf Gunvald, 2012, 'Adivasis in and against the State Subaltern Politics and State Power in Contemporary India', in *Critical Asian Studies*, vol. 44, no. 2, pp. 251-82.

——, 2013, 'Adivasi Mobilization in Contemporary India: Democratizing the Local State?', in *Critical Sociology*, vol. 39(4), pp. 615-33.

——, 2015, 'Subalterns and the State in the Longue Durée: Notes from "The Rebellious Century" in the Bhil Heartland', in *Journal of Contemporary Asia*, vol. 45(4), pp. 1-22.

——, 2016, 'Democratic Struggles in the Bhil Heartland: Historical Trajectories and Contemporary Scenarios', in Uday Chandra and Daniel Taghioff (eds.), *Staking Claims: The Politics of Social Movements in Contemporary Rural India*, New Delhi: Oxford University Press, pp. 31-63.

——, 2016, 'Real, Practical Emancipation? Subaltern Politics and Insurgent Citizenship in Contemporary India', in *Focaal—Journal of Global and Historical Anthropology*, vol. 76, pp. 31-45.

Ramkuwar, 2009, 'We Will Never Forgive the Government', in Lyla Mehta (ed.), *Displaced by Development: Confronting Marginalization and Gender Injustice*, New Delhi: Sage Publications, pp. 270-81.

Rahul, 1998, 'Bhil Women of Nimad: Growing Assertion', in *Economic and Political Weekly*, vol. 33, no. 9, pp. 445-6.

Sah, D.C., 2003, 'Social Capital and Governance Evidences from Southwestern Tribal Belt of Madhya Pradesh', in *Review of Development and Change*, vol. VIII, no. 1, pp. 41-70.

——, 2010, 'Migration as a Coping Strategy: Evidence from Central Tribal Belt of India', in S.N. Chaudhary (ed.), *Tribal Economy Crossroads*, Jaipur: Rawat Publications, pp. 55-83.

Shah, Mihir, 2005, 'Ecology, Exclusion and Reform in Madhya Pradesh: Introduction', in *Economic and Political Weekly*, vol. 40, no. 48, pp. 5009-13.

Sharma, B.D., 2010, *Unbroken History of Broken Promises*, New Delhi: Sahyog Pustak Kuteer.

Shilpi Kendra, 2007, *Destined to Die: Report of Silicosis in Jhabua, Madhya Pradesh*, Indore: Shilpi Kendra.

Shraddha, 1994, *Gavleen Gatha: Adivasi Astitva ki Ladai* ('Battle for Tribal Existence'), Indore: Press release issued by Sarvodaya Press Service.

Shukla, H.L., 1986, *Tribal Heritage of Madhya Pradesh*, Delhi: B.R. Publishing Corporation.

Sinha, A.K., 1999, 'The Birhor of Madhya Pradesh: As They are Today', in *Indian Anthropologist*, vol. 29, no. 1, pp. 77-101.

Sundar, Nandini, 2011, 'At War with Oneself: Constructing Naxalism as India's Biggest Security Threat', in Michael Kugelman (ed.), *India's Contemporary Security Challenges*, Washington DC: Woodrow Wilson International Centre for Scholars, pp. 1-23.

Sunil and Smitha, 1996, 'Fishing in the Tawa Reservoir: Adivasis Struggle for Livelihood', in *Economic and Political Weekly*, vol. 31, no. 14, pp. 870-72.

Swaminathan, Srilata, 2001, 'Tale of Continued Oppression Government Atrocities on Tribals in Dewas', in *Economic and Political Weekly*, vol. 36, no. 18, pp. 1510-12.

Tandon, Indrakshi, March 2020, Working Paper—*Postcoloniality and Bhil Identity—perpetuating tribal stereotypes in India* (Preprint), downloaded from WorkingPaper-PostcolonialityandBhilIdentity-perpetuating tribal stereotypesinIndia.pdf on 17 September 2021.

Tapan, Neeta, 2010, 'Economics of Borrowing in Tribal Areas', in S.N. Chaudhary (ed.), *Tribal Economy Crossroads*, Jaipur: Rawat Publications, pp. 288-300.

Tripathy, S.N., 2010, 'Globalization and the Plight of Displaced Tribes in India', in S.N. Chaudhary (ed.), *Tribal Economy Crossroads*, Jaipur: Rawat Publications, pp. 205-26.

Venkatesan, V., 2011, 'A Tale of Two Dams', in *Frontline*, 17 June, pp. 32-4.

Western India Rainfed Farming Project CNTR 04 5752 Final Report, October 2005, Department for International Development India, downloaded from https://assets.publishing.service.gov.uk/media/57a08c92e5274a31e00012d0/India_Rural_Livelihoods.pdf on 24 September 2021.

CHAPTER 4

Fight inside the Red Corridor

Tribal Movements in Chhattisgarh

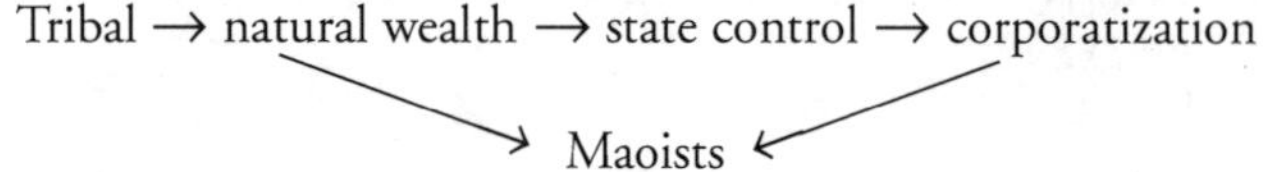

> Contrary to the dominant narrative that areas where Naxalites are strong are where the State has been absent, for the last 100-150 years, there has been a gradual expansion of the State in tribal areas regardless of whether the people want it or not. . . . The problem here is that the State only wants to take a military approach towards ending Naxalism. . . . It is evident that the *Adivasis* are not only under relentless attack, but are also becoming paupers. (Sundar, 2012)

There are a series of tribal revolts which took place in the region since colonial era. In those days tribal movements were essentially described as peasant rebellion guided by religious reforms. There was nothing specific 'tribal' detected in these movements. They have either been documented by their name like Santhal *hul*, Munda *ulghulan*, Kol or Bhil uprising or in the garb of socio-religious peasant rebellion like Sardari movement, Devi movement, Kherwar movement, etc. But in recent times there is a propensity to view the tribal movements from a more extremist gaze. They have been frequently termed as Maoist or left- wing movement. These kinds of approaches deliberately deny the exclusivity of tribal resistance developed within its own skin. They fail to contemplate the tribal political consciousness growing around democratic rights and social justice. Tribals are in no way a naïve and apolitical entity who reside in the lap of nature and do not care for the world outside. Rather, they are in no way less serious than any citizens who have lost their means of livelihood at the hands of the corporate power. Though there are attempts to discredit their political representation and agency, my field visits have uncovered their knowledge of today's political development quite clearly.

It is a well known fact that tribal movements in recent times have been time and again influenced, modified and directed by the left-wing extremist development in the eastern central part of the country, called the Red Corridor. This region comprises mainly of Bihar, Jharkhand, eastern Uttar Pradesh, southern Odisha, eastern Madhya Pradesh, Andhra Pradesh, Telangana, southwestern Bengal, southern Maharashtra and Chhattisgarh. There were three elements in the Red Corridor—tribals, Maoists and the state. This complex scenario has transformed the hitherto sublime equation and dynamics of the tribal society into an intertribal and intratribal conflict. This area has experienced a considerable amount of Maoist violence since the inception of Naxalite movement and Srikakulam movement in 1967 in West Bengal and Andhra Pradesh respectively. Since 2005-6, the state deployed paramilitaries to augment combing operations as a part of tackling Maoist guerrillas, which instead escalated violence and widespread human rights abuses, but could neither justify the violence emanating from the war nor bring peace.

The state of Chhattisgarh was carved out from Madhya Pradesh in the year of 2000. Though Chhattisgarh was created as a tribal state it has yet to give the tribals constitutional rights of reservation in government jobs or local self-governments. This indicates the marginalization of the tribals who constitute 32 per cent of the total population of the state. They started with 34 reserved seats in the year of 2000, but later during post-delimitation in 2008, they were left merely with 29 seats in a house of 90, which was about 32 per cent of representation. The Constitution of India has granted proportionate share of the government jobs to both the Scheduled Castes and Scheduled Tribes. When Madhya Pradesh was bifurcated it had 20 per cent Scheduled Tribes and 16 per cent Scheduled Caste population which was changed into 32 per cent and 12 per cent respectively. In the new state of Chhattisgarh, an additional 12 per cent reservation for tribals was required. But after more than ten years the targets remained untouched. In protest of this injustice the tribals formed Sarva Adivasi Samaj and staged a demonstration on 1 November 2011 (Sharma 2012).

Tribals of Chhattisgarh have witnessed colonial subjugation and fought against its suzerainty. Bastar was a battle ground where the colonial power faced a fierce challenge from the denizens as early as in 1866. Muria rebellion of 1876 and Bhumkal rebellion of 1910 in Bastar was well documented by Nandini Sundar. The tribal movements against British oppression and policies gave birth to a fledgling consciousness of separate tribal identity in Bastar. The demand of a separate statehood was as old as 1920s when it was first raised. Later it was again raised during the Tripuri Congress. Chhattisgarh was created mainly due to its distinct socio-cultural and ethnic identity which is separate from Madhya Pradesh. Poverty was another reason because of which demands were strong in favour of the bifurcation of Madhya Pradesh so that the new state could prosper.

Shivaji Mukherjee has traced the origin of the Maoist insurgency in the Red Corridor from the colonial era. He said that, *zamindari* land tenure system gave birth to inequality which led to underdevelopment in certain regions which were under indirect control of the British. The princely states, which were the feudatory native states and had a subsidiary alliance with the British, had a comparatively low grade bureaucracy and state capacity which led to the exclusion of tribes from the process of the formation of a modern nation-state, for example, Bastar, Kanker, Surguja, and Jashpur in Chhattisgarh. This structural unevenness of the society got carried into the post-colonial era which was exploited by the Maoists in order to mobilize the tribals. These districts still do not have modern institutions and state machineries. But on the contrary, the regions which were under the direct colonial rule or administration and land revenue system had a greater degree of development and were outside the Maoist influence, like Raipur and Bilaspur. Tribals of the Dandakaranya region always maintained their indigenous customary laws and institutions and resisted any attempt of centralized state formation since the historical times. British rule made use of these regions first for timber and then for other forest resources, introduced stringent forest laws and imposed taxation on the tribals for collecting non-timber forest products without taking much interest in initiating development or administration. Tribals rebelled against such exploitation during the colonial times, but their grievances were never addressed or demands met leaving them without an alternative other than joining more violent struggle launched by the Maoists (Mukherjee 2018).

Bastar in south Chhattisgarh has two subregions: Abujhmar is a part of Dandakaranya comprised of Odisha, Jharkhand, Andhra Pradesh and Maharashtra. About 70 per cent people of this region are Gond who have a rich history of rebellion. According to K.S. Singh, Gonds did not have a tradition of militant struggle waged in defence of their rights over land and forest. Though the Gond landlords led the 1857 rebellion in their area like other landlords did elsewhere, the Gond peasants as a whole were not involved in any movement. Bastar rebellion of 1911 was caused by the forest question, forced labour and incompetent administration. But from 1940s, cases of Gond resistance against encroachment on their forest rights gradually came to the forefront. After Independence their political structure broke down, new outsiders flooded their region and Gonds migrated to Adilabad and Chanda districts in search of work in the industrial sector. The Dandakaranya surroundings made them protest against encroachment of forest rights and not against land rights (Singh 2015). In the late 1980s, a number of small movements arose in Bastar-Gadchiroli-Adilabad tri-junction. They asserted the tribal's natural rights to manage all their affairs in accordance with their customs and traditions. A small gathering of tribals in Sangam village on the bank of Kotari river near Abujhmar in Bastar on 10 November 1989 resolved *Mava Nate, Mava Raj* (Our Village, Our Rule) which became a universal slogan of the tribal struggle for self-rule (Sharma 2010: 64-5).

Singh has recorded some Gond movements after Independence and one of them was led by Hira Singh during late 1950s which reached its zenith in 1962-3 before it died down. Hira Singh founded an organization called Adibasi Kalyan Samiti to promote the welfare of the Gonds. The organization used to help tribals to get government benefits, encourage cultivation and construct shrines for Gond deities like Gaura Deo and Burha Deo. At the local level, he set up Majhi Sarkar which used to work like an invisible government. He founded Bharatiya Gondwana Sangh in August 1959. He was arrested and later acquitted in 1962. Some described the movement as a secret insurgency. Singh has also recorded forest *satyagraha* led by

Fetal Singh in 1957. He formed Bhagat Party in the then Kherwar region of Madhya Pradesh. Another forest *satyagraha* developed in Ambikapur-Surguja district of Chhattisgarh involving the Kherwar tribes under the leadership of Chuni the same year. Both the movements were interlinked. Fetal was arrested, incarcerated and later acquitted. Both the movements failed to achieve their goals of forest rights for the tribals (Singh 2015).

Some other tribal movements were also documented by scholars. For example, the movement of Gahira Guru in Surguja, Raigarh and Bilaspur districts of Chhattisgarh in mid-fifties. The movement was called the Sant Samaj movement and it had no avowed political goals. Its main aim was to elevate the socio-cultural status of the tribals of that region (Danda 2015). Another example should be Rajmohini Devi's Bapu Dharma movement of Surguja distrct in 1951 which was a socio-religious movement. Bapu Dharma Sabha Adivasi Seva Mandal was formed to spread the message of the movement. The movement was a propagation of Hinduism and aimed to stop conversion to Christianity (Ekka 2015). A more recent Bhagat movement started in 1970 in Chapka village of Bastar under the leadership of Baba Bihari Das. By mid-1971 the Bison-horn Maria, Dhurwa and Dorla tribals joined the movement. The hill Marias remained untouched by the movement. It was a socio-religious movement as well. In August 1975 Bihari Das was arrested under MISA and imprisoned after which the movement lost its strength. He was accused of exploiting the tribals and encroaching government lands. Later Bihari Das supported Congress Party in assembly elections, but in the end he fled to Odisha (Bhatt 2015).

Therefore, it can be said that the tribal resistance movements of Chhattisgarh have not always been guided by extremist violence rather they had their own set of pathways to flourish, expand and achieve their goals since historical times. There are remarkable differences between the tribal and Maoist movements and both cannot be equated in any way, though attempts have been made to define tribal movements in the light of Maoist activism in order to curb the growing dissatisfaction of the tribals against the state. Nevertheless, the state's counter-insurgency response has nothing but worsened the situation and deepened the process of domination-subjugation propagated once made by British colonialism. With the introduction of economic liberalism, new forces and actors appeared on the scene that helped to shape the course of both the tribal resistance and the Maoist insurgency movements. Corporatization of natural wealth has not only provided forces against which tribals now have to fight but with this the advent of modern technology and foreign funding brought new opportunities for the Maoists to get levies and recruit disgruntled tribals as guerrillas. Maoists have become a potent force who extract money from the industrialists, miners and other development contractors in the form of commission. They need money for spreading their activities farther and deeper which could lead them to organize themselves better and this has nothing to do with the plight of the poor tribals who do not get any benefit from their insurgency per se. It is interesting to note that the sites of resource extraction have become the new battle ground for the state and the Maoists. Tribals on the other hand are caught between them. The role of the Maoists does overlap as well. In some cases they play the role of the agent who actively participate in making tribals conscious about their rights, and sometimes they take advantage of the marginality of the local tribals, manipulate them and use them against the state.

Chhattisgarh has been the heartland of tribal rebellions since the colonial era and gradually emerged as the site of India's biggest 'internal threat'. It is argued that, the excess of Maoist activities are the result of virtual invisibility of governance and development which isolated the historically deprived tribals and forced them to live at the edges of modern society and made them fall prey to the ideology of revolutionary violence. But this argument cannot be corroborated as the other parts of the country being in a similar socio-economic deprivation and poverty did not seek the same route of violence. Maoism is a more recent phenomenon which is concentrated along the Red Corridor and grew in absence of a strong presence of the state as the tribal areas are mostly situated in remote and inaccessible areas devoid of any communication and road networks. With the coming of the corporate companies for the greed of the mineral resources, the state started to develop roads and other means of communication which faced severe resistance from the local tribals as it was leading to displacement and plunder of their natural wealth. This led the state to demean the tribal movement as anti-development and anti-modern. In this context, the issue of 'tribal development' needs to be understood separately. State led development that talks about economic growth and modernization should not be confused with the concept of tribal development.

The Mineral Policy of Chhattisgarh in 2001 promoted large scale private mining sector investment which affected the subsistence economy of the tribals. In the coal bearing districts of Surguja, Raigarh and Bilaspur, more than 72,000 acres of cultivable lands were given on lease to South Eastern Coalfields Limited (SECL), a subsidiary of CIL. In Bastar and Durg districts more than 20,000 acres of lands were acquired for iron ore mining in Bailadila and Dalli Rajhara areas. Bailadila Iron Ore Mines in Bastar, the largest in Asia, was established in 1957. The project displaced only six tribals, but actually it devastated 50 villages in its margin within a decade. The tribal chiefs who were invited for the inaugural ceremony returned the best quality woollen shawls given to them by Nehru. After that Nehru promised them that he would exchange them with sturdy blankets which never arrived as the promises were never kept. A big paper mill was established in Chadrapur, Balharshah in 1952 amidst a rich bamboo forest, the abode of the fabled Murias of Bastar-Gadchiroli range. The Murias retreated to Marh and adjoining areas and their land was taken by the people of the plains for modern development. This changed the entire demography of the region (Sharma 2010: 20-21).

Apart from this, the Chhattisgarh government reportedly granted 18,652 acres of land on lease for various mining purposes and 26,410 acres for the setting up of various industries such as cement, steel, ferro-alloys, re-rolling mills and rice mills. It indicates, a total of 137,062 acres of land was leased by the government for mining and mineral based industries. This land could have sustained at least 34,265 families or around 180,000 people with an average distribution of four acres of land per family (Meher 2009). Dandakaranya project made serious inroads into their forest. 3,310,06 acres of reserved forests and 78,127,17 acres of protected forests were cleared and given to the Dandakaranya Development Authority for rehabilitating the refugees from East Pakistan. Nehru himself inaugurated the

Authority in 1958. The vision of tribal development in Dandakaranya backfired. A hundred thousand acres of land each at Pakhanjor in Bastar, Umarkot and Malkangiri in Koraput was allotted for reclamation and rehabilitation of the Bangladeshi refugees without any resistance. But the refugees moved to Calcutta (Kolkata) leaving their resettlement camps. The local tribals in neighbouring Abujhmar were not impressed by the reclamation of the land as they were mainly shifting cultivators. They refused to take the cleared lands. Then the landless tribals were brought from other areas in Bastar which created more problems for the locals (Sharma 2010: 34-6). The exclusive region, according to B.D. Sharma, naturally attracted the Maoists who were just to earn the confidence of the people with no adversaries of any kind around to deal with. Their very presence neutralized some of the adverse forces whose demeanour hurt their democratic sensibility and sense of honour to the core (Sharma 2010: 34-6 and 126).

The impact of mining and industrialization on tribals is multifarious. Chhattisgarh was an isolated area and largely outside the colonial rule and even after Independence very little industrialization took place which was limited mostly in Jagdalpur. The chimera of development faded away soon when the Dandakaranya Resettlement Project was declared where initially 7,330 Bengali refugees were allotted 60,000 hectares of forest land. They soon brought 40,000 hectares of land under cultivation. The Indian Bureau of Mines decided to exploit the vast reserve of iron ore in 1961. National Mineral Development Corporation (NMDC) took over in 1963. Located south of the river Indravati, in Dantewada tehsil, the mines started operating in 1968. Almost all of the production from these mines was exported to Japan which became India's largest foreign exchange earning unit. But Gonds of Kirandul bore the brunt of development and paid for it as with the inception of the construction work about 40 Dandami Maria families were evicted from Kirandul. Now Kirandul has just about two per cent tribal population. The environmental costs are also heavy. For example, red slime overburdens of Bailadila mine were dumped into Sankhini river which joins Dankhini at Dantewada and then flows further south causing water pollution. Some 40,000 people living in about 51 villages were immediate victims who did not even have drinking water. The project also led to the establishment of the district's first and only railway track from the port city of Vishakhapatnam on the east coast, to the Kirandul mining township through which the ore is exported to Japan (Bastar 1989, Part I). The colony which was constructed near the mining area was named Kailashnagar. To meet the full quantities under the long term contract entered into with the Japanese Steel Mills in 1970 for supply of iron ore to Japan between April 1971 and April 1980, a second deposit at Bailadila was taken up for exploitation. The mine started production in January 1977. After Kirandul, another township was erected at village Bade Bacheli at the base of the hill where the deposit was located and the colony near the mining area was named Akashnagar. With the passage of time tribals became almost strangers in their homeland and the migrants became the new natives and the former were stripped of their claims to indigeneity. The lack of a coping mechanism made Maria women, in particular, vulnerable to burden of dislocation. They not only lost their livelihood intimately related to the forest collection, but also diluted opportunities in the newly emerged employment sector dominated by men. Thus mining and industrialization restricted the mobility of Maria women and compromised their survival, leaving them with the gigantic task of earning two square meals for their families (Mukherjee 2014). In the early 1980s illegal tin mining at a massive scale was reported in Sukma and Dantewada districts of south Bastar. Giant trading and mining companies were seemingly involved in purchasing tin from the tribals, who smelted it and sold it in their *haat* (weekly markets). Fierce fulmination compelled the government to take stern action to stop this. In 1983, about 112 cases involving 141 people, mostly tribals, were launched under the Mining and Minerals Regulation and Development Act (Bastar 1989, Part I).

Bhilai Steel Plant (BSP) acquired around 300 acres of agricultural land for its captive iron mine in 1963. Before the introduction of the mining project the land of this region was not that fertile and agriculture was dependent on monsoon rain. But still the tribals were eking out a standard livelihood supplemented by forest resources. But after BSP, the tribal land was taken in exchange of a meagre cash compensation and employment for one person per family. A very small number of people got the job, though the number of heirs to the land were more than one. Moreover, the deposits of red laterite soil and iron oxide got carried away along with the rainwater from the mines to the agricultural land below and the fertility of the soil was lost. The trauma of displacement, loss of agricultural land due to pollution and a wobbling opportunity of jobs drew the tribals to the habit of alcoholism. It was found that the employment level of BSP declined from around 64,000 in 1980s to around 33,000 in 2007 due to increasing automation and mechanization. The condition of the tribals displaced due to HINDALCO bauxite mines at Samri in Surguja was no less miserable. HINDALCO signed an agreement with the government of Madhya Pradesh in May 1997 and obtained mining leases for bauxite mining. In spite of the fact that Surguja district was situated in the Scheduled Five area where tribal land cannot be taken away, no *gram sabha* meeting was held to take the consent of the suffering tribals for the land alienation, granting of mining lease or compensation. The land of over 200 tribals had been forcefully acquired since 1997 and given to HINDALCO. The oustees were compelled to take a very little amount of compensation money and that was also not based on the market value of the land. Many even were not paid. The jobs were of wage labour type with no medical leave or holidays (Meher 2009).

The state of Chhattisgarh has a forest cover of as much as 45 per cent. In Dantewada 52 per cent of the forest is reserved and another 31 per cent is 'protected' (Government of Chhattisgarh 2005). It has a variety of mineral resources like iron, coal, bauxite, dolomite, platinum, corundum, limestone, gold, diamond, manganese, quartzite, tin ore, tin metal, granite, marble, beryl, uranium, alexandrite, copper, silica, fluorite, garnet and many more amongst which Dantewada's iron ore is one of the best in quality and dolomite deposit is the largest (around 24 per cent). The tribal population of Chhattisgarh is around 32 per cent who depend largely on the collection of non-timber forest products such as tamarind, *mahua*, *sal*, *tendu* leaves, fruits, honey, herbs, lac, gum and the like. Primitive mode of subsistence like hunting-gathering, fishing and shifting cultivation are also their means of livelihood. Natural resources contribute about 10 per cent of domestic product in the state. In the early 1970s, plans were tabled for industrial forestry in Bastar. Jagdalpur, Barsur and some parts of Bijapur tehsil were designated as the industrial catchment areas constituting 25 per cent of the district. Against this background the much hyped pine plantation scheme was proposed which was funded by the World Bank with a plan to establish 15 paper and pulp mills. The project was called Madhya Pradesh Forestry Technical Assistance Project which paved the way for the formation of Madhya Pradesh State Forest Development Corporation (MPSFDC). In Kurundi, closed to Jagdalpur 3,100 hectares of forest land was freed and replanted with pine in July 1975. But after strong resistance of the tribals under the leadership of Baba Bihari Das the scheme was cancelled in 1981. Another scheme for dolomite mining in a different forest zone (about 2,450 hectares) was terminated in the wake of tribal protest. A chain of eight to nine hydel projects on Indravati was put forward which accounted for around 31,000 hectares submergence area and a sum of 1,500 megawatt power generating capacity. These development projects were virulently opposed by the tribals. The Bodhghat Project work over Indravati in Bastar was started in 1984 without consulting the local Maria Gonds. The Marias refused to give their land and could not be allured by apparently attractive resettlement package which was prepared in conformity with the MP Rehabilitation Act of 1985 and Narmada Sagar Project. The package included house and jobs, monetary compensation, a model rehabilitation colony at Bodhli (Kundri), etc. but failed to win over the Marias' trust. Their movement received a wholesome support from across the country. Later the project was stalled (Bastar 1989, Part I).

The foundation stone of a steel plant at Mavalibhata (M/s S.M. Dichem) was laid on 5 December 1992 by the then Chief Minister. It was praised by all as a development watershed for Bastar. But the government did not consult the tribals living there for ages. The Murias challenged the state in their own way by breaking the stones into pieces and throwing them away untraced till date. After facing stiff resistance the state withdrew from the project. The tribals in Mavalibhata Declaration made it clear that community ownership has to be recognized and they would prevent privatization of public sector enterprises. Another attempt to set up a steel plant at Hiranar near Dantewada was also abandoned in the face of tribal resistance (Sharma 2010: 65-6). Gaare village in Raigarh district was the foci of a non-violent struggle against Jindal Power and Steel Company. It dug out two open-cast coal mines and built the world's largest sponge iron factory in Raigarh. On 5 January 2007 the tribals of Khamariya village of Tamnar tehsil were subjected to brutal lathicharge when a public hearing was going on where they refused to give up their lands to Jindal Coal Mines. In January 2008 people of Gaare were lathicharged at a public hearing. In September 2008 a road blockade by hundreds of tribals of the Jameen Bachao Sangharsh Samiti successfully resisted land acquisition and foiled the proposal for handing over an area of 105 sq. km. situated in 30 villages of Kunkuri tehsil of Jashpur district (with more than 80 per cent tribal population) to the Jindal Power and Steel Limited. Jashpur is the only district that held a procession in favour of tribal rights which was attended by 50,000 tribals and forced the government to delay the mining plans. The resistance in Dharamjaigarh block of Raigarh where DB Power, a subsidiary of the *Dainik Bhaskar* group, a media conglomerate, displaced 524 families from six settlements comprising 350 acres of land to extract two million tonnes of coal every year. This was to fuel the 1,320 megawatt thermal power plant that the company proposed to build in Janjgir-Champa. 438 Gond and Oraon tribal people voted against the DB Power. There was no comprehensive rehabilitation package in Raigarh and Janjgir-Champa (*Frontline* 2011). The public hearing for environmental clearance for AES Chhattisgarh Power (A joint venture with the American energy giant) was stalled by the villagers. The Indian Farmers Fertilizer Cooperative Ltd. had to withdraw its proposal of setting up a 1,000 megawatt coal based thermal power plant in Premnagar in Surguja district after strong protest. The villagers organized themselves in the Gram Sabha Parishad and protested the diversion of the Atem river for the plant (Update 2010: 69-71). It is interesting to note that tribal resistance was enough to protest and prevent privatization and displacement in Bastar and there was no presence of the Maoists in these attempts. It was to their credit that mining leases were not signed in 1960s after Bailadila experience and one after another the so-called industrialization and 'development projects' were thwarted.

According to Amita Baviskar, for a long four decades the Mines Shramik Sangh in Chhattisgarh has been fighting for the rights of employees who work in public sector mines and private ancillary industries. The workers' union is fighting not only for security of their employment but also for ecological protection for their health and safety. Shankar Guha Niyogi, who led the organization, and was killed in 1991, formed the Chhattisgarh Mukti Morcha (CMM) which summoned small and marginal farmers against the environmental depletion of agricultural land and the contamination of water because of mining related activities. Local people supported the organization and its candidate was elected to the state legislative assembly. The CMM mobilized tribals for right to natural resources and a harmless and non-polluting industrial process (Baviskar 2005). The CMM steered the formation of the state in 2000 out of a handful of tribal dominated districts of eastern Madhya Pradesh.

In spite of the fact that Samatha Judgement (Supreme Court of India, Samatha *vs.* State Of Andhra Pradesh And Others on 11 July 1997) reassured the rights of the tribals in the scheduled areas, bauxite mining is taking a big role in the privatization process of country's mineral wealth. According to Patrik Oskarsson, the move to extend the area of the project came from the collaboration between Indian and Hungarian governments that finally established BALCO at Korba in1965. Due to some technological glitches BALCO could not operate its company appositely for many years. When it resumed work it was found that the bauxite ore reserve was not sufficient. In the meantime Vedanta Alumina International Ltd. entered the scene and purchased BALCO. The vicinity of Vedanta at BALCO in Chhattisgarh was a huge one which could devour a whole aluminium smelter with the associate coal based power plant. The old Hungarian smelter and the new Chinese built smelter continue to operate together. The Government of India planned to privatize BALCO situated in the scheduled areas of Chhattisgarh. The concern is that privatization of BALCO hinted at the transfer of tribal land in the scheduled area to private hands or better say non-tribal hands. By using Public Interest Litigation the BALCO union of employees filed a petition against the Government of India to the Supreme Court which challenged the sale on the basis of being against the Madhya Pradesh Land Transfer Legislation. After the creation of Chhattisgarh it inherited this legislation in 2000. But unfortunately the court allowed the sale to proceed by observing that BALCO was the same company and same owner of the lands although it had been privatized. The court decided that the case did not involve any transfer of land from tribals to non-tribals (Oskarsson 2010). Thus the privatization was given a green signal,

> The land was validly given to BALCO a number of years ago and today it is not open to the State of Chhattisgarh to take a somersault and challenge the correctness of its own action. Furthermore even with the change in management the land remains with BALCO to whom it had been validly given on lease. (Supreme Court of India 2001)

This was the reason of a steady and steep rise of Maoist activities which began in the early 1980s. It is telling that when Chhattisgarh was created, that is in 2000, the Government of India amended the Mines and Minerals Regulation and Development Act which facilitated the extraction of minerals from the tribal regions. The amendments entrusted licensing powers to the individual state governments for mining, ended foreign equity limits and removed 13 minerals that were reserved for the public sector. Chhattisgarh did not have a legacy of tribal movement for self-representation or autonomous statehood, but still its demand for a separate statehood was supported by the local elite who wanted to control the mineral flow without state intervention in the guise of ethnic identity and cultural distinctiveness. The inclusion of Bastar in Chhattisgarh was justified exclusively on the grounds of forest regulations. Under British rule Dantewada was part of the Princely State of Bastar. In 2007 and 2012, parts of Dantewada were cut off from the district for administrative purpose. This has created a sense of isolation, distrust and doubts in tribal minds which is reflected in the opposition and rejection of state authority.

There is no dearth of land in Bastar. The region is arid and dusty, but a large area of land remained uncultivated due to shortage of water. This is the principal cause of dull agricultural production which happens to be severe want of water and which leads to the seasonal outmigration and endemic poverty. Water scarcity made tribals go to the nearby riverside for defecation. Tribals of these inaccessible terrains also ensconced in some indelible beliefs and taboos regarding defecation. The Ministry of Rural Development initiated Nirmal Gram Yojana funded by the central government in 2007 under poor villages identified by state governments were provided with toilets and sanitation facilities. The programme was aimed at improving the supply of water along with an extension of sanitation facilities, especially for women and children. But this programme was planned without the consultation of the tribals for whom it was completely a new thing. They were forced to use the toilets which they later deserted mainly due to water scarcity and lack of maintenance. Thus, the scheme became a meaningless attempt to 'modernize' the tribals who were not even involved in the planning. The primary demand of the tribals has always been an uninterrupted supply of water but the scheme did not show any interest in water supply and emphasized only on the sanitation provisions. When tribals did not use the toilets they were treated with impunity and coerced to pay fines; their household items and agricultural equipment were seized by the local administration. The imposition of such thoughtless measures foiled the actual objective of a participatory development. Jhabua in Madhya Pradesh experienced similar kinds of failures when toilets were first introduced in the tribal areas (Mehrotra and Patnaik 2008).

Tribals have refused to comply with the state model of development and resisted attempts of commodification of their mineral and other natural wealth through violence. Maoists have manoeuvred this sphere of discontent and annoyance of the local tribals, oriented them into the left-wing ideology of revolutionary violence, and formed organizations to reshape their movements. In response to this the state has also unleashed repressive counter-insurgency violence that has aggravated the crisis and deployed military and local militia in order to check the growing revolutionary violence. The Government of India declared the 'Integrated Action Plan to Develop Tribal and Backward Districts in Left-Wing Extremist Areas' in 2010. The scheme provided funds sanctioned by the central government for infrastructural building for example schools and health centres in the Maoist affected districts to gather people's support in favour of the state. Thus, the civil war in Chhattisgarh has speedily and qualitatively changed the character of tribal movement.

The Chhattisgarh government has contracted the Border Roads Organization (BRO), a wing of the armed forces responsible for building and maintaining infrastructure along India's volatile borders with

Pakistan and China, to construct a network of all-weather, paved roads in the south western part of the state where the Maoists have established a significant presence. The Industrial Policy, 2004-9 of the Government of Chhattisgarh (2004) stressed on the private businesses that should proffer impetus for introducing mega development projects in the underdeveloped tribal areas. It was aimed at doubling profits through revenue and generating employment through development. The total forest land diverted from 1980 to 2003 was 17,166.501 hectares, of which 67.22 per cent was diverted for mining. Almost 90,000 hectares of land is under mining of major minerals and coal. The top five most mined districts are Korba, Koriya, Surguja, Raigarh and Durg. Dantewada has around 2,010 hectares of land under mining for iron ore, tin and corundum. The Dantewada District Report indicates that one-third of its forest cover has already been degraded. In spite of industrialization the iron bearing districts of Dantewada and Bastar are among the top ten most backward districts in the country (Update 2010: 16). It has been estimated that by 2004, more than two lakh acres of land were acquired for implementation of ten major projects which affected around 238 villages and all were tribal, leaving them waiting for the compensation which never arrived (Ray 2019).

Interestingly, the counter-insurgency operation began in June 2005 when a militia called Salwa Judum, means a 'purification hunt' in Gondi dialect, now declared disbanded by the Supreme Court, was formed by the local tribal people. In the same month Tata Steel and ESSAR signed Memorandums of Understanding with the Chhattisgarh government for new iron ore mines and steel plants on the tribal land. Delhi High Court rescinded the grant of a prospecting licence to Tata Steel to mine iron ore in an area spread over 2,500 hectares of forest in Dantewada. According to Navlakha, 'it is the criminal negligence of our people's welfare that is responsible for causing the Maoist led rebellion' (Navlakha, 2008). After the formation of the state, Maoist activities got intensified. Outside Abujhmar, in the village of Dhurli and Bhansi SEZ has become a dirty word. The Chhattisgarh government sanctioned 1,500 acres of land for ESSAR Steel Project, but tribals were restive (*India Today* 2008). From 2000 to 2013 a total of 1,416 people including security men, Maoists and ordinary people have been killed in Maoist related violence and on the current count of casualties, Chhattisgarh is the worst Maoist affected state in the country (Saxena 2013). The penetration is viewed by both the state and the Maoists as an expression of retaliation against the Salwa Judum, and ergo cannot be taken as a causal justification for counter-insurgency. This has led to the destruction of the ecosystems with which the tribals have always reciprocated and breathed in and caused a colossal loss of livelihood as well.

NMDC had in the late 1990s, announced plans to set up a steel plant at Nagarnar for which it was to manage the Romelt technology, used for extracting iron from any iron bearing wastes of mines, from its foreign collaborator—Moscow Institute for Steel and Alloys (MISA) (*The Economic Times* 17 July 2006). Nagarnar was a tribal inhabited region in Chhattisgarh. Initially, the local tribals did not oppose the project but were unsatisfied as the project authority and the government wanted to acquire their agricultural land. They were willing to offer the barren forest land for the project, but the authorities were determined. The tribals objected in the *gram sabha* meeting and unanimously opposed the land acquisition work. But the administration grabbed the minutes of the meeting and tampered with it. After forging the minutes the administration revealed to the media that the tribals had given their consent in favour of the plant. When the local tribals got to know about the conspiracy they complained to the ST/SC Commissioner in Delhi. An enquiry started against the local administration which decided to take the revenge. Within few days three people were booked under false charges, one of them was a tribal boy. In protest against the concocted arrests the tribals gathered in front of the police station. Police first lathicharged and when the tribals began pelting stones police charged teargas shells and opened fire on the protesting tribals. Three people were injured amongst whom two were men and one was a tribal woman. But police brutality could not supress the movement. All arrested tribals were released. But on 10 March 2002 police again unleashed terror. For three to four days hundreds of tribal people of Nagarnar were beaten, apprehended and sent to Jagdalpur Jail so that the inaugural ceremony of the plant could be held peacefully. The administration called the programme 'Mission Possible'. The administration and the police forced the people to accept the compensation money and the land acquisition went on unabated. The government finally handed over 403 hectares land to the NMDC in 2002 (Anonymous 2004).

According to Sundar, the dispossession of village headmen and landlords by the Maoists led to a reaction in the form of an anti-Maoist movement known as the *Jan Jagran Abhiyan* of 1990 which started in West Bastar, and unrolled further south. This movement, led by an influential tribal leader, Mahendra Karma, was the blue-print for its infamous successor, the Salwa Judum, and involved arson and various scorched earth tactics. Later *Jan Jagran Abhiyan* was reintroduced as Salwa Judum. It was claimed that this militia was a spontaneous rebellion against Maoist violence. But there is no scope for doubts that this was created, mobilized and sponsored by the state itself essentially by the strongmen of Mahendra Karma who was an MLA of the Congress Party. He was later gunned down by the Maoists in a roadside ambush in May 2013. Villagers were coerced into attending rallies, on pain of beating or fines, and then forcibly taken to camps or 'strategic hamlets' or 'concentration camps'. Several hundred villages refusing to join were burned, and their residents, especially those known to be active in the *sanghams*, were killed, beaten, or arrested. Women were raped. Property, especially livestock, was looted, and grain was burned (Sundar 2011).

Salwa Judum terrorized and intimidated tribal people, forcefully displaced them and sent to their camps erected alongside the national highway of Bastar. More or less 40,000 tribals were uprooted due to the operation of Salwa Judum which has set one of the biggest and infamous examples of internal displacement. 'Relief' camps did not bring any relief to the impoverished tribals. The displaced tribals were not provided with any jobs by the government and were made dependent on wage labour in the adjacent villages. People in the 'relief' camps were suffering from severe malnutrition and diseases, especially the children in the Baangapal and Dorapal camps suffered from Grade 4 malnutrition. UNICEF identified hundreds of such children in the camps. Nevertheless, tribals fled from the camps in fear of losing their land lying vacant in their respective villages, because of which several camps, like Karkeli camp, remained empty on the Nelasnaar-Bedre road. The official records of April-May 2006 reveals that 45,958 tribals from 644 villages were displaced and forced to live in 22 detention camps run by the state government. When the reports came out that the tribal women were being sexually exploited and abused in the camps an all-India fact-finding team was set up by the Committee against Violence on Women (CAVOW) that went to Dantewada twice between September and November 2006. The team investigated the incidents of rape and violence against women perpetrated by Salwa Judum during the evacuation of the villages and also inside the 'relief' camps. Reports showed that tribal women were arrested on false charges amongst whom 21 were murdered and 3 had their breasts cut off and genitals mutilated. Thirty-seven were molested sexually amongst whom 23 were gang raped. Ten women were sexually exploited in the camp and 4 inside the police station (Punwani 2007).

The tribal villagers were removed to the camps so that the Maoists could not enter the villages for any supply and secondly, internal displacement helped Salwa Judum get resources and free labour force for building roads and other constructions in exchange of food only. The government enacted one of the most oppressive Chhattisgarh Special Public Security Act in 2005 to expedite the process. The act gave the state arbitrary powers to decide who is unlawful. The rehabilitation camps were kept under the control of the Special Police Officers (SPOs). The SPOs were recruited from the local unemployed tribal youths, trained and armed with guns, who called themselves as 'Koya commandos'. Tribal women were also recruited as the SPOs. The state police along with the Central Reserve Police Force (CRPF) and Indian Reserve Battalions (IRBs) of Naga and Mizo forces—were all engaged in the battle. It was a new version of the divide and rule policy once taken up by the Britishers by which tribals were pitted against tribals. This time militarization of a section of the tribals against the other is a more brutal version of the colonial policy. Whoever had opposed this cowardly act of the state was incarcerated, tortured and tagged as Maoists, like Binayak Sen and Soni Sori. The SPOs were forced to work in a very difficult situation. They were not given any holiday, made to work in dead of the night, not permitted to go home and not even paid for months. When this operation was stopped these tribal youths came back empty-handed. They were neither given permanent jobs as was promised nor recognition. Thus, the state funded counter-insurgency strategy of Salwa Judum was nothing but a despoliation of resources functioning under the auspices of big fat local influential Mafioso. After disbandment Salwa Judum lost its previous role and now it is used for resolving disputes among influential commanders of different camps which are viewed as a safe and secure zone controlled by the state (Spacek 2014).

But it was unfortunate that the Chhattisgarh government evaded the materialization of the Supreme Court order regarding disbandment of the SPOs and changed their designation to the Armed Auxiliary Forces to District Reserve Group. The reports which bear extensive data regarding the terror of Salwa Judum are: Report of People's Union of Civil Liberty (2006), Report of Independent Citizen's Initiative (2006), Report of International Association of People's Lawyers (2007), Report of Human Rights Features (2008), Government Report of Expert Group to Planning Commission (2008) and many more. When counter-insurgency boomeranged by increasing civilian support for the Maoists, instead of ending the paramilitary operations and atrocities the government of India launched an official war against the Maoists which was euphemistically called Operation Green Hunt in November 2009 by deploying army to Bastar and Dantewada. The state often glorified this civil war and the death of the CRPF men were immoratalized as martyrdom in the war between the state and Maoists. Tribals were persuaded, seduced and threatened to join Bastar Battalion of the CRPF and the state is planning to recruit the local tribal youth in the armies mostly from the Maoist affected regions so that a division can be created or a polarization can be drawn within the tribal communities and thus pull away the support base of the Maoist insurgency and detach the tribals from joining the rank and file of the Maoist organizations. Kennedy and King have commented that, before the inception of Salwa Judum campaign, the choices available to the tribals of Maoist affected areas were either to side with the insurgents or to protest quietly. After the creation of Salwa Judum, they had to take part actively either in the Maoist insurgency or buttress Salwa Judum and if they refuse to comply with any one of them, the other might surmise that they belonged to the opposite side (Kennedy and King 2009).

Maoist insurgency has been viewed by scholars as a resistance movement against neoliberal development policy of the state which encompasses exploitation of natural resources and massive displacement in the wake of mining and industrial boom. It has been explained in terms of an outburst of subaltern discontent which emerged from the historical negligence and deprivation meted out to the tribals. Arundhati Roy (Roy 2011) has vividly written about the fight of the Maoists for the dignity of the tribals. The report of the Expert Group to the Planning Commission of the Government of India (Government of India 2008) also delineated the causes of the people's support for the Maoists. The report said that, it was the injustice, failure and inadequate measures of the government which gave space to the Maoists to grow. They have taken full advantage of the unequal distribution of wealth and opportunity among different regions and maladministration to inflame the anger brewing inside the underbelly of India shining (Shah 2013). They have raised consciousness among the tribals about their rights. Illegal felling of trees caused large scale deforestation in the tribal forested belt of Bastar. The tribals were given safeguard by the Madhya Pradesh Protection of Aboriginals (Interest of Trees) Act 1959.

Though the tribals have the ownership right on some specific trees, but the timber mafias with the connivance of the forest officials, tactfully arranged thumb impressions of the illiterate tribals and cleared the entire forest area which led to the eventual abolishment of the system in 1975. In order to compensate for the degradation of the forests, the government began afforestation programme by implementing commercial forestry and mono cultural plantations, like *sal*, Eucalyptus, Caribbean pine, pines, teak and the like which had a devastating impact on the tribals. From the early 1980s, four environmental and wildlife protection projects were implemented and they were: Kanger Valley National Park (200 sq km), Bairamgarh Game Sanctuary (139 sq km), Pamed Game Sanctuary (262 sq km) and the biggest among all Indravati Abhyaranya Tiger Project (3,000 sq km) situated close to Kutru, Bijapur tehsil. There were 57 villages having a population of 6,000 in the reserve. The villagers were displaced with a meagre amount of compensation. The growing dissatisfaction among the displaced favoured the rise of the Maoists in Kutru and Bhopalpatnam. This brought the establishments of the armed police camps in those villages which were transformed into a never-ending battle between the state and the Maoist insurgency (Bastar 1989 Part I).

Maoists organized the tribals for increasing the wages against the notorious forest or labour contractors and against the extraction of heavy fines from the poor tribals for collecting minor forest produce. They have raised awareness among the tribals about the growing corruption, harassment and intimidation, poverty and landlessness. The Maoists also took money in large amounts from the *tendu* leaf contractors to finance their activities. In all this rigmarole the tribal were the worst sufferers. Thus, the Maoist movement evolved in Chhattisgarh, and gave them support to till the *patta*less lands and led them to encroach upon forests to bring more land under cultivation. Their front organization Adivasi Kisan Mazdoor Sanghathan (AKMS) raised the issue of irrigation time and again in its demands (Bastar 1989 Part II). Maoists have protected the tribals not only from the rapacious forest officials, police and other state agents, but also undertaken various ameliorative measures like opening up of schools, mobile health facilities, redistribution of lands and helping the tribals to sell their forest collection at reasonable price at the local market and banning illegal liquor shops. The Maoists have become an integral part of the tribal life and share everyday living with them. This feeling of togetherness has made them more proximate to the joy and grief, gain and loss, fortune and misfortune of the poor and deprived. They have successfully fulfilled the vacuum that should have been filled by the state representatives and machineries. The revolutionary characteristics of Maoists and their sympathizers define them as self-sacrificing political actors who speak for the exploited. In Arundhati Roy's term the Maoists are 'Gandhians with a Gun' (Roy 2010). But Maoist insurgency brought forth a large contingent of armed police force in the interior tribal areas which transformed their life forever. Neither was their aspiration fulfilled nor was their consent respected by any of the party. No effort was made to engage them in the decision making process. Rather it shut down all the other alternatives, previously open for their survival.

According to Jonathan Kennedy, insurgency should be considered as a state building enterprise rather than a mafia or social movement. It is pertinent to note that state violence in areas under insurgency is much more indiscriminate (Salwa Judum) than the insurgents (Maoists). But at times insurgent violence crosses the apparently obscured boundary between private and collective interests. A more important requirement for the insurgents is to secure the compliance of local people in order to ensure the plethora of resources essential for guerrilla warfare, like shelter, food, intelligence and recruits. Since 1995, insurgents' governance in base areas, particularly in southern Chhattisgarh where political institutions are strongest, is referred to as *Janatana Sarkar* (People's Government). This operates through two institutional forms, which perform both belligerent and benevolent functions. *Sanghams* (committees) belong to peasants' and workers' front organizations, such as the Dandakaranya Kisan Adivasi Mazdoor Sangham (Dandakaranya Peasant Tribal Worker League) live separately from the villages. They undertake military operations against the state, use violence to punish real or potential opponents in areas under their control, and back up the *sanghams'* activities with the credible threat of violence (Kennedy 2014). The traditional tribal power structure like *manjhi pargana* had slowly gotten extinct.

Maoists gradually started strengthening their party, guerrilla army and the front in order to protect the *Janatana Sarkar* which was essential for the advancement of the revolution. People's Liberation Guerrilla Army (PLGA) was formed to fight the state forces. Tribal women were recruited in the party and in the army as well. Women constitute 40 per cent of the PLGA. Apart from the army many mass organizations were built, like a cultural organization called Chetna Natya Manch and a women's organization called Krantikari Adivasi Mahila Sangathan (KAMS). It is telling to note that the Maoists have even mobilized tribal children into a children's organization called Krantikari Adivasi Bala Sangathan (KABS). However, children do not participate in combating activities, but work as 'informers' in the Maoist intelligence network at the base level (Kumbamu 2017 also see *Open* 2010).

There are other aspects of the Maoist insurgency as it can be rightly detected that all Maoists are not tribals and all tribals do not support Maoists. For example, Gonds are more prominent in the Maoist movement in Bastar. They are even promoted to local and regional party leadership. But smaller tribal groups like the Murias and Dhurwas keep themselves away from the Maoists. Maoists' claim of being an indigenous movement attached to land, forest and water is a misrepresentation of indigeneity and thereby tribal movement. Furthermore, it is also interesting to note that Maoist insurgency is not an integral and inseparable part of tribal life. It does not occur among the tribals alone. Displacement can be a reason of the predominance of Maoist activities, but it is not the only reason. There are a lot of places where tribals have not been displaced or tribal lands have not been alienated, but are under Maoist influences, like Bihar and Andhra Pradesh. In some places customary right over the forest resources and forest management play a more crucial role in attracting tribals towards Maoists who protect them from the extortion and torture of the forest guards when they go for collection of minor forest produces. The private traders were complicit in forcing the tribals to sell their forest collection at a low price and the state did not take action against them. This impacted the tribal livelihood pattern and immiserated further compelling them to protest against the injustice and lawlessness. Besides, the socio-economic condition of the tribals in Chhattisgarh has not transformed qualitatively. This static situation has made them support the Maoists. It is also true to say that there are many tribal dominated places where Maoist violence is not at all an issue, like the northeastern states of India. The non-tribal Maoist leadership try to mould their insurgency according to the needs of the tribals which could provide them with a stimulus to give them a backup. According to Uday Chandra,

> In eastern and central India alike, Maoist groups attempted to capture the hearts and minds of target populations, especially young and willing combatants, by promising to overturn traditional class, caste and gerontocratic hierarchies. In doing so, they displayed a clear willingness to think in local or regional terms, thereby shelving temporarily their long-term goal of capturing state power throughout India. (Chandra 2013)

While the state's contribution towards ensuring rights and entitlements of the tribes is undoubtedly very meagre, the Maoists, on their part, had also added more trouble to it. Under the pretext of giving greater autonomy to the tribals, the Maoists intended to take political control over land and other forest resources. The Maoists or the Maoist backed groups have been functioning as middlemen between the tribals and the corporates. On the one hand, the nexus between the corporates and the Maoists and on the other the prolonged struggle between the state and the Maoists exposed the tribals to exploitation and deprivation. Both are crucial instruments in sustaining the conflict and alienation of the tribal people. There were tribals who did not support the Maoist activities which impaired their voice and agency and imposed things according to its own analysis. The Maoists turned against the tribals who did not subscribe to their ideology. Sustaining violence, both by the state and the Maoists, shrouded genuine socio-economic issues. The state starts concentrating on how to distance people from the Maoists, not how to deliver justice to the tribal people (Behera 2019). The collapse of government structures at the local level disrupted the supply line of the crucial amenities which fail to reach to the tribals at times of need. Thus, tribals have been ensnared by the vicious cycle of conflict which always leaves them at the receiving end. It is the state or the Maoists who reside at the giving end. Tribals are not given adequate say whether it is about the issues or demands of the Maoists or about the leadership or organizational structure or course of the movement. For both the state and the Maoists, they remain as actors not leaders; subjects, not rulers; receivers not givers; sufferers not perpetrators.

The question remains, why are the Maoists successful in getting such a huge amount of support from the tribals? Is development-induced-displacement the sole reason behind their inclination towards the Maoist ideology of insurgency? Why are the tribal people supporting the non-tribal (*diku*) led Maoist movement who exploited and vilified them since historical times? Do the tribals comply with the application of violence? Poverty is often explained as a leading cause of the Maoist insurgency in the tribal areas. But it is also pertinent to remember that a huge proportion of rural mass is poverty stricken people and are unaffected by the insurgency. One should remember that tribals support the Maoists basically for two reasons. One, they support the Maoists who defend their interests which the state could not do. Maoists help them in getting justice in the nature of gunning down the brutal forest guards and police who exploit tribals and secondly, it was the Maoists who forced the state in a way to highlight tribal cause and thus helped them to negotiate their demands. They ventilate their grievances through them and fulfil their agendas at times. Land grabbing and development-induced displacement is one of their grievances. Maoists have chosen tribal areas because they are backward, remote, underdeveloped, inaccessible and surrounded by deep forest and mountainous terrain and therefore, suitable for ambushes and secret organizational activities. The presence of state machineries or representatives are very few and rare in these areas, thus favourable for creating a guerrilla zone. But then also geographical positions do not always adequately analyze the growing Maoist activities. For example, there are large forest cover and mountainous areas in the Western Ghats along India's western coast in Karnataka, where Maoists could not make a dent and Bihar where they could, was not a thick forested area. There are places where natural resources are abundant, but no sign of insurgency till date. Marginality, poverty or geographical isolation can be sufficient but not necessary corollary for understanding tribals' resistance movements which have generally been both violent and non-violent in nature, not particularly Maoist violence.

The Maoist movement envisages a stereotypical conceptualization of tribals being violent, rebellious and armed. Instead the tribal movement outside Maoist influence are more ethnic and righteous in nature and composition, because Maoists are comprised of both non-tribals and tribals and interestingly the leadership always lies with the non-tribals most frequently, urban, well-educated, dominant and upper caste. In fact, non-tribals are more predominant than the tribals under whom they have historically been subjugated and humiliated. The prospect of making a classless society does not go with a society that is torn apart by caste hierarchies. Another basic structural feature of the conflict observed by Felix Padel is that Maoists, like the police, receive a lot of their funding through the mining investment. When they attack mines, they do not try and check operations but grab explosives only and the attack functions as a negotiation over protection money. The ESSAR had paid 'protection money' to the Maoists which prove the extensive funding system of the Maoists. In this sense,

Padel continues, the Maoists have unfolded a 'warlord' character which is similar to terrorist groups in countries like Afghanistan, Syria or Iraq where ideology merges into a tussle for power and resources (Padel 2017).

Tribals of Chhattisgarh have been caught between two warring parties for a long time, one is the state and other is the Maoists which have brought unending miseries for them. A field survey was conducted in 2018 in Mangalnaar village of Bhairamgarh block in Bijapur district of southwest Bastar which was remotely located and severely affected by Maoist insurgency. Mangalnaar village was a predominantly Gond village whose sources of livelihood were forestry, hunting, fishing and shifting cultivation, though shifting cultivation has been prohibited by the government. Gonds also collect minor forest produces like *tendu* leaves, *mahua* flower, leafy vegetables, *tora*, *chironji* and *tendu* fruits from the adjoining forest. The study recorded that, in 2005 the local tribals were recruited in Salwa Judum campaign, imparted with training and given weapons against the Maoists by the state government. It has also noted that one of the key factors of illiteracy among the Gonds in the region has been the Maoist interference, lack of awareness, inaccessibility and the like. However, after the setback of the Maoists' a good number of them are sending their children to school (Sanyal and Ramyash 2020).

There is little doubt about the fact that the tribals participated, supported and sympathized with the Maoists for their dedication and commitment in delivering tribals with justice and a sense of dignity. The Maoists have definitely played a decisive role in organizing and mobilizing tribals against the discrimination, exploitation and state repression. The state on the other hand muzzled their voice of dissent and made them feel like the 'others'. According to Nandini Sundar, one of the causes why the tribals support the insurgency was that the Maoists have developed indigenous Gondi literature and formed cultural groups who perform songs and dances in Gondi, their indigenous language. Thus, they have successfully disseminated their messages across the tribal regions in Bastar. Sundar has opined that, RSS set up organizations like Vanvasi Kalyan Ashram for the tribals which worked towards converting the tribal children into Hindus. This drive was conducted through the educational institutions like schools and specifically through the hostels. The tribal children of the hostels were taught to chant Hindu *bhajans* and hymns (Sundar 2010). But the growing influences of Hindu fundamentalist elements in Chhattisgarh have failed to make their impact on the tribals the way Maoists once had. This is because right wing politics do not oppose capitalist development agenda and caste system inherent in it. Hinduization of the tribal communities is not a new phenomenon and this could never become a powerful mobilizing force to be accepted by the tribals. The state even forbids the media from reporting and covering the atrocities perpetrated by the security forces. Incidents of false encounters of the tribals are justified in the name of gun battle between Maoist and army.

Sundar visited a camp of Salwa Judum on the Andhra Pradesh and Chhattisgarh border at Maraigudem in 2007 where she was told by a teacher incharge of the residential school that the number of children in the hostel kept changing due to the disturbances as their parents brought their children in the school when situation was fraught with troubles, and took them back when it was comparatively peaceful and under control. This happened because school buildings were targets of the war going on between the Maoist insurgents and counter-insurgency forces. The paramilitary forces use the school buildings as their camps as these are built with concrete. Maoists usually exploded the school buildings as an act of revenge which either way affects the education of the innocent tribal children. Maoists preferred to bring people from nearby villages to demolish the schools as tribals of that very village would have felt disheartened to raze their own school buildings which they themselves once built for their own children. The state on the other hand built one thousand seated residential schools next to Salwa Judum camps and police stations where it could keep an eye on the tribal children so that they could not be persuaded by the Maoists. This has been the reason why there is a constant inertia on the part of the teachers to go to the interior of the tribal areas to teach the poor tribal children. It keeps the tribal literacy rate still lingering far below the expected level (Sundar 2010).

It has been time and again reported that the Maoists frustrate and play havoc with any kind of government initiatives that aim to develop the tribals and that purports the inner conflict of interest between the tribal cause and that of the Maoists. In many areas tribals fall prey to the Maoist violence as they are being killed on regular basis on the pretext of being either an informer or supporter of another political party. Tribals who were promised government service and recruited as SPOs later became invariable enemies of the Maoists. They could never dare to come back to their village, when the disillusionment of government jobs happened, for the obvious reason of being killed by them. Tribals who were once part of the Maoist movement but were later caught and coerced to join counter-insurgency forces became targets of Maoists as well. Thus, tribals are becoming the victims of the Maoist violence though they claim to be their saviours. They have no other option other than continue to be with the counter-insurgency movement in order to save their own lives. Their choices are limited as there is no coming back for them ever. According to Jonathan Kennedy and Lawrence King, insurgent activity is most likely to occur in areas where tribals retain control of their land. They try to structure the insurgency in terms that are relevant to tribals and to provide a blending of collective and selective incentives. They said that the likelihood of being engaged in insurgent activity is highest in areas where tribals till their own land. It corroborates the argument that rural inhabitants with higher levels of communal unity and organizational autonomy are more likely to get involved in insurgent activity. Tribals do not always favour the Maoists and do not support their ideology of violence every time. This is the reason why they move to the Salwa Judum camps and support the counter-insurgency, though very little (Kennedy and King 2009). Sundar's analysis has seconded this argument as she wrote that, it is not unusual in Chhattisgarh to have one sibling with the Maoists and the other working as an SPO. Tribals need both the Maoists and the state but definitely for different reasons. They want parliamentary parties and civil liberties groups to help them if they get arrested and also the Maoists who can help them secure their land rights (Sundar 2013).

Kennedy and King think that those tribals who support Salwa Judum tend to have benefited from collaboration with the dominant state, while those who support the Maoists tend to have suffered as result of it (Kennedy and King 2009). They conducted a field survey in Dantewada and observed that,

It was apparent from talking to Adivasis in Salwa Judum camps that they all had reason to resist or fear the insurgents. In many cases they previously held a privileged status as a result of descending from a particular lineage or collaborating with dominant society. But, in the process of establishing control, the insurgents challenged and undermined their authority. They include *kotwars*, the traditional administrators in the village who have a reputation for demanding bribes for services such as registering births, and *sarpanches*, the elected community leaders who are often said to embezzle a proportion of money from government projects. Adivasi teachers and forest guards, who are seen by the insurgents as agents of the state and are often involved in local level corruption, also form a sizeable proportion of Salwa Judum sympathizers. It is, however, not possible to depict all Adivasis opposing the insurgents as having vested interests that are harmed by an otherwise popular insurgency. (Kennedy and King 2013)

Since the Maoists believe that any state efforts like communication building, infrastructure building, employment generation, construction of roads, schools or health centres could bring development to the tribals and could segregate them or make them withdraw their support from the Maoists, they create obstruction and those people who seek work in those projects are treated like class enemies. They do not endorse democratic parliamentary institutions like panchayats and boycott people's representation in the elections (Morrison 2012). These are banned in their political ideology of revolutionary overthrow of the establishments. This is sometimes tantamount to thuggery. They want tribals to be in lifelong penury which will in turn ensure their own survival and sustenance and serve their political agenda as well. On the other hand, the tribal rebellion was and is very much associated with democratic process and hardly believes in the revolutionary violence the way Maoists do. Tribals do not share the ideology that believes 'political power flows from the barrel of the gun'. Besides, the steady growth of an elite class in the Maoist leadership has caused dissatisfaction among the rural poor. Tribals are more of a collective entity who fight together with traditional weapons.

Election boycott by the Maoists as part of their ideology and political strategy of insurgency and state sponsored counter-insurgency forced tribals to flee into the deep forests on the day of the election to be saved by any means from giving vote or to not vote.

These uncertainties and risks make the tribals more frightened, unguarded and weak. For Maoists, elections are like wars and the security forces and party agents are their enemies. Nandini Sundar has written that, in the 2013 assembly elections, there was one armed security man for every nineteen residents in Bastar. In 2014, seven poll officials were killed in Bastar along with five security personnel. Electronic voting machines were looted. It was deliberately planned to create the booths at a distant place in order to avoid any violent activity, but then also very few tribals could actually reach such a distant place to cast their votes. She has further stated that, democracy becomes a juncture of no escape and no return, a moment when democratic actions and ambitions are deceitful in overturning democratic outcomes and fetishize the electoral process. The failure of the Maoist's own strategy of armed struggle to give a better alternative to democratic means and its subsequent retrogression into brutality, the frequent incrimination of alternative mechanisms for implementing self-governance and most importantly the inability to establish a true democratic system through representative election, that demands a huge expenditure and media coverage, give birth to the contradictions and clashes in democracy itself and foil its actual goals (Sundar 2018).

It is crucial to remember that since late sixties, government downturned the development programmes and withdrew from the tribal heartlands as a gesture of allowing the tribals to develop without interference from the outsiders suggested by B.D. Sharma who was then the District Collector of Bastar (1971-2). If noticed mindfully then it is quite clear that in south Bastar there was no tribal land acquisition by the state or any corporate companies, as happened in case of Odisha, either for industrialization or for mining or for any dam building in recent times. Therefore, there were no such issues like tribal resistance against land acquisition. In fact, in the interior rural Bastar, the state hardly has had any existence. There are rather more incidents of development disasters in the central parts of the state which is not a tribal area or in northern Chhattisgarh which is fairly populated by various tribal communities. For example, the Chhattisgarh government initiated a lot of developmental schemes during the Eleventh Five-Year Plan period, i.e. from 2007 to 2012 with a huge budget of Rs. 108.70 lakhs. They were, Chief Minister Security Plan for availing free rice, Indira Awas Yojana, Antyodaya Anna Yojana, Social Security Schemes like widow pension, etc. But the schemes misfired badly due to lack of proper implementation by the state government. The condition of the Birhors who have been designated as the Particularly Vulnerable Tribal Group could not be changed by these schemes (Mathew and Kasi 2021). The introduction of LPG policy in the nineties, creation of Chhattisgarh in 2000 and subsequent expansion of the Maoist activities from Andhra Pradesh made the situation difficult and complicated. Clashes between the security forces and Maoists led to a large-scale outmigration from Bastar which is shooting up day by day culminating in the drain of indigenous tribals of Bastar. The Maoists are manipulating the deprivation of a section of the masses as an excuse to perpetuate their growth and fulfil their agenda at the cost of denial of peace in the Red Corridor. It is true to say that violence is inbuilt in the quest for dominance and, therefore, counter-violence emerges in the process of challenging it. The repercussion of this was disastrous for the tribals who actually lost the battle between the state and the Maoists (Roy 2017).

Supriya Sharma, a journalist, who visited Bastar, had stated that, tribals act as party cadres but are hardly placed at the top leadership and people who got killed by the Maoists as informers or collaborators of the state are mostly tribals. Local tribals feel, she said, that the Maoists tried to impose their ideas on them which they dare to accept or reject at times. She has observed that, while south of Chhattisgarh was beleaguered by the Maoist violence, the northern part is more greatly stormed by the corporate aggression. Here Maoists are not that active and this is the reason why one should not equate investment-induced displacement with Maoist insurgency in Chhattisgarh. Districts such as Raigarh and Janjgir-Champa in the north which witnessed massive displacement by companies like KSK Energy to set up a 3,600 megawatt power plant, Videocon Power and Vandana Vidyut are far from the reach of the Maoists. These districts are populated both by the tribals and dalits and they are fighting for their rights together. The Maoists are more prominent in Bastar, south of Chhattisgarh where displacements are caused by the Salwa Judum campaign which was launched to curb the Maoist violence. Thus, tribals are surrounded by three powerful contenders, the state, Maoists and corporate companies who are not ready to allow them to express themselves (Sharma 2012). Therefore, it is pertinent to note that there was no such interrelationship between Maoist insurgency and extraction of mineral resources. Not a great number of tribals were affected by the ESSAR or Tata projects and the cases of tribal dispossession and land grabbing are not so high in Chhattisgarh in general and Bastar in particular. Very recently in 2018 one bauxite ore mine, though low grade, has been opened in Chhattisgarh. The places where displacement has taken place very lately are outside the Maoist influence and the number of displaced is also moderately low. Tribal support for Maoists in Chhattisgarh, ergo, cannot be defined in terms of mining or development-induced displacement.

Apart from the development-induced displacement, the difference and contradictions within the legal measures regarding the forest rights are also causing hardships for the tribals. For example, the Scheduled Tribes and other Traditional Forest Dwellers (Recognition of Forest Rights) Act of 2006 has recognized the right of the forest dwelling people over the forest, but its provisions are not applicable for the parks and wildlife sanctuaries. By the 1980s, it was becoming quite clear that the push to create parks and sanctuaries was going in vain in order to protect forest cover per se. The reported decimation in forest cover was the highest in Madhya Pradesh, which had lost a large amount of teak, *sal*, and bamboo forests. Furthermore, the state planned to bring significant pockets of the remaining forests under developmental programmes. But the development projects could not perform well or meet their goals, the forest communities lost their access to fuel wood, fodder, forest foods or other minor forest produce, which went to a selective settled gentry (Sharma 2020).

This makes one question, is the legal system really pro-tribal? Or, it is just an instrument of homogenization of diverse cultures by denying the plurality inherent in it and bringing them all under one umbrella of the so-called 'mainstream culture'. The impact of such thoughts is the disappearance of rich knowledge systems that preserve different untapped and unutilized practices like ethnomedicine. This is a way to justify the displacement of the tribals as happened in Lormi and Mungeli blocks of Bilaspur district where the Baigas living in 25 forest villages out of 42 villages within the Achanakmar Wildlife Sanctuary of Bilaspur were evicted and resettled in a non-tribal and non-forest area. Achanakmar Wildlife Sanctuary was a central government sponsored scheme which was established in 1975 as an important part of Achanakmar-Amarkantak Biosphere Reserve. The sanctuary is spread over 551.552 sq. km. The steering committee of Project Tiger proposed that Achanakmar Wildlife Sanctuary should be created as a critical tiger habitat in 2003 and thus the sanctuary was directed to enlarge. The Baigas were convinced to sign the required documents which stated that they are being voluntarily evacuated and relocated for common good. After the displacement when no reassurance came on the part of the state to compensate the oustees and their access to the forest resources was restricted, the tribals resisted which received nothing but an outright ignorance by the government. This displacement caused disaster for the Baigas as they could not cope with the new environment and lost their traditional livelihood resources in forms of forest collections (Azeez 2016). Later only six villages comprising of 245 families relocated from Achanakmar were said to have received a paltry amount of Rs. 50,000 per family, but no land and no access to forest. Nineteen more villages were to be displaced later. Baiga Mahapanchayat claimed that they have resettled 390 villages over the past 20 years which were evicted from Bhoramdeo Sanctuary in Kabirdham and Bilaspur districts. None of the families were compensated with cash or land. Vedanta's BALCO bauxite mines started functioning in the Bodai Daldali hills of Kabirdham in 2003. The project displaced 262 families officially out of which 71 families were compensated and unofficially 150 families were forced to evacuate their lands since they could not show any legal titles of their land. Vedanta gave them Rs. 4,000 and resettled in Indrapani. About 980 hectares of land was leased out to BALCO for a period of 90 years for the Korba plant which aimed at mining 40 million tonnes of bauxite per annum. Bilaspur and Kabirdham lost 4,600 hectares and Chhattisgarh lost 32,400 hectares of forest cover between 2003 and 2011 (Bera 2012).

The Baigas also rely on rich traditional source of ethno-medicine for antenatal and postnatal care which they inherited from their ancestors. Due to development-induced displacement the forests were lost from where they used to collect the herbs. When the displaced Baigas were relocated they lost the access to the forest and unable to get the traditional medicines at the time of illness. For example, the Baigas in Achanakmar Wildlife Sanctuary were popular for their traditional medicinal practices. But after moving to the rehabilitation colonies, they met with a lot of hurdles when it came to avail of the modern treatment and medicinal services, like distance, language barrier, costing and the like. A study revealed that Baiga women in Jalda rehabilitation colony expressed their fear about visiting the hospital (Sahoo and Pradhan 2021). The disarticulation of their socio-economic life and culture made them vulnerable and prone to many diseases which they used to prevent by their magnificent knowledge of medicinal practices rooted within the forests and inherited from ancestors. Baigas believed that the medicinal plants were gifted with supernatural powers. It includes higher fungi, lower and higher plants, roots, rhizome, bark, bulb, tuber, gum, leaves, stem and fruits. It is used for curing skin diseases, rheumatism, sexually transmitted infections, snake bite and other poison intake, headache, typhoid, paralysis, gastric troubles, body ache, infertility, family planning, etc.

Apart from the extinction of traditional knowledge of ethno-medicine, water resources are also under severe threats due to privatization. Gautam Navlakha, in a recent article, has reported the case of privatization of Sheonath river in 1998. The Public Accounts Committee submitted a report in the legislative assembly in March 2007 criticizing the mode of privatization, but of no avail. It was the unyielding local tribals' movements that forced the government to set up the committee in 2003. Navlakha said that, when the movement was on, Radius Water, a company established by Kailash Engineering, that won the contract to carry out the project, became the owner for 22 years of the river's water. The move was advocated as a necessity for industrialization which was related to the denial of water for irrigation. Radius started walling the land along the river. They fenced 22.7 kms of river, took over thousand acres of land, as well as 176 acres along the river bank by 2000. The company acquired assets amounting to Rs. 5 crore by paying a sum of Re. 1 to the Madhya Pradesh Udhyogik Kendra Nigam and collected Rs 1.84 crore from the Chhattisgarh

State Industrial Development Corporation in the very first year of its operation. Coincidentally, a large part of the Sheonath river flows through Dantewada, is currently under occupation of ESSAR Steel Chhattisgarh. The selling of rivers went on after that. Rivers like Kelo, Kurkut, Shabri, Kharm and Maand were handed over to corporate companies (Navlakha 2008).

Nicolas Prévôt, in a recent research on the Muria dance of Bastar, has discussed the tribal situation there. He said that, the tribals are torn between the Hindu nationalists and Maoists and caught in the crossfire between the state sponsored vigilantism or counter-insurgency and the Maoist guerrillas. Their miseries are growing due to the industrialization which brings grisly travails for the tribals in Chhattisgarh. This political crisis began in 2005 when the Salwa Judum operation was first launched. Gradually the war was intensified leading to the victimization of the tribals who were caught in the slugfest and stuck between the two competing camps for power. The Chhattisgarh government, as a strategy to cover up the war, invented a new idea of promoting local tribal culture by underscoring tribal identity in the media and representing it with a 'close to nature' colour. By doing this the state covertly assisted the corporate companies to set up their business and exploit natural resources engrained in the tribal heartlands. The state also attempted to hide the war with the Maoists by showing extra interest in tribal art and craft so that the tribal mind can be won over. Maoists have been fighting for the tribal rights and also recruiting tribals in their guerrilla army which indirectly helped the Murias preserve their culture. But in a war zone Maoist behaviour was getting more and more vague and ambiguous. They are becoming like a threat for the Muria culture in general and for the *ghotul* (dormitory) in particular. During his field survey, Prévôt also heard that the Maoists have started to close the *ghotul* because of the mobility they allow to the tribal youth and also due to the fear of losing control over them. The Maoists have also boycotted the Folk Dance Competition that has been organized for at least fifteen years in the small town of Kondagaon between different dance groups representing different village *ghotul* of the region. On the other hand, the state, politicians, and parties—are all trying to shift the attention of the tribals from the ongoing gory combats between the military and the guerrillas by locating a stereotypical concept of the tribals in the wilderness of Bastar through boosting tribal tourism (Prévôt 2014).

Ramchandra Guha travelled through the district of Dantewada in the summer of 2006 and found that the Salwa Judum polarized the tribal society, fuelled very many murders and killings and displaced at least 60,000 people from their homes. He said that, the Maoists had also contributed to escalate the cycle of violence by beheading alleged 'informers', assassinated village headmen and set off land mines that killed civilians as well as police men. They had also blown up schools, transmission lines and railway tracks and stopped paramedics from working in villages under their influence. He confabulated with a former Muria schoolteacher who became homeless in the course of the civil war. He stated clearly that the Maoists do not have the courage to keep their weapons outside the village and engage in discussion with the lay tribals. The Maoists, according to him, are afraid of democratic debate with poor and unarmed tribals. Guha while analyzing Maoist violence, observed that the Maoists attacked school buildings as they do not want children to be exposed to pedagogy other than their own. They kill village headmen because they see electoral democracy as a threat to their one party system. In Guha's words,

> . . . the Maoists may sometimes provide the tribal succour against the exactions of the forest guard or moneylender. In the medium and long term, they provide no real solution. For them, the tribals are essentially cannon fodder, as a stepping stone in a larger war against the Indian State . . . they will further escalate the violence and expose the adivasis to even more suffering and discontent. (Guha 2011)

The tribals of the war zone have repeatedly tried to bring peace. They came together and formed Sarva Samaj committees which demanded justice (Sundar 2014). Sudeep Chakravarti, the writer of the famous novel called *Red Sun: Travels in Naxalite Country*, said that,

> The climate is poisoned in Bastar, and the times vicious. For deterrence and revenge, people have been raped, beaten, murdered by the state. . . . The Maoists too have done their dance, hacking to death suspected informants, blowing up both police personnel and members of Salwa Judum, as well as innocents who happen to be at the wrong place at the wrong time. (Chakravarti 2008)

The repertoire of development has always been meant for the tribals in a uniform way, i.e. to 'modernize the primitive man'. The nature of government's policies towards tribals has never changed since the colonial times. It aims at mainstreaming the traditional communities, colonize their resources and corporatize their subsistence economy to such an extent that could assimilate the tribals with the urbanized, industrialized and monetized class. One has already started seeing the growing creamy layer in the tribal community with a marching of a middle class which supports the recent model of development and who are enticed with government jobs, like joining the military and paramilitary forces for making the path of corporate exploitation easier. Tribals do not oppose state or state policies, but the agents of the state who exploit them, who try to impose things from above, who deprive them of their rights and justice. They do not want to go back to the primitive life or remain backward and poor, rather they want to keep contact with the larger society and get full advantage of development, modern education and healthcare facilities. It will be a gross mistake to think that tribals want to remain isolated and they oppose development. Instead they do desire government jobs, participate in the policymaking, contest the elections, and the like. But at the same time it is also true to say that tribals are even more in need to be free from outside pressure for development. Exploitation, iniquitous socio-political opportunities, depressed wages, inadequate employment, lack of access to forest resources, primitive methods of agriculture, geographical isolation, faulty policies of land reforms, poor quality of government services like healthcare and education, lack of awareness and most importantly poverty—all have contributed to the growth of Maoist movement in tribal regions. When the state fails to ensure real progress and justice, they often choose to turn to the Maoists for conveying their dissatisfaction and dissent. Thus, it is evident that in the conflict of the state and the Maoists, the poor tribals who are fighting against each other without even being 'class enemies' suffer most. Poverty cannot be an alibi for violence or terror and violence cannot be an answer to deprivation and injustice. Bullets cannot bring peace likewise corporatization is not the other name of development.

REFERENCES

Anonymous, 1989, 'Bastar: Development and Democracy', in *Economic and Political Weekly*, A Report published by Madhya Pradesh unit of the People's Union for Civil Liberties, Part I, vol. 24, no. 39, pp. 2188-90.

——, 1989, 'Bastar: Development and Democracy', in *Economic and Political Weekly*, A Report published by Madhya Pradesh unit of the People's Union for Civil Liberties, Part II, vol. 24, no. 40, pp. 2237-41.

——, 2004, 'Human rights violation in the context of the displacement of project affected people: A report on five case studies of State-sponsored terror in India', in *Social Change*, vol. 34, no. 4, pp. 107-21.

——, 2006, *Salwa Judum* (in Bengali), Kolkata: Muktikami Prakashani.

Azeez, Abdul E.P. and Ajeesh Sebastian, 2016, 'Development and Cultural Distortion: Assessing the Impacts of Development Programmes and Policies on Medicinal Practice of Baiga Community of Chhattisgarh', in *Contemporary Voice of Dalit*, 8(1), pp. 82-9.

Baviskar, Amita, 2005, 'Red in Tooth and Claw? Searching for Class in Struggles over Nature', in R. Ray and M. Katzenstein (eds.), *Social Movements in India: Poverty, Power, and Politics*, Lanham, MD: Rowman and Littlefield, pp. 161-78.

Behera, Anshuman, 2019, 'Politics of Good Governance and Development in Maoist Affected Scheduled Areas in India: A Critical Engagement', in *Studies in Indian Politics*, 7(1) pp. 44-55.

Bera, Sayantan, 29 July 2012, 'Baigas in Exile', in *The Statesman.*

Bhatt, Vikas, 2015, 'A Baba in Bastar', in K.S. Singh (ed.), *Tribal Movements in India*, vol. 2, New Delhi: Manohar, pp. 223-41.

Bhattacharyya, Amit, 2007, *Janaganer Unnayan: Dandakaranyer Avigyata* (in Bengali), Kolkata: Radical Publications.

——, 2010, 'Maoist Movement in India and the Alternative Model of Development in Dandakaranya', in Pradip Basu (ed.), *Discourses on Naxalite Movement*, Kolkata: Setu Prakashani, pp. 268-80.

Chandra, Uday, 2014, 'The Maoist Movement in Contemporary India', in *Social Movement Studies*, vol. 13, no. 3, pp. 1-6.

Chakravarti, Sudeep, 2008, *Red Sun: Travels in Naxalite Country*, New Delhi: Penguin India.

Danda, Ajit K., 2015, 'Gahira Guru and his Sant Samaj Movement', in K.S. Singh (ed.), *Tribal Movements in India*, vol. 2, New Delhi: Manohar, pp. 197-208.

Dasgupta, Shubhendu and Sujata Bhadra, 2011, *Operation Green Hunt* (in Bengali), Kolkata: A.G. Enterprise.

Dash, Dillip Kumar, 2021, 'Diverse and Contra-Sectional Subjectivities in Social Movement Unionism: A Study of Chhattisgarh Mukti Morcha (Mazdoor Karyakarta Samiti)', in *Sociological Bulletin,* 70(1), pp. 76-93.

Ekka, William, 2015, 'Reform Movement of Rajmohini Devi', in K.S. Singh, (ed.), *Tribal Movements in India,* vol. 2, New Delhi: Manohar, pp. 209-21.

Frontline , 17 June 2011, 'Standing up to the State', pp. 9-18.

Frontline, 6 November 2009.

Government of Chhattisgarh, 2005, *Human Development Report,* Raipur: Government of Chhattisgarh.

Government of India, 2008, *Development Challenges in Extremist Affected Areas,* Report of an Expert Group to the Planning Commission, New Delhi: Government of India

Guha, Ramchandra, 31 January 2011, 'A Nation Consumed by the State', in *Outlook,* pp. 30-44.

India Today, 11 February 2008, 26 October 2009, 9 November 2009, 19 April 2010.

Industrial Policy 2004-2009, 2004, Raipur, India: Government of Chhattisgarh, Commerce and Industries Department.

Kumbamu, Ashok, 2017, 'Bury My Heart in Bastar: Neoliberal Extractivism, the Oppressive State and the Maoist Revolution in India', in *Kairos: A Journal of Critical Symposium,* vol. 2, no. 1, pp. 15-34.

Kennedy, Jonathan, 2014, 'Gangsters or Gandhians? The Political Sociology of the Maoist Insurgency in India', in *India Review,* vol. 13, no. 3, pp. 212-34.

Kennedy, Jonathan J. and Lawrence P. King, 9 March 2009, 'The Sociology of Insurgency in Indigenous Communities: Moral Economy, Class Analysis, Geopolitical and Political Economy Explanations of "Naxalism" in Chhattisgarh, India', in *Faculty of Politics, Psychology, Sociology and International Studies Working Paper Series,* University of Cambridge, pp. 1-61.

——, 2013, 'Adivasis, Maoists and Insurgency in the Central Indian Tribal Belt', in *European Journal of Sociology,* vol. 54, no. 1, pp. 1-32.

Mathew, Gladis S. and Eswarappa Kasi, 2021, 'Livelihoods of Vulnerable People: An Ethnographic Study among the Birhor of Chhattisgarh', in *Asia-Pacific Journal of Rural Development,* 31(1), pp. 127-42.

Meher, Rajkishor, 2009, 'Globalization, Displacement and the Livelihood Issues of Tribal and Agriculture Dependent Poor People: The Case of Mineral-based Industries in India', in *Journal of Developing Societies,* 25 (4), pp. 457-80.

Mehrotra, Nilika and S.M. Patnaik, 2008, 'Culture versus Coercion: Other Side of Nirmal Gram Yojana', in *Economic and Political Weekly*, vol. 43, no. 43, pp. 25-27.

Morrison, Chas, 2012, 'Grievance, Mobilization and State Response: An Examination of the Naxalite Insurgency in India', in *Journal of Conflict Transformation & Security*, vol. 2, no. 1, pp. 53-75.

Mukherjee, Shivaji, 2018, 'Colonial Origins of Maoist Insurgency in India: Historical Institutions and Civil War', in *Journal of Conflict Resolution*, vol. 62(10), pp. 2232-74.

Mukherjee, Sonali, 2014, 'Mining and Women: The Case of the Maria of Chhattisgarh', in *Social Change*, 44(2), pp. 229-47.

Navlakha, Gautam, 2008, 'Savage War for "Development"', in *Economic and Political Weekly*, vol. 43, no. 16, pp. 16-19.

Open, 2 July 2010.

Oskarsson, Patrik, 2010, 'The Law of the Land Contested: Bauxite Mining in Tribal, Central India in an Age of Economic Reform', A thesis submitted to the School of International Development, University of East Anglia, in partial fulfilment of the requirements for the degree of Doctor of Philosophy.

——, 2018, *Landlock: Paralysing Dispute over Minerals on Adivasi Land in India*, Acton: ANU Press.

Padel, Felix, 2017, 'A Resource War to Die For: Is the Conflict Over Minerals Centred in Chhattisgarh the Worst war there has Ever been in India?', in *Journal of Peoples Studies*, vol. 2, issues 1-4, pp. 36-48.

Prévôt, Nicolas, 2014, 'The "Bison Horn" Muria Making it "More Tribal" for a Folk Dance Competition in Bastar, Chhattisgarh', in *Asian Ethnology*, vol. 73, nos. 1-2, pp. 201-31.

Punwani, Jyoti, 2007, 'Traumas of Adivasi Women in Dantewada', in *Economic and Political Weekly*, vol. 42, no. 4, pp. 276-8.

Ray, Panchali, 2019, 'Towards a Politics of Pain: Building Solidarities, Breaking Silences in Contemporary Chhattisgarh, India', in *Journal of International Women's Studies*, 20(2), 271-84.

Raychaudhuri, Diptendra, 2011, *A Naxal Story*, New Delhi: Vitasta Publishing.

Roy, Arundhati, 29 March 2010, 'Walking with the Comrades', in *Outlook*, India, pp. 1-26.

——, 2011, *Broken Republic*, New Delhi: Hamish Hamilton.

Roy, Himanshu, 2017, 'Interrogating the Maoists and the Indian State: A Study of Salwa Judum in Bastar', in *Indian Journal of Public Administration*, 63(2), pp. 284-301.

Sahoo, Madhulika and Jalandhar Pradhan, 2021, 'Reproductive Healthcare Beliefs and Behaviours among Displaced Tribal Communities in Odisha and Chhattisgarh: An Analysis Using Health Belief Model', in *Journal of the Anthropological Survey of India*, 70(1), pp. 87-102.

Sanyal, Srabani and Ramyash, 2020, 'Livelihood Sources of Gond Tribes: A study of village Mangalnaar, Bhairamgarh Block, Chhattisgarh', in *NGJI An International Peer-Reviewed Journal*, vol. 66, no. 2, pp. 174-85.

Saxena, Anupama and Dhammshil Ganveer, 2013, 'Whither are the Tribals in Chhattisgarh', in *Contemporary Voice of Dalit*, vol. 6, no. 1, pp. 91-7.

Sen, Binayak, 2012, 'An Appeal for Peace in South Bastar', in Biswajit Roy (ed.), *War and Peace in Junglemahal*, Kolkata: Setu Prakashani, pp. 269-72.

Shah, Alpa, 2013, 'The Intimacy of Insurgency: Beyond Coercion, Greed or grievance in Maoist India', in *Economy and Society*, vol. 42, no. 3, pp. 480-506.

Sharma, B.D., 2010, *Unbroken History of Broken Promises*, New Delhi: Sahyog Pustak Kuteer.

Sharma, Supriya, 2012, 'Adivasi Predicament in Chhattisgarh', in *Economic and Political Weekly*, vol. 47, no. 2, pp. 19, 21-22.

Sharma, Varun, 2020, 'Pardhi Criminality in Postcolonial Chhattisgarh: of Tigers, Tribals and Misfits', in *Studies in History*, 36(1), pp. 98-120.

Singh, K.S., 2015, 'The Gond Movements' and 'A Forest Satyagraha', in K.S. Singh (ed.), *Tribal Movements in India*, vol. 2, New Delhi: Manohar, pp. 177-85, 187-95.

Spacek, Michael, 2014, 'Revolutionary Maoism and the Production of State and Insurgent Space in Eastern and Central India', in *Geopolitics*, pp. 1-23.

Sundar, Nandini, 2010, 'Educating for Inequality: The Experiences of India's "Indigenous Citizens"', in *Asian Anthropology*, vol. 9(1), pp. 117-42.

——, 2011, 'At War with Oneself: Constructing Naxalism as India's Biggest Security Threat', in Michael Kugelman (ed.), *India's Contemporary Security Challenges*, Washington DC: Woodrow Wilson International Centre for Scholars, pp. 1-23.

——, 2012, 'The Path to a Conflict-free State', in Biswajit Roy (ed.), *War and Peace in Junglemahal*, Kolkata: Setu Prakashani, pp. 266-8.

——, 2013, 'Reflections on Civil Liberties, Citizenship, Adivasi Agency and Maoism: A Response to Alpa Shah', in *Critique of Anthropo-logy*, 33(3), pp. 361-8.

——, 2014, 'India's Million Mutinies: The Paths to Reconciliation', in

Amitabh Matttoo (ed.), *The Argumentative Indian*, Melbourne: Australia India Institute.

——, 2018, 'Hostages to Democracy', in *Critical Times*, vol. 1, no. 1, pp. 80-98.

Supreme Court of India, 2001, Judgement in the Case of 'Balco Employees Union versus Union of India and others'.

Update Series 18, 2010, *Adivasi in India*, Kolkata: Update Publications.

Epilogue

Systematic and structural violence of tribal rights began with the inception of colonization which never ended and renewed itself in the form of an internal colonization under the euphemism of globalization. The neo-colonial or neoliberal exploitation is the root cause of tribal uprisings in recent times. The tribal movement is closely linked to the question of tribal identity and existence. This is the reason why they do not even think twice before going even against the state. The state response to the tribal movements is basically two-fold: either submit to development based on mainstream notion of large scale industrialization and commercialization or be ready to be forced to do so by the security forces. Arbitrary arrests, torture, abuse, implicate with false charges and fake encounters, are some of the weapons with which the tribal movements are being choked again and again. Violation of human rights and atrocities have become the order of the day. Most importantly, the tribal middle class is divided and can not provide an able representation at the national level of political development. The local militant groups also do not raise questions like tribal land rights and fail to give a better alternative as well. This has caused a big disillusionment on the part of the tribals who feel betrayed as they once supported them in creating bases in their interior areas. The chief problems of tribals in the area under study are: hunger, indebtedness, land alienation, displacement, migration, environmental degradation, resource conflicts, human rights and identity assertion. There is an immeasurable sense of exclusion, marginalization and deprivation among the tribes of India which give birth to various reasons of their movements let alone poverty. Some of the broad causes are, clear lack of a well thought tribal policy, land policy, excise policy, forest policy and environmental policy; denial of giving self-governance by the state; assault on tribal culture, tradition, customary rights and religious beliefs; economic deprivation, social marginalization and political disenfranchizement. The existing laws are poorly implemented in the scheduled areas and rampant corruption has aggravated the crisis in the tribal world (Kujur 2016).

The fate of the tribals has always been poignant. Tribals have shunned any model of destructive development that threatens to disrupt their traditional means of livelihood by advocating and propagating business and related eviction. They have every right to decry 'development' and ask for better rehabilitation which is a legitimate expectation from the perspective of law as they are to sacrifice their life and livelihood for the greater good. About extremism it can be said that Maoists belong to a specific political school of thought and have an extremist ideology which can only claim to represent the tribals or at the most champion their cause, but they cannot lead them for long because tribal mobilization has its own dimensions, ideology and pathway. Maoists are not successful in providing a better alternative to the tribals.

The market driven reform is gradually losing the focus from the non-market subsistence economic institutions. Large scale industrialization forgets to value intensive cultivation and take land as only for business which is affecting traditional farming practices like swidden which can be a good alternative and a backup policy for crop failure in those areas where severe droughts and starvation deaths are common. It has been proved time and again that tribals take up arms only when they are under oppression, their freedom is curtailed; outsiders interfere in their everyday life or there is violation of their age old right to land and forest. Tribals are adaptable and tolerant by nature. They even tolerated the incursion of *dikus* and state oppression. They only react when things cross the limit of toleration which is true of almost all the tribal movements since colonial times. The onslaught of acculturation and influx of consumerist culture is gradually eroding the mainstay of tribal activism to a great extent (Dubey 1998).

The book tries to analyze the impact of liberalization on the vulnerable tribals and identify the inherent arguments postulating the structural violence emanating from it and the resultant recurrent extremist violence which gave birth to counter-violence and proved to be a potential threat to the tribals. The main thrust of the theme of the book remains the accentuation of problems of land grabbing, displacement, impoverishment and cultural genocide of the tribals in the neoliberal regime. Opening up of the interior tribal areas which are rich in mineral and natural wealth to the giant corporate agencies in collaboration with an authoritarian state forced the tribals to watch the great loot helplessly and deal with the exploitative capitalist forces and consumerist culture. The state has become just a puppet in the hands of the global corporate system. In short, tribals are not only being alienated physically due to the ongoing corporatization and commercialization, but also losing their distinct indigenous identity. The hegemony of neoliberal development is gradually eroding the collective existence of the tribals of India.

Tribal movements cannot be analyzed or documented in a single book. There are numerous and variegated forms and categories of tribal movements across the country. The book is a small attempt to write a history of only a few tribal movements which made their presence felt and left a lasting impression as far as tribal activism is concerned. There are a host of books and articles on tribal movements and theories related to the everyday forms of resistance, both in colonial and postcolonial periods. But in this book an attempt has been made to write a simple history of tribal movements going beyond complex academic theories and mainstream historical discourses in which tribal voice remain unheard perpetually and slowly but steadily they get more and more vulnerable, finally extinct. This is the reason why the tribals, the indigenous inhabitants of our country cry and say, 'leave us alone without exploitation; just be grateful and respect us from a distance' (Rama 1999: 17).

REFERENCES

Dubey, K.C., 1998, 'Tribal Uprisings and Social Movements in Madhya Pradesh', in K.S. Singh (ed.), *Tribal Movements in India: Antiquity to Modernity in Tribal India*, vol. IV, New Delhi: Inter-India Publications, pp. 205-317.

Kujur, Joseph Marianus, 2016, 'Adivasi Militancy and Land Relations: The Context of Central and Eastern India', in K.B. Saxena and G. Haragopal (eds.), *Marginalization, Development and Resistance*, New Delhi: Aakar, pp. 328-46.

Rama, Swami, 1999, *Living with the Himalayan Masters*, Pennsylvania: Himalayan Institute Press, Honesdale, USA.

Glossary

Balahar	take-home ration
Bandh	strike
Bhajans	religious songs
Bustees	colony areas
Daroga	sub-inspector of police
Dehatis	people who live in villages
Dikus	hostile aliens
Dongar	shifting cultivation land
Ghotul	dormitory
Gram sabha	village assembly
Gram swaraj	village self-reliance
Haat	weekly markets
Hul	rebellion
Jal, zamin and jungle	water, land and forest
Janata	common people
Jhum	shifting cultivation
Khorkar	the right to clear the wastelands in the village
Khuntkatti	joint ownership or holding of land by tribal lineage
Mahua	madhuca longifolia used to brew country liquor
Manjhi parganait	traditional village administration system among the tribes
Mankis	head of parha
Mukkadams	local agents
Mulk ki ladai	fight for the country
Nevad	shifting cultivation
Panchayati raj	local self-government of village
Parha	traditional village administration system among the tribes
Patta	land deed

Podu	shifting cultivation
Sanjha Chulha	combined kitchen
Sarna	sacred groves
Sasandiri	cremation grounds
Satyagraha	non-violent resistance movement
Thana	police station
Zamindari	landlordism

Bibliography

Primary Sources

Centre for Science and Environment, 2008, 'Rich Lands Poor People: Is "Sustainable" Mining Possible?', *The State of India's Environment: The 6th Citizen Report*, New Delhi: Centre for Science and Environment.

Central Water Commission (CWC), 1996, Status of Projects Monitored by the Central Water Commission 1993-94, New Delhi: CWC.

Government of Bihar, 1986, 'Rehabilitation Plan for Displaced and Affected Families of Koel-Karo Hydro-Electric Project', mimeo, Department of Energy, Directorate of Rehabilitation and Land Acquisition, Patna.

Government of Chhattisgarh, 2005, *Human Development Report*, Raipur: Government of Chhattisgarh.

Government of India, 2008, *Development Challenges in Extremist Affected Areas*, Report of an Expert Group to the Planning Commission, New Delhi: Government of India.

Government of Orissa, 2000, *Status Report on Rehabilitation and Resettlement and I.P.D.P of Rengali Irrigation Project*, Department of Water Resources, Bhubaneswar.

Human Development Report, 2004, Government of Orissa, Published by Planning and Coordination Department Bhubaneswar: Government of Orissa.

Industrial Policy 2004-2009, 2004, Government of Chhattisgarh, Raipur: Commerce and Industries Department.

Ministry of Home Affairs, 1985, 'A Report of the Committee on Rehabilitation of Displaced Tribals due to Development Projects', New Delhi: Government of India.

National Land Reforms Policy, 8 June 2017, Committee on State Agrarian Relations and Unfinished Task of Land Reforms, Ministry of Rural Development, New Delhi: Government of India, https://dolr.gov.in/sites/default/files/Committee%20Report.pdf downloaded on 30 October 2021.

PUCL, September 2003, 'Pachwara Coal Mining Project', *Enquiry Report*, Dumka: Jharkhand Unit.

Shah Commission, 2013, *First Report on Illegal Mining of Iron and Manganese Ores in the State of Jharkhand*, vol. IV, Ministry of Mines, New Delhi: Government of India.

Supreme Court of India, 2001, Judgement in the case of 'Balco Employees Union *vs.* Union of India and Others'.

The Chota Nagpur Tenancy (Amendment) Act 1938 (Bihar Act 2 of 1938), Bihar Legislative Department, Superintendent, Bihar: Government Printing.

Secondary Sources

Agarwal, P.K., 2010, *Naxalism: Causes and Cure*, New Delhi: Manas Publications.

Ananthamurthy, U.R. (ed.), 2011, *Re-imagining India and Other Essays*, New Delhi: Orient BlackSwan.

Basu, Pradip (ed.), 2010, *Discourses on Naxalite Movement*, Kolkata: Setu Prakashani.

Behura, N. and N. Panigrahi, 2006, *Tribals and the Indian Constitution: Functioning of the Fifth Schedule in Orissa*, New Delhi: Rawat Publications.

Bose, Nirmal Kumar, 2019, *Tribal Life in India*, New Delhi: National Book Trust India.

Bhattacharyya, Amit, 2007, *Janaganer Unnayan: Dandakaranyer Avigyata* (in Bengali), Kolkata: Radical Publications.

Bhattacharjya, Manjima (ed.), 2009, *Sarpanch Sahib*, New Delhi: Harper Collins Publishers India.

Chakravarti, Sudeep, 2008, *Red Sun: Travels in Naxalite Country*, New Delhi: Penguin India.

Chandra, Uday and Daniel Taghioff (eds.), 2016, *Staking claims: The Politics of Social Movements in Contemporary Rural India*, New Delhi: Oxford University Press

Chaudhary, S.N. (ed.), 2010, *Tribal Economy Crossroads*, Jaipur: Rawat Publications.

Dasgupta, Shubhendu and Sujata Bhadra, 2011, *Operation Green Hunt* (in Bengali), Kolkata: A.G. Enterprise.

Dias, Anthony, 2012, *Development and its Human Cost*, Jaipur: Rawat Publications.

Ekka, Alex, 2011, *A Status of Adivasis/Indigenous Peoples Land Series-4, Jharkhand*, Delhi: Aakar Books.

Ekka, A. and M. Asif, 2000, *Development-induced Displacement and Rehabilitation in Jharkhand*, New Delhi: Indian Social Institute.

Evans, G., James Goodman and Nina Lansbury (eds.), 2002, *Moving Mountains: Communities Confront Mining and Globalization*, London: Zed.

Fernandes, Walter and Mohammed Asif, 1997, *Development-induced Displacement in Odisha 1951 to 1995: A Database on its Extent and Nature*, New Delhi: Indian Social Institute.

Ganguly, V.B. (ed.), 2015, *Land Rights in India: Policies, Movements and Challenges*, New Delhi: Routledge.

Gellner, David N. (ed.), 2009, *Ethnic Activism and Civil Society in South Asia,* New Delhi: Sage.

George, Ajitha S., 2014, *Status of Adivasis/Indigenous Peoples Mining Series-2, Jharkhand*, Delhi: Aakar.

Guha, Ranajit, 1983, *Elementary Aspects of Peasant Insurgency in Colonial India*, Delhi: Oxford University Press.

Kugelman, Michael (ed.), 2011, *India's Contemporary Security Challenges*, Washington DC: Woodrow Wilson International Centre for Scholars.

Kumar, Kundan, 2011, *A Status of Adivasis/Indigenous Peoples Land Series—2, Orissa*, New Delhi: Aakar.

Mahana, Rajakishor, 2019, *Negotiating Marginality: Conflicts over Tribal Development in India*, New Delhi: Social Science Press.

Mattoo, Amitabh (ed.), 2014, *Deconstructing the Argumentative Indian*, Melbourne: Australia India Institute.

Mehta, Lyla (ed.), 2009, *Displaced by Development: Confronting Marginalization and Gender Injustice*, New Delhi: Sage Publications.

Mishra, Sujit Kumar and R. Siva Prasad (eds.), 2018, *Displacement, Impoverishment and Exclusion: Political Economy of Development in India*, Delhi: Aakar.

Mohanty, Aliva, 2016, *Socio-political Harmony and Displaced Women of Odisha*, New Delhi: Abhijit Publications.

Munshi, Indra (ed.), 2012, *The Adivasi Question: Issues of Land, Forest and Livelihood*, New Delhi: *EPW* and Orient BlackSwan.

Narayan, S. (ed.), 1992, *Jharkhand Movement: Origin and Evolution*, Delhi: Inter-India.

Oskarsson, Patrik, 2018, *Landlock: Paralysing Dispute over Minerals on Adivasi Land in India*, Acton: ANU Press.

Padel, Felix and Samarendra Das, 2010, *Out of this Earth: East India Adivasis and the Aluminium Cartel*, New Delhi: Orient BlackSwan.

Pati, Sikta, 2012, *Industrialization and Displacement: An Economic Impact*, New Delhi: Concept Publishing Company.

Patra, Himansu Sekhar, 2014, *Status of Adivasis/Indigenous Peoples Mining Series—5, Odisha*, New Delhi: Aakar.

Prakash, Anjal, V.S. Saravana and Jayati Chourey (eds.), 2012, *Interlacing Water and Human Health: Case Studies from South Asia*, New Delhi: Sage Publications.

Rao, M.G. and P.K. Rama, 1979, *East Coast Bauxite Deposits of India*, New Delhi: Report by the Geological Survey of India.

Ray, R. and M. Katzenstein (eds.), 2005, *Social Movements in India: Poverty, Power, and Politics*, Lanham, MD: Rowman and Littlefield.

Raychaudhuri, Diptendra, 2011, *A Naxal Story*, New Delhi: Vitasta Publishing.

Roy, Arundhati, 2011, *Broken Republic*, New Delhi: Hamish Hamilton.

Roy, Biswajit (ed.), 2012, *War and Peace in Junglemahal*, Kolkata: Setu Prakashani.

Roy, S.C., 1912, *The Mundas and their Country*, Calcutta: Kuntaline Press.

Saxena, K.B. and G. Haragopal (eds.), 2016, *Marginalization, Development and Resistance*, vol. II, New Delhi: Aakar.

Scott, James C., 1976, *The Moral Economy of the Peasant: Rebellion and Subsistence in Southeast Asia*, New Haven: Yale University Press.

——, 1985, *Weapons of the Weak: Everyday Forms of Peasant Resistance*, New Haven: Yale University Press.

Sen, Asoka Kumar, 2018, *Indigeneity, Landscape and History: Adivasi Self Fashioning in India*. New York: Routledge.

Sharma, B.D., 2010, *Unbroken History of Broken Promises*, New Delhi: Sahyog Pustak Kuteer.

Shukla, H.L., 1986, *Tribal Heritage of Madhya Pradesh*, Delhi: B.R. Publishing Corporation.

Singh, K.S. (ed.), *Tribal Movements in India: Antiquity to Modernity in Tribal India*, vol. IV, New Delhi: Inter-India Publications.

——, 2015, *Tribal Movements in India*, vol. 1 & 2, New Delhi: Manohar.

Singha Roy, Debal K. (ed.), 2010, *Dissenting Voices and Transformative Actions: Social Movements in a Globalizing World*, New Delhi: Manohar.

Sinha, S.P., 1990, *Tribal Leadership in Bihar*, The Bihar Tribal Welfare Research Institute for the Government of Bihar, Ranchi: Welfare Department.

Somayaji, Sakarama and Susmita Dasgupta (eds.), 2013, *Sociology of Displacement: Policies and Practice*, New Delhi: Rawat Publications,

Tharakan, S. (ed.), 2002, *The Nowhere People: Responses to Internally Displaced Persons*, Bangalore: Books for Change.

JOURNALS AND PERIODICALS

Asian Anthropology
Asian Ethnology
Asia-Pacific Journal of Rural Development
Business Standard
Commonwealth and Comparative Politics
Contemporary Voice of Dalit
Contribution to Indian Sociology
Critical Asian Studies
Critical Sociology
Critical Times
Critique of Anthropology
Cultural Anthropology
Development
Down to Earth
Economic and Political Weekly
Economy and Society
European Journal of Sociology
Focaal—Journal of Global and Historical Anthropology
Frontier
Frontline
Gender, Technology and Development
Geopolitics
Indian Anthropologist
India International Centre Quarterly
Indian Journal of Public Administration
India Review
Journal of the Anthropological Survey of India
Journal of Asian and African Studies
Journal of Conflict Resolution
Journal of Conflict Transformation & Security
Journal of Contemporary Asia
Journal of Developing Societies
Journal of Gender Equality and Sensitivity
Journal of International Women's Studies
Journal of Land and Rural Studies
Journal of Peoples Studies
Kairos: A Journal of Critical Symposium
Mainstream

Open
Outlook
Politics & Society
Review of Development and Change
Seminar
Social Change
Social Movement Studies
Sociological Bulletin
South Asia Multidisciplinary Academic Journal
South Asia Research
Studies in History
Studies in Indian Politics
Tehelka
The Indian Economic and Social History Review
The Indian Historical Review
The International Journal of Community and Social Development

NEWSPAPERS

Daily Pioneer
Dainik Bhaskar
Hindustan
Indian Express
India Today
The Statesman
The Times of India

Index